THE CRIMEAN WAR
THEN & NOW

THE
CRIMEAN
WAR
THEN & NOW

DAVID R. JONES

Frontline Books

**THE CRIMEAN WAR
THEN AND NOW**

This edition published in 2017 by Frontline Books,
an imprint of Pen & Sword Books Ltd,
47 Church Street, Barnsley, S. Yorkshire, S70 2AS

ISBN: 978-1-84832-491-6

For more information on our books, please visit
www.frontline-books.com
email info@frontline-books.com
or write to us at the above address.

Printed and bound in India by Replika Press Pvt. Ltd.

Typeset in 10/12.5 Avenir

Contents

Introduction

The war in the Crimea of 1854-56 was fought against Russia by an alliance of the armies of Britain, French, Turkey and Sardinia. It has been described as either the last conflict in the old era or the first in the modern. It was a time when British Guard regiments still went into battle wearing scarlet tunics and bearskins, and when round-shot cut bloody channels through tightly-packed columns of advancing soldiers. However, it was also a time when the first ironclad vessels were being tested as gun platforms and politicians at home could communicate with their generals using the new electric telegraph.

The Crimean War was one of the first in which newspaper correspondents were despatched to the front to report on progress first hand. It was when photographers, as well as more traditional artists, were present to record the scene for those at home. Their work provides a rich legacy in the way of a verbal and visual record of a significant international event of the Victorian era. We are indebted to those who reported events at the time with pen and paper and who captured the scene with cameras, sketch pads and watercolours.

I became interested in the Crimean War in my retirement and visited the Crimea in 2010, 2011 and 2012 to acquaint myself with the battlefields and other locations that I had seen in contemporary photographs and paintings. Armed with a camera, maps and copies of relevant images, I began to replicate the old scenes as they appear today after identifying the location where the artists so long ago would have stood or sat. This publication is the result of this work. As well as contrasting contemporary images with the same landscape today, the book also reveals, with the aid of maps and aerial photographs, where important military actions within battles occurred and where these places can be found on the modern landscape. In addition, this book identifies where the artist stood to record the scene and the significance of the location. Each contrasting pair of 'then' and 'now' images is also accompanied by an account of the historical significance of the site. The illustrations are supported by an account of the invasion of the Crimea and subsequent events up until the final departure of allied troops.

Many of the landscape photographs taken by Roger Fenton and James Robertson or his assistant Felice Beato in 1855-56 are shown together with modern views of the same scene. Some of the works of the war artist William Simpson are also included. In addition, there are images of battlefields captured by Colonel Vladislav Klembovsky at the turn of the twentieth century before they were changed forever by urban and more recently tourist developments. The reader will also be taken to where Fenton's iconic image of the 'Valley of the Shadow of Death' was taken and the site where Lord Raglan, the British Commander-in-Chief, had his headquarters.

The writings of others, notably Alexander William Kinglake and William Howard Russell, have been drawn upon for facts and figures concerning the war. All major references have been included in 'Sources of Information' and recommended for further reading or perusal by those whose interest in this fascinating topic may have been stimulated. The book serves as an illustrated guide to the battlefields where epic struggles for supremacy took place 160 years ago. It would be of especial interest to those who want to know how sites that have historical significance have changed over the years and where they can be found today.

The British monument to the Battle of Balaklava at the site of the unfinished No. 5 Redoubt on the Causeway Heights. It was here that the Russian cavalry moved from left to right shortly before its encounter with the British Heavy Cavalry Brigade on the slopes leading down into the South Valley of Balaklava. The British Light Cavalry Brigade later advanced from near here to its bloody encounter with the Russian guns and cavalry in the North Valley of Balaklava, which lies behind the trees on the left.

The idea for a book based on contrasting images made during the time of the Crimean conflict with those of the same scenes as they appear today was suggested to Martin Mace of Frontline Books in 2015. The response from him and his colleague, John Grehan, was enthusiastic and led to the rapid completion of a first draft. The encouragement shown by John and his editing of the manuscript is especially appreciated.

Manita Mishina of Sevastopol is thanked for organising accommodation and transport for the author during his photographic visits to the Crimea. Manita or her husband Yuri also acted as interpreters on various field trips and this help was greatly appreciated.

Many of the contemporary photographs taken by Roger Fenton and images of watercolours painted by William Simpson came courtesy of the public domain website of the Library of Congress in Washington, USA. All photographs taken by James Robertson/Felice Beato and some by Roger Fenton were reproduced with the permission of the Royal Collection Trust in London. The Walter Havighurst Special Collections, Miami University Libraries, Oxford, Ohio in the USA is thanked for kindly providing copies of the photographs of Colonel Vladislav Klembovsky. Additional images have been reproduced by permission of the National Army Museum, the Victoria and Albert Museum and Manuscripts, Special Collections of the University of Nottingham in the UK, and The Art Institute of Chicago in the USA. Adrian Lipscomb, a descendant of William Simpson, is thanked for allowing a portrait of Simpson to be reproduced and Darryl Lundy of 'The Peerage' website for permission to use an image showing George Shaw-Lefevre in later life. Images that are not accredited to a source in their captions were downloaded from websites in the public domain.

Google Earth is thanked for its policy of allowing its aerial views to be reproduced in books. Tony Margrave is acknowledged as the source of the date of the arrival of Mary Seacole in Balaklava.

David R. Jones
Callala Beach, New South Wales, Australia
31 March 2016

Invasion

The Landings at Kalamita Bay

The Allied invasion fleet gathering offshore at Varna in present-day Bulgaria steamed off into the Black Sea on 5 September 1854, with orders to re-group off the Crimean coast. Because the beach at the Katcha estuary originally chosen for the landing was now deemed unsuitable, another reconnaissance of the coast began on 10 September 1854 by high-ranking officers on board the steamship HMS *Caradoc*. Eventually it was agreed that disembarkation should take place at Kalamita Bay on a beach about thirteen miles to the southeast of the port of Eupatoria. The fleet anchored two to three miles off Eupatoria just after 15.00 hours on 13 September 1854 and soon afterwards the local governor surrendered the virtually defenceless port to a landing party. At 20.00 hours that evening, orders were issued for the fleet to move during the night to locations opposite the landing beaches prior to disembarkation the next day. The long awaited invasion would then begin in earnest. How had it come to this?

The drift towards war in the Crimea began as a result of Russia's perceived weakness of the Ottoman Empire and its likely imminent collapse, plus the opportunities such a collapse presented for the expansion of its own influence and territory. Russia sought to control the Black Sea and to gain access for its ships to the Mediterranean through the Bosphorus and Dardanelle Straits. To achieve this goal, it needed to change the political landscape in the Balkans. Czar Nicholas I referred to Turkey as the 'sick man' of Europe in conversations with the British Ambassador Sir George Hamilton Seymour in 1853 and tried to persuade Britain to collaborate and cooperate with Russia when the time came to 'carve-up' the region. However, Britain was immediately hostile to Russia's plans as it would upset the balance of power that kept mainland Europe in check and threaten its overland and sea routes to India and the Far East.

Since 1740, France had been the protector of the Roman Catholic Church in the Holy Lands, which was part of the Ottoman Empire, and this gave it custody of the keys to the Church of the Holy Sepulchre and the Church and Grotto of the Nativity. However, the situation changed when Christians were allowed to visit the Levant in the 1830s, as Russian saw itself as a protector of Christians in Turkish dominions though the Orthodox Church. France did not want Russia meddling in Turkish domestic affairs and, in 1850, decided to re-stake its claim to the keys of Christian antiquities. This led to a quarrel between Russia and France, who both strove to influence the Turks.

Louis-Napoleon Bonaparte, the elected president of France, was the nephew of Napoleon Bonaparte. As Napoleon III, he was eager for military victory and argued for a combined European action against Russia. When Turkey decided that France should retain its possession of the keys to the holy places and subsequent negotiations between Russia and Turkey broke down, the Czar then issued Turkey with an ultimatum – it either backed down or Russian would invade its provinces of Moldavia and Wallachia. This demand was unacceptable to Turkey and the Pruth River border was duly crossed by Russian forces in July 1853. War between Turkey and Russia seemed inevitable.

In early October, Turkey finally declared war on Russia. The Czar then ordered the Russian fleet to sail from Sevastopol in the middle of November and on 30 November 1853 its warships attacked a Turkish squadron in the harbour of Sinope on the southern shore of the Black Sea. Admiral Pavel Nakhimov caught the Turkish warships at anchor and modern explosive shells fired from Russian guns did much damage. The fight was one-sided and became even more so when Vice-Admiral Vladimir Kornilov arrived with steamships. The Turkish squadron was destroyed with the estimated loss of 4,000 lives. The only surviving ship was sent to Constantinople with the news, which reached London and Paris on 11 December. The Sinope incident outraged Britain and France, who had pledged to protect Turkey, and the public of both countries wanted revenge. Lord Aberdeen, the British Prime Minister, ordered the British fleet into the Black Sea in January 1854.

Britain and France Join Turkey in Declaring War on Russia

On 27 February 1854, Britain and France issued an ultimatum to the Czar to the effect that Russia must agree within six days to the withdrawal of all Russian troops from the Danubian provinces of Turkey by 30 April 1854 or there would be war. The Czar did not send a reply and his refusal only became known on 19 March 1854. War was declared on 27 March 1854. However, fearing the worst, the first British troops had already left Britain for Malta the previous month. By May 1854, most of those in the British expeditionary force had arrived in Turkey and had established camps in either Gallipoli or at Scutari across the Bosphorus from Constantinople.

Meanwhile, the Turks had confronted the Russians in its Danubian provinces shortly after their declaration of war in 1853. Prince Mikhail Gorchakov led the invading Russian army of 80,000 men, while the Turks deployed behind defensive positions in towns along the Danube. About 20,000 Turkish troops under Omar Pasha also advanced over the river to engage the Russians. After a few clashes, the Russians were held in check just before the onset of winter.

An advance by Russia in January 1854 to Citate was countered by Turkey. Nevertheless, the Turks under Ahmed Pasha fell back on Kalafat. In the spring of 1854, the Russians captured two towns to give them a foothold on the Upper Danube. In April 1854, Silistria was besieged by 40,000 Russians, who attacked the town a number of times, but failed to overcome the garrison. After Turkish reinforcements arrived, the Russian position was weakened and they abandoned the siege on 23 June 1854. By this time, British and French troops in Turkey had been moved up to Varna on the western coast of the Black Sea and were preparing to throw their weight behind the Turks further north, who had been successful in defending their territory. Faced with an ultimatum from the King of Prussia to vacate the Danubian provinces or else, the Czar wisely decided to give up the struggle on 24 July 1854 and, by 7 September 1854, most Russian troops were back across the Pruth River. About half of the original force of 80,000 Russians were now dead, most through sickness.

The Russian army was not the only one to have health problems. Cholera had reared its ugly head in the British and French armies camped around Varna and took its toll on the as yet untested Allied soldiers. Over 200 men of the British Light Cavalry Brigade were sent on a patrol on 24 June 1854 to determine if the Russians really were pulling back. They returned from their so-called 'sore-back reconnaissance' much the worse for wear on 11 July 1854, with both men and horses exhausted. However, it was confirmed that the Russians had indeed gone. A French force of cavalry followed by infantry also went raiding and engaged some Russians before being decimated by cholera with hundreds dying in one day alone. The expedition was rather pointless with an estimated 7,000 troops being affected by disease.

With the retreat of the Russians back over their borders, a diplomatic initiative may well have ended the war. However, this was not a desired outcome for the Allies, who wanted to teach the Czar a lesson. With navies and armies in place, the mood was for the war to continue with the objective of severely diminishing Russia's military capabilities in the Black Sea region. In particular, revenge had to be extracted for the destruction of the Turkish ships at Sinope by Russia's Black Sea fleet. This fleet's base at Sevastopol was the obvious target. On 19 July 1854, the steamship HMS *Fury* left Varna in the company of protecting warships to reconnoitre the Crimean coast for a suitable landing place in preparation for an invasion. The embarkation was planned for the end of the month or the beginning of the next, but it was delayed by cholera spreading to ships' crews.

In early August, there was a great fire in Varna with many shops and most of the commissariat stores burnt. Looting also occurred. The cholera became worse with all hospitals full and new marquees having to be erected. Troops sickened and died within hours. However, conditions began to improve later in the month and, on 24 August 1854, British and French troops camped in the countryside began to converge on Varna prior to boarding transports.

The Crimea was not the only object of offensive moves against Russia. British and French fleets also attacked Russian possessions in the Baltic with isolated actions also taking place in the White Sea and on the Kamchatka Peninsula in the Far East. However, it was the war in the Crimea peninsula that gripped public attention.

Disembarkation

William Howard Russell, the war correspondent for *The Times*, described the landing site at the 'Old Fort' location on Kalamita Bay as follows:

> The place thus selected for our landing was a low strip of beach and shingle, cast up by the violence of the surf, and forming a sort of causeway between the sea and a stagnant salt-water lake. The lake is about one mile long and half a mile broad … frequented by vast flocks of wildfowl. The causeway was not more than two hundred yards broad, leading, at the right or southern extremity of the lake, by a gentle ascent, to an irregular table-land or plateau of trifling elevation, dotted with tumuli or barrows … Towards the sea this plateau presented a precipitous face of red clay and sandstone, varying in height from a hundred to a hundred and fifty feet … Thence towards the south there was a low sandy beach, with a fringe of shingle raised by the action of the waves above the level of the land, and saving it from inundation … The post carriage from Sevastopol to Odessa was also seen rolling leisurely along, and conveying probably, news of the great armament with which the coast was menaced.

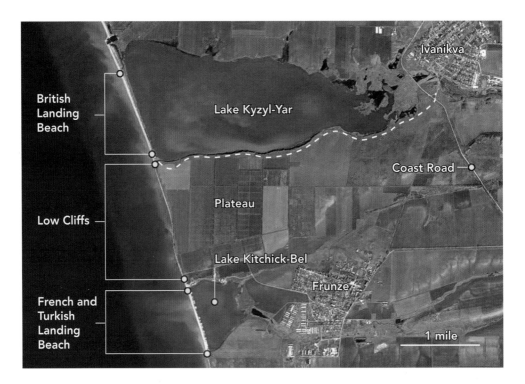

Aerial view of the landing beaches and hinterland today. The isthmuses between the salt lakes and the Black Sea where the British, French and Turkish armies landed are indicated. The low plateau, where the British army bivouacked uncomfortably in the rain the first night of the invasion, forms low cliffs on the Black Sea coast. Today's dirt track to the British landing beach from the main coastal highway near Ivanivka is indicated by a white dashed line to the south of Lake Kyzyl-Yar. A four-wheeled drive vehicle would be needed to reach the beach in wet weather. (Adapted from Google Earth™ image).

It was arranged for a buoy to be placed off shore at the centre of the beach to separate French and British landing sectors. The French and Turks were to land to the south while the British were to land to the north. However, during the hours of darkness, the French placed the buoy at the extreme north end of the beach. As to land at the chosen location would now result in confusion and, rather than move the buoy and possibly annoy the French, a similar beach to the north of the low cliffs that stretched for one and two thirds of a mile north from the 'Old Fort' beach was quickly decided upon as a suitable alternative landing site by the British. This too was an isthmus behind which was another salt-water lake.

According to Russell, the French were the first to get a boat ashore soon after 07.00 hours on the morning of 14 September 1854. A flagstaff was quickly erected and soon a tricolour was flying over the scene. There was no enemy in sight. A gun was fired by the French admiral at 08.00 hours and the French began landing troops in earnest. As more men reached the shore, the troops began to reconnoitre the ground and spread out over the hinterland like a fan. About 6,000 troops were ashore in little under an hour.

At about 09.00 hours, one black ball was run up to the fore of HMS *Agamemnon* and a gun was fired to draw attention to this signal, which meant the first stages of disembarkation of the British infantry and artillery should begin. Russell recalled that almost immediately, 'the sea was filled with launches, gigs, cutters splashing through the water, some towing flats.' As this flotilla was approaching the shore, a Russian was seen observing the goings-on from the cliff top and making a sketch of the fleet. This Russian stayed for an hour and was joined during that time by several Cossacks, who were seen gesticulating towards the French advancing from the coast about half a mile away further south.

The very first British boat landed on the isthmus to the north of the low sea cliffs and was soon followed by more. Lieutenant General Sir George Brown, Commander of the Light Division, and Brigadier General Sir Richard Airey, who had recently been in command of the 1st Brigade of the Light Division, but was now Quartermaster General, were in this first wave of boats and among the first to disembark. They walked south along the beach and began to ascend the low cliffs. A number of native carts were seen on the brow of the plateau beyond and it appears Airey turned back at this stage, possibly to organise their capture. Five minutes later, Brown was observed running down the coastal bluff. Cossacks hidden less than a hundred yards away from him had attempted an interception. Brown was short-sighted and most likely unaware of the danger until the Cossacks were close. He was saved by fire from men of the nearby 7th (Royal Fusiliers) Regiment, who caused the Cossacks, already concerned about their path to safety being cut off by the French, to rapidly retreat. A local youth attending the carts on the plateau was shot in the foot at this time. He was the first casualty of the war in Crimea. The fourteen carts abandoned by the Cossacks were found to contain fruit and firewood. The landings continued unabated all through the morning.

Brigades were assembled in contiguous columns along the beach. By 11.00 hours, the 2nd Battalion of the Rifle Brigade and the 7th and 23rd (Royal Welch Fusiliers) regiments in the Light Division had been inspected and marched from the left to the right across the front of the other regiments and up the slope onto the low plateau. By noon, the previously empty and isolated beach was full of soldiers. By 13.00 hours, most regiments of the Light Division had moved inland across the plateau. The 2nd Battalion of the Rifle Brigade with skirmishers ahead eventually reached a village four-and-three-quarters-of-a-mile from the beach. By 15.00 hours, 14,200 men had landed and two batteries of artillery.

Against the general flow of troops inland, long strings of soldiers were winding their way down the hillside and back onto the beach in twos carrying horizontal burdens. These were sick or dying soldiers lying on ambulance stretchers. Graves were dug at the bottom of the bluff for those who didn't survive long enough to be rowed back to the ships. Tartars began arriving with food stuffs to sell. Some begged Fitzroy James Henry Somerset, better known as Lord Raglan, the Commander-in-Chief of the British Army, for muskets and powder to help fight their Russian masters.

The morning had been sunny and calm. However, the wind increased in the afternoon and by evening the surf made the disembarkation increasingly difficult, if not hazardous. Nevertheless, by the time night fell, the 1st, 2nd and 3rd Divisions of the French infantry and eighteen pieces of their artillery were landed while the British had put ashore all its infantry divisions plus part of its field artillery. The first night was particularly miserable for the soldiers of the British army on shore as no tents had been landed and it rained heavily.

The Allied army stayed in the area for four more days. The local Tartars reported that about 15,000 Russians were encamped at the River Alma, which was about twelve miles away on the road to Sevastopol. A troop of the 11th Hussars was sent to investigate, but was forced to return when pursued by a regiment of Cossacks. Some Cossacks approached quite close to the Allied lines on reconnoitring missions. That night, their watch-fires to the south turned the sky red.

The First Clash – The Affair on the Bulganak

It wasn't until 09.00 hours on the morning of 19 September 1854, that the Allied army started its march south towards the River Alma and Sevastopol. The French, followed by the Turks, marched closer to the coast while the British were further inland and a little to the rear. The combined forces moved in echelon with the French in front. The army's right flank was covered by the fleet ready to fire two miles inland should the Russians attempt any action, but the left flank, where the British marched, was open to a surprise attack.

Russell was very impressed with the sight of the Allies advancing through a countryside he described as being destitute of tree and shrub. He recalled:

> The troops presented a splendid appearance. The effect of these grand masses of soldiery descending the ridges of the hills, rank after rank, with the sun playing over forests of glittering steel, can never be forgotten by those who witnessed it. Onward the torrent of war swept, wave after wave, large stately billows of armed men, while the rumble of the artillery and the tramp of cavalry accompanied their progress.

Alexander William Kinglake, the author of the eight-volume text *The Invasion of the Crimea*, wrote:

> In each of the close-massed columns, which were formed by our four complete divisions, there were more than 5,000 foot-soldiers. The colours were flying; the bands at first were playing … But more warlike than trumpet and drum was the grave quiet which followed the ceasing of the bands. The pain of weariness had begun: Few spoke - all toiled … Yet now, before the first hour of march was over, the men began to fall out from the ranks. Some of these were in the agonies of cholera. Their faces had a dark, choked look; they threw themselves on the ground and writhed, but more often without speaking or a cry. Many more dropped out from mere weakness.

Smoke from burning farmhouses and villages ahead signified that the enemy knew of the advance and were adopting a scorched-earth policy. As the leading units of the army topped a hill in the early afternoon, a wide valley became visible with a distant ridge. On the left of the plain between the hill and the far ridge lay a large village in flames. Along the bottom of the valley ran a small stream called the Bulganak.

Raglan, who was riding in advance of the infantry, observed a group of Cossacks on the brow of the far ridge. He ordered Major General Lord Cardigan, who commanded the Light Cavalry Brigade, to take the 11th Hussars and the 13th Light Dragoon forward and reconnoitre the ground. The four squadrons of the two regiments advanced up the slope towards the ridge and over the first rise. After traversing a slight depression they crested

The isthmus where the British army landed on 14th September 1854 taken by Klembovsky in the early 1900s. The view is roughly to the northwest from the edge of the low plateau where the track shown on the aerial view reaches the beach. A salt water lake is on the right and the Black Sea on the left. The various regiments assembled on the beach would have marched towards the camera and then up on to the plateau behind and to the right. (Walter Havighurst Special Collections, Miami University Libraries, Oxford, Ohio).

The British landing beach today. Vehicular access is only possible by driving along a four mile-long dirt track from the main coastal highway.

The isthmus where the French and Turkish armies landed on 14 September 1854 taken by Klembovsky in the early 1900s. The view is roughly to the south-southeast from the north end of the isthmus with a salt lake on the left and the Black Sea on the right. The land rises to a low plateau behind and to the left of the cameras. (Walter Havighurst Special Collections, Miami University Libraries, Oxford, Ohio).

The French and Turkish landing beach today. The isthmus here is more accessible by road than the British landing beach and stalls selling food and drink line a promenade here making it popular with holidaymakers.

a second low rise, and halted before the final hollow in front of the high ridge. Here they formed a line.

The Cossacks came forward a little, then halted, threw out skirmishers and tried some long-distance and ineffective shooting with their carbines. Cardigan also threw out skirmishers and it appeared he may charge his enemy. However Raglan, who had remained with his staff further back, could see a mass of Russian cavalry on the crest of the ridge that was out of sight of Cardigan. Airey, who was with Raglan, could also make out the glint of sunlight on bayonets, which indicated that there may also be several infantry battalions just behind the ridge. Cardigan and his two regiments were greatly outnumbered and it looked like a trap.

Raglan ordered up the Light and 2nd Divisions together with the 8th Hussars and 17th Lancers of the Light Brigade. Later, the 9-pounder batteries attached to the Light Division were also summonsed. Airey was sent by Raglan to Cardigan to order the withdrawal of 11th Hussars and 13th Light Dragoons. Cardigan's cavalry retired in good order with alternate squadrons stopping every fifty paces to face the enemy.

A Russian field battery then appeared on the ridge with more mounted men and opened fire on the retreating Light Brigade. The first round shot grazed the ground and flew over the cavalry. A second shot bowled into the 11th Hussars knocking over a horse and taking off the rider's leg. More shots followed, but C Troop of the Royal Horse Artillery under Captain John Brandling and then I Troop under Captain George Maude had come forward rapidly with their guns and commenced firing from the rear and left flank of the Light Brigade. They were later joined by E Field Battery led by Captain John Anderson.

The first shell fired by the British artillery exploded over a Russian gun and put it out of action. Another burst in the centre of a Russian column of light infantry brought up to support their cavalry. After fifteen minutes bombardment, the Russian forces retreated back over the ridge in the direction of the River Alma.

After a short break, the army pushed on with the rest of the artillery crossing the stream on the undamaged bridge. In front and to the left of the road just beyond the bridge was a white building that was not on fire, although its outhouses and yard were burning. This was the Imperial Post-House of Bulganak and it was where Raglan chose to spend the night. It was at the Post-House that Raglan met Marshal Armand-Jacques Leroy de St. Arnaud, the Commander-in-Chief of the French forces, in the evening to discuss tactics for the following day when the Allies would reach the Russian defences on the Alma River. St. Arnaud presented a sketch map that showed the French 2nd Division under General Pierre Bosquet plus the Turks turning the Russians on their left flank near the sea with the main attack consisting of the French 1st Division under General François Canrobert and 3rd Division under General Prince Jéröme Napoleon, the cousin of Napoleon III, going in at the centre.

The French envisaged the British army carrying out a flanking movement on the Russian right. Raglan was not convinced that St. Arnaud was correct in his assumption that the main body of the Russian army would be opposite the French lines. Although not challenging St. Arnaud at the time, Raglan had made up his mind to wait until he was sure of enemy's deployments before committing himself to any French plan devised without full knowledge of situation.

The French army were more advanced than the British when night fell and the Allied position formed an oblique line from the coast back to the Bulganak. Raglan was said to

Above: The watercolour by William Simpson entitled *The Cavalry Affair on the Heights of the Bulganak - The First Gun, 19th Sepr. 1854.* It depicts the moment when a troop of Royal Horse Artillery seen at the lower right moved forward to support the 11th Hussars and 13th Light Dragoons seen in the centre. The 8th Hussars are shown in the left foreground with the 17th Lancers just beyond. The Russians are in possession of the ridge in the background and are firing their field guns. (Library of Congress, Washington).

Opposite top: The view today looking south from the Bulganak stream towards the ridge on the skyline with a row of trees that was the high ground held by the Russians. The undulating ground on the upward slope causes rises and depressions. One such rise is visible in the foreground. The tree-lined highway between Eupatoria and Sevastopol is behind the line of trees on the left. In 1854, the post house where Raglan spent the night would have been on the other side of the road on the far left with the village that was on fire just beyond.

Opposite bottom: The view today north from the Russian-held ridge south of the Bulganak stream. The main road from Eupatoria to Sevastopol is behind the trees on the far right with today's village beyond. The Bulganak stream flows from right to left near the bottom of the upward slope seen in the distance. The final hollow before the top of the ridge is in the foreground. The Light Brigade under Cardigan may have advanced as far as the line of trees now seen on the far side of this hollow.

have personally supervised the army's bivouac for the night because of its exposed left flank and the nearness of the Russian army. He also wanted the army to be able to move off in the correct order and without much reorganisation for the battle on the River Alma that was expected the next day.

The main body of the army was positioned south of the Bulganak stream on the high ground to the east of the burning village and on the ridge that the Russians had vacated. Rations of rum and meat were distributed to break a ten hour fast. Casks were broken and, together with nettles and long grass, used to start fires. The 4th Light Dragoons, who were bringing up the rear, caught up with the rest of the army and camped north of the Bulganak with the 4th Division.

The River Alma lay almost five miles to the south of the Bulganak. The enemy's watch-fires could be seen to the south and east that night. Those marking the Russian bivouac positions on the River Alma illuminated the sky. The scene was set for the first major collision of the adversaries since the invasion.

The Battle of the Alma
An Allied Victory on the Road to Sevastopol

The men of the French 2nd Division, who were up and moving at 05.30 hours on the morning of 20 September 1854, reached the plain of the Alma an hour later. Generals Canrobert and Prince Napoleon were astonished that the British had not begun to advance as planned and rode to the British 2nd Division, which was the closest to the French, to investigate. The two generals were told by its commander, Lieutenant General Sir George de Lacy Evans, that he had not been acquainted with the plan of the attack agreed by Raglan and St Arnaud the night before on the Bulganak and had not yet received his orders.

Because of the delay, the French were obliged to stop the advance of General Bosquet's 2nd Division on the right flank. Colonel Louis Trochu, who was on St Arnaud's staff, was sent to Raglan to find out what was happening. At 07.30 hours, he was assured by the British Commander-in-Chief that the orders to march were at that moment being issued to the British army. To allow more time for the British to catch up, the French forces stopped for coffee at 09.00 hours. When the British army eventually began to move, it advanced obliquely to the right so as to gain contact with the French left.

Allied steamers off the coast began to fire on the Russian left flank at 10.20 hours. One or two missiles at very long range reached the Russian positions opposite the French centre. At 11.30 hours, the British right made contact with the French left and the British Light and 2nd Divisions marched on in alignment with the French 3rd and 2nd Divisions. They halted about one and a half miles from the River Alma. From this position, they faced Russian skirmishers on the north bank.

Raglan rode across the front of Prince Napoleon's men to meet St. Arnaud. It was now evident that the British army, instead of facing the extreme right flank of the Russians, was opposite a force superior in numbers to that which faced the French. St. Arnaud realised that his initial battle plan was no longer applicable and asked Raglan if he would attack either the Russian positions directly ahead of his troops or try and turn the Russian right flank. Although a frontal assault on the enemy's main defences was a risky strategy, Raglan decided on this course of action because the Russian cavalry, which greatly outnumbered the Light Cavalry Brigade, controlled the high ground opposite the extreme left of the British line and he considered that a flanking movement may run into serious trouble. The advance was sounded along the lines at 13.00 hours. St. Arnaud rode off to the centre of his front.

At 13.25 hours, eight French steamers and one British steamer, which had moved further south, began to fire on four Russian field guns at a village near the coast. These artillery pieces had been placed at this location to deter a landing behind Russian lines. Fire from the ships was also maintained on Russian troops opposite the French on the high ground south of the River Alma.

At about 13.30 hours, two battalions each of the Belostoksky and Brestsky regiments and then four battalions of the Tarutinsky Chasseurs Regiment plus their guns positioned on a low narrow ledge at the base of the escarpment in front of the French 3rd Division moved back to higher ground. These troops had not yet been fired upon and their withdrawal was without orders. It went unchallenged by the Russian generals. This move was later suggested by Lieutenant General Vasily Kiriakov, who commanded this sector of the battlefield, to have been a tactical retreat and prompted by common sense because the concentrations of Russian troops in these areas made them easy targets. Kiriakov was obviously defending himself after the battle. It was not a good beginning for the Russians.

The Battlefield

In front of the Allies was a wide and flat valley through which the River Alma flowed roughly from east to west to the sea. The ground fell gradually towards the river from the north. Down this slight incline the Allies approached the battlefield. The French and Turks were to the west and the British to the east.

Three settlements lay on the north side of the river. The village of Almatamack was located almost a mile east-southeast of the Alma River estuary. Bourliouk with its fifty houses had its centre about two miles further east. The village of Tarchanlar, which was also on the north bank of the Alma, was a further two miles to the northeast of Bourliouk. A landmark building known as the White Homestead had been built on the river flats on the north side of the Alma half way between Almatamack and Bourliouk. The advancing Allied infantry stretched from the coast to the northeast of Almatamack, past Bourliouk to almost as far as Tarchanlar with the British light cavalry on the left flank; a front of approximately five miles. The French and Turks were to attack from the sea to the western outskirts of Bourliouk with the British attacking east of the western outskirts of Bourliouk.

Gardens and vineyards, which were differentiated by low stone walls, lay on the flood plain to the north of the River Alma. Although deep in places, the Alma was fordable by men and horses along much of its length. The bank at the southern edge of the Alma flood plain was steep in many places, but was no great obstacle.

The land was much hillier on the south side of the river. West of Bourliouk, in the French sector of attack, an escarpment broken by ravines stretched to the sea. In general, this escarpment became steeper and less broken the closer it got to the coast. In places, the slope was so steep that red-coloured cliffs were exposed. The attacking force would need to scale this barrier to engage the Russians positioned on the high ground.

On the high ground opposite a point about half way between Bourliouk and the White Homestead, a Russian semaphore turret known as the Telegraph Station was under construction. This area of the plateau became known as Telegraph Height. The plateau tended to increase in altitude from west to east. Near the coast, the highpoint was about 130 feet above sea level. This rose steadily to 270 feet in the east. The undulating land behind the crest of the plateau fell gradually away to the south.

On the south side of the River Alma opposite Bourliouk, a side valley or hollow recess cut southeast into the plateau. Kinglake referred to this valley as 'the Pass' in his account of the battle. The eastern escarpment of Telegraph Height was to the west of the Pass and

Klembovsky's image taken in the early 1900s that looks south towards the high ground that was left virtually undefended by the Russians at the Battle of the Alma. The estuary of the Alma River is in the middle distance just before the land begins to rise. It was here where General Bouat's troops gained the plateau after fording the river. (Walter Havighurst Special Collections, Miami University Libraries, Oxford, Ohio).

The same beach west of the site of Almatamack is popular with holidaymakers today.

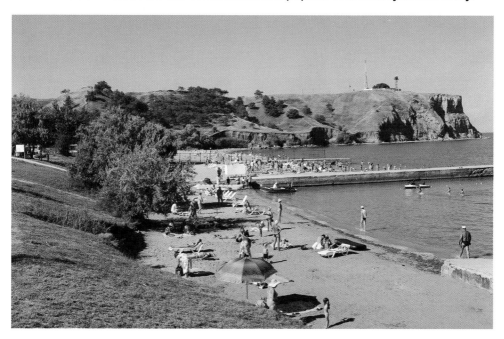

Looking west-northwest along the edge of the escarpment towards the Black Sea. The course of the River Alma follows the trees at the base of the escarpment. General Bosquet's 1st Division attacked between here and the coast.

Looking northwest from the escarpment above the site of Almatamack. A track in this ravine was the route by which guns of the French 1st and 2nd Divisions gained the top of the plateau. General d'Autemarre's brigade in Bosquet's 1st Division attacked in this immediate area.

An engraving from an 1872 watercolour by the French artist Isidore Pils entitled **La Bataille de l'Alma**. The scene depicts French field guns being forded across the River Alma at Almatamack prior to taking the track up the ravine to the top of the escarpment. (Public domain work of art).

Kourganè Hill uplands to the northeast. Ravines dissected the edge of the escarpment at the southern end of the Pass. The Eupatoria-Sevastopol Post Road crossed the River Alma on a wooden bridge to the southeast of the village of Bourliouk. After passing over the bridge and the flood plain, the Post Road ascended a slope up a broad ridge or 'rib', which extended west-northwest from Kourganè Hill. The distance from the bridge to the crest of the ridge was about 500 yards. Kinglake called the route of the Post Road in this locality the Causeway. After crossing the ridge at the end of the Causeway, the Post Road dropped in altitude before crossing the valley floor and ascending a ravine on the far side of the valley onto the plateau.

Kourganè Hill, which lies on the east side of the Pass, was another major geographical feature. The edge of the flat summit lay about 1,300 yards southeast of the road bridge over the River Alma. Between the Alma and the summit, the slope upwards was at first gentle and then became gradually steeper. The high ground to the southeast and east of the summit formed a plateau. This plateau overlooked a large 'hollow recess' formed by the downward slope north and a low ridge before the steep bank down to the Alma flood plain. To the southwest of the plateau, the uplands descended into the floor of the Pass as it curved around to the southeast.

The French Attack
While Bosquet was left waiting on the French right flank for the rest of the Allied army to catch-up, he took the opportunity to reconnoitre the steep-sided escarpment across the

River Alma that lay before him. He found two routes up the slope that gained the heights of the plateau. One was a path near the estuary of the River Alma and the other was a track opposite the village of Almatamack.

Prince Alexander Menshikov was the Russian Commander-in-Chief. He had left the coastal area only sparsely defended because the steep slopes were deemed an impediment to a serious assault and the heights were within range of the guns of the off-shore Allied fleet, which would endanger any concentration of his troops deployed in defence. Instead, he had concentrated most of his army further to the east on the plateau opposite the French and also on and around Kourgané Hill east of the Pass opposite the British. Menshikov's defensive preparations in the way of earthworks had been minimal. He was so confident of victory at the Alma that Russian ladies from Sevastopol had been allowed as spectators to view the much anticipated defeat of the Allies.

The two brigades of the French 2nd Division under Bosquet were the first to move forward on the virtually undefended left flank of the Russians. General Bouat's brigade on the right with support from the Turks waded in waist deep water in single file along a sand bar that crossed the river estuary and scrambled unopposed up the escarpment on to the plateau. However, the route was too steep for the brigade's artillery to follow.

To the east, the brigade of General d'Autemarre, preceded by skirmishers, advanced on the village of Almatamack and the vineyards on either side. The time was just before 14.00 hours. By 14.10 hours, d'Autemarre's men were fording the River Alma. Soon afterwards, troops of the 3rd Zouave Regiment scrambled to the top of the escarpment and regrouped.

A track in a ravine that dissected the slope in d'Autemarre's sector was found suitable for the movement of artillery. The French force assembling on the plateau moved forward to secure the immediate area and the guns of d'Autemarre and then Bouat were brought forward across the river and up the escarpment. There was little opposition and a foothold had been gained on the vulnerable Russian left flank.

A battalion of the Minsky Regiment and half a Russian battery were stationed in the coastal village of Ulukul Akles about a mile away to the west-southwest, but the Russian troops did not show themselves. However, the four pieces of Russian artillery were moved to Ulukul Tiouets, the next village to the east of Ulukul Akles, and opened fire on the French at long range. When Kiriakov heard the guns, he posted two battalions of the Moskovsky Regiment further east on the upper and lower slopes of the escarpment above the White Homestead and lined up eight pieces of artillery to sweep the plateau should the French advance from the west. The guns that had been with the infantry, which had retreated back onto the plateau before the battle started, were relocated near the Telegraph Station.

Menshikov was taken by surprise and may even have been shocked by the French advancing so quickly on to the plateau to flank his army. He departed his position on Kourganè Hill opposite the British front to reconnoitre his extreme left flank. It was here that he was fired upon by Allied ships and four members of his entourage were struck down.

Menshikov attempted to counter the French, who were in the process of establishing themselves on the plateau, by relocating two light batteries each of eight guns to silence their artillery and also to cover the advance of four battalions of the Moskovsky Regiment, including the two that Kiriakov had deployed above the White Homestead, and three battalions of the Minsky Regiment. All in all, he now had a total of thirty-six guns, which

View east along the face of the escarpment towards where General Canrobert's troops advanced onto the plateau.

opened a barrage on the twelve French guns. However, accurate fire from the Minié rifles of French sharpshooters took their toll on the Russian gunners. No French guns were disabled and they were even advanced to a more commanding location. Menshikov then ordered the Moskovsky and Minsky battalions, which were under his personal command, back to the centre of the plateau as they could not advance against the French guns without suffering severe losses. The result was that Bosquet's men were left to consolidate their position on the western end of the plateau.

Earlier, seeing that Bosquet's forces would make it to the top of the escarpment, St. Arnaud ordered the 1st Division under Canrobert in the centre and 3rd Division under Prince Napoleon on the French left flank to advance. This force consisted of a total of 15,000 men. The Russian artillery now relocated near the Telegraph Station began to fire at the new French threat over the heads of their own defending infantry regiments. In response, the French artillery was brought forward to the edge of the vineyards and directed fire on the Belostoksky and Brestsky battalions positioned on the upper slopes of the escarpment. The French skirmishers crossed the River Alma into an area of broken ground at the foot of the incline.

Canrobert's skirmishers pushing forward in the vicinity of the White Homestead crossed the river and scaled the escarpment virtually unopposed. However, his division did not

Looking south-southwest across the Alma flood plain at the escarpment west of Bourliouk that was attacked by the French 3rd Division under General Prince Napoleon.

A 1856 painting of the Battle of the Alma by the French artist Horace Vernet. General Prince Napoleon is depicted issuing orders in the centre right foreground while 'thankful' British soldiers exit the scene of battle on the left. The River Alma runs through trees at the base of the escarpment that leads up to Telegraph Height. In the left middle distance, French troops of the 3rd Division advance up the escarpment towards the Russians. In the centre middle distance, General Canrobert's 1st Division is shown as advancing upwards just below the top of a rounded spur. The White Homestead is visible on the flood plain of the Alma on the far right with Almatamack and the Black Sea beyond. (Public domain work of art).

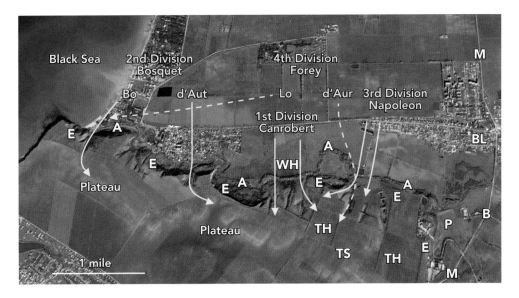

An aerial view of the French sector of the Alma battlefield with arrows showing the approximate initial movements of French infantry brigades on today's landscape. North is at the top of the image. Key; A = course of the River Alma; B = bridge over the River Alma; BL = Bourliouk; Bo = General Bouat's attack; d'Aur = General d'Aurelle's attack; d'Aut = General d'Autemarre's attack; E = slope of the escarpment attacked by the French; Lo = General de Lourmel's movement in support of Bouat's brigade; M = main highway from Eupatoria to Sevastopol; P = the valley known as the Pass; TH = Telegraph Height; TS = Telegraph Station under construction; WH = White Homestead. (Adapted from Google Earth™ image).

advance over the edge of the plateau because of fire from the Moskovsky Regiment and artillery. Instead the attacking French regiments, which included the 1st Zouaves and the 7th de Ligne, took shelter on the upper and lower slopes or under the lip of the escarpment. The Russian artillery controlled the top of the plateau and swept it with fire that kept French heads down. Canrobert was also unwilling to advance until he had artillery. Because there was no suitable route for his guns to reach the top of the plateau and support his regiments in this sector, Canrobert had to send them via the only known route up the escarpment suitable for artillery at Almatamack. It would take some time for these guns to become available.

The French Hesitate

For an hour and a half, the Allies had been under fire without taking on any of the enemy's battalions at close hand. While most of Canrobert's forces had crossed the river and reached the escarpment slopes, the 9,000 men under Prince Napoleon hung back on the flood plain with many of them still on the north bank of the Alma. These troops, together with Canrobert's men on the lower slopes of the escarpment, had no shelter and were exposed to plunging fire from Russian guns on Telegraph Height. They began to feel discouraged.

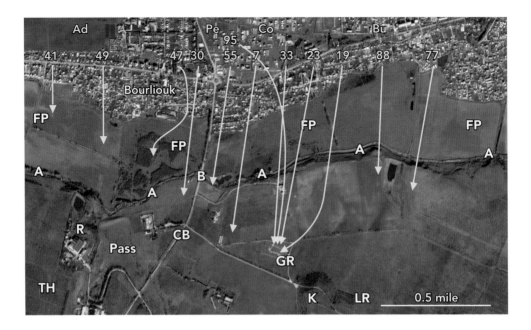

An aerial view of the British sector of the Alma battlefield with arrows showing the approximate movements of the British infantry regiments during the first phase of the battle on today's landscape. North is to the top of the image. Regiments are identified by their numbers. Key: A = course of the River Alma; Ad = Brigadier General Adams' brigade; B = bridge over the River Alma; Bu = Brigadier General Buller's brigade; Co = Major General Codrington's brigade; CB = Causeway Batteries; FP = flood plain of the River Alma; GR = Great Redoubt; K = Kourganè Hill; LR = approximate position of the Lesser Redoubt; Pe = Brigadier General Pennefather's brigade; R = approximate position of Lord Raglan's viewpoint or knoll; TH = Telegraph Height. (Adapted from Google Earth™ image).

Bosquet, who was with d'Autemarre's brigade on the plateau further to the west, was isolated. He had guns, but only one infantry brigade. All he could do was to hold his ground at this stage. Bouat's men were even further to the west on the coast where they could not easily participate in the battle. Like Canrobert, Bouat had no artillery, which limited his capabilities. All along the French front, the battle was languishing and the initiative was being lost. If the Russians made a determined push, defeat was a possibility.

Raglan, who had been delaying the attack in the British sector until the plateau had been secured in accordance with the battle plan, was asked by the French to begin his attack immediately to provide relief. Raglan, whose troops had been waiting under fire, obliged.

The Zouave regiments were battle experienced and the elite of the French infantry. The French 1st, 2nd and 3rd Divisions each had its own Zouave regiment to act as a spearhead. The 3rd Zouaves of d'Autemarre's brigade in the 2nd Infantry Division had been the first to scale the escarpment opposite Almatamack. Now, the frustrated 2,000 men of the 2nd Zouave Regiment in Prince Napoleon's 3rd Division, stormed obliquely up the escarpment to finish next to the 1st Zouave Regiment in Canrobert's 1st Division. Although Canrobert's guns had still not arrived, his men cautiously began to edge onto the top of the plateau.

The French Call on their Reserves

The situation was serious enough for St Arnaud to call up his reserves, and the two brigades led by generals de Lourmel and d'Aurelle in General Élie Forey's 4th Division were committed to battle. De Lourmel's brigade, with Forey in overall command, marched to the coast in support of Bouat where, far from the main action, it achieved little. The brigade led by d'Aurelle pushed through the bulk of Prince Napoleon's men and up a small ravine that led to the top of the escarpment. However, the ravine became crowded with troops unable to fight effectively. Instead, of moving forward, they hung back under the lip of the escarpment. At this stage, Kiriakov commanded two batteries, four battalions of Tarutinsky Chasseurs and two battalions each of the Belostoksky and Brestsky. On the upper slopes and along the edge of the escarpment, the latter two regiments were exposed to the French artillery and were steadily being reduced in number. Nevertheless, firing over the heads of the Tarutinsky on the plateau, Kiriakov's guns still controlled the ground over which the French needed to advance in order to attack his main Russian position at the Telegraph Station.

The seven battalions from the Moskovsky and Minsky regiments under the personal control of Menshikov had now been joined by the extra battalion of the Moskovsky Regiment from near the coast making eight battalions in total. These were positioned to the right rear of the Telegraph Station and were being prepared for an onslaught on Canrobert's 1st Division. However, Menshikov then chose to ride off because of impending threats in the British sector, leaving his regiments behind for Kiriakov to command. Kiriakov marched the men forward in two columns; each comprised of four battalions. This move threatened the centre right of Canrobert's Division, which was still without its guns. French soldiers fell back over the edge of the escarpment as the Russians advanced towards them.

Canrobert's artillery, which had recently arrived on the plateau via the track from Almatamack, was at this moment moving east along the heights with some of guns of Bosquet's Division. The enemy battalions were spotted by the advancing French artillerymen in slightly lower ground that lay ahead and they moved their guns into position on the Russian left flank. 'Shot and shell' were soon 'inflicting a dreadful slaughter' within the dense ranks of the men in the Russian columns.

Kiriakov ordered his infantry to retreat and his now decimated columns retired in good order back to the right rear of the Telegraph Station without having fired a shot. Although this was the critical moment on the French front, the Russians were not immediately followed by Canrobert's infantry, who were cautiously remerging over the edge of the escarpment on to the plateau.

Kiriakov was by now conscious that the battle was not going well for the Russians in the British sector. Because of this and the flanking fire coming from the encroaching French artillery, he decided to move his men back out of range. However, Kiriakov's account of the battle has been questioned because he was trying to save his reputation. The French version is that its Zouave regiments and the 39th de Ligne from d'Aurelle's brigade, rushed forward and fought fiercely with Kirakov's battalions in the vicinity of the Telegraph Station, which forced the Russians to withdraw The French suffered casualties in this action. Although Kinglake put this down to fire from Russian soldiers remaining at the site and also the retiring Russian artillery, other authors, such as Colonel Julian Jocelyn (*History of the Royal Artillery [Crimean Period]*), give more credence to the French version of events.

Kinglake calculated that, in the French sector, the French with 37,000 men and sixty-

Today's view south towards the twin bridges that now carry the Eupatoria-Sevastopol Highway over the River Alma. The wooden bridge of 1854 crossed the river at approximately the same location. The Russian guns in the Causeway Batteries were situated on the ridge visible on the skyline just to the left of centre

The view north to the twin bridges that carry the Eupatoria-Sevastopol Highway over the River Alma today from the ridge where Russian guns in the Causeway Batteries controlled the river crossing during the first phase of the Battle of the Alma. The village of Bourliouk was located in the left background.

eight guns had faced the Russians with 13,000 men and thirty-six guns. This was in contrast to the British sector, where the British with 25,400 men and sixty guns had faced the Russians with 26,000 men and eighty-six guns. This equated to the French facing one-third of the Russian army at the Alma while the British faced two-thirds.

The Russian Defensive Positions in the British Sector
British soldiers looking south down the gentle incline towards the River Alma could see the high ground at the north-eastern edge of Telegraph Height to the west, the low land at the entrance to the Pass and the steadily rising land that led to the summit of the Kourganè Hill at centre and a 'hollow recess' or basin to the left of the Kourganè Hill with a high plateau beyond to the east.

The Great Redoubt, which lay on the steepening upward incline towards Kourganè Hill, was the main defence position at the centre of the Russian line in the British sector. It consisted of an earth breastwork about three feet high and 200 yards long behind which were positioned twelve guns. These guns in the main controlled the ground on both sides of the river east of the river bridge. The low parapet was curved at both ends like the bottom of a hockey stick so that some guns could project enfilading fire on any troops attempting to flank the position. Indeed, artillery located on the left of the redoubt could throw missiles on either side of the river bridge. The only part of the approach to the guns out of their direct line of fire was the ground under the steep south bank of the food plain of the River Alma. Shallow trenches had been made between each gun in the Great Redoubt so that sharpshooters could be placed as cover for the artillery. On either side of the position ran a protective ditch that could accommodate infantry. The Great Redoubt was formidable and the key to the Russian defence in the British sector.

Seven hundred yards to the west of the Great Redoubt, Menshikov placed light batteries of the 16th Artillery Brigade on a ridge either side the Post Road. These sixteen guns controlled the flood plain either side of the bridge and became known as the Causeway Batteries. The village of Bouliouk to the northwest was also in their line of fire. Like the Great Redoubt, this defensive position was also a significant barrier to any forward movement in this sector.

To the east of the Great Redoubt, facing northeast on the northeast side of the Kourganè Hill, stood the Lesser Redoubt. This may have had a low earth parapet similar to the Great Redoubt and is suspected to have originally contained eight guns, though only five were in action later in the battle. The guns positioned here controlled the rising land in the hollow recess before the plateau to the east of Kourganè Hill on the right flank of the Russian line.

The British Wait for the Right Moment to Advance
From 13.30 hours onwards, the advancing British had begun to encounter poles with pieces of canvas tied to them. These were range markers set in place by the Russians so that the gunners would have an appreciation of the distance between themselves and their target. This is when the British front line received the first round shot from the Russians. When the fire became brisk, the leading companies were halted and told to lie down in the walled-vineyards north of the river.

The initial plan was for the 2nd Division, commanded by Lieutenant General Sir George De Lacy Evans, to form up on the west of the Light Division in the first line of attack. However, as a result of the Light Division not taking enough ground to its left, the boundary between its right flank and the left flank of the 2nd Division overlapped to such an extent that they became entangled and jammed together at the convergence. The second or support line of attack was to have had the 1st Division, under Lieutenant General HRH Prince George Charles, Duke of Cambridge, aligned with the 3rd Division. However, when the 1st Division advanced into position with the Guard regiments to the west and the Highland regiments to the east, its line extended from behind the 2nd Division to further east than the Light Division. Because practically the entire support line was now occupied by the 1st Division, Raglan ordered Lieutenant General Sir Richard England to bring up the 3rd Division behind the right flank of the 1st Division and act in support of the Guards. The 4th Division under Lieutenant General Sir George Cathcart, which was still incomplete because it had been the last to move from the Bulganak, was held in reserve behind the left flank. The Light Brigade was to the east of the 4th Division and protected the left flank of the army.

While the infantry waited at a range known by the Russian artillery, the British batteries fired back at the Russians. However, the fire was ineffective given the long range and was stopped until the guns had an opportunity to advance closer. With most of the infantry lying down, the officers on horseback wearing plumed hats were conspicuous. Raglan and his entourage became a target at this stage. Having seemingly little luck striking him down with round shot, the Russians changed to shells, which burst in small white clouds sending showers of shrapnel down on those below. However, Raglan was unharmed.

Russian skirmishers in Bourliouk set fire to the village, which was soon engulfed in flames. A faint breeze from the sea blew the smoke towards the river bridge. For hours afterwards, the thick cloud hung over the immediate area, but did not affect the rest of the battlefield. However, for hundreds of yards to the east and west directly ahead of the 2nd Division, the front was ablaze and impenetrable. To the north of the village, De Lacy Evans had had to position Major General John Pennefather's brigade before Brigadier General Henry Adams's brigade because of the lack of space, but there was still a substantial overlap with the Light Division on the left.

The Advance to the River Alma

At about 15.00 hours, Raglan ordered the 2nd and Light Divisions forward when the French, who were in difficulties, sought British help in distracting the Russians. British forces had by then been waiting patiently for an hour and a half under fire so were probably eager to move. The front line arose in two ranks and advanced towards the river. Russian round shot at extreme range was described as 'bounding along the ground like cricket balls'. When the men saw them coming, they opened their ranks and the balls went hissing past. Some of the rolling round shot was chased by a furiously barking greyhound belonging to a captain in the 2nd Battalion of the Rifle Brigade.

The British 2nd Division to the immediate left of the French army approached the blazing village of Bourliouk with Pennefather's brigade to the fore and Adams's behind. De Lacy Evans was forced to divide his troops so that the 47th (Lancashire) Regiment, the 55th (Westmorland) Regiment, the 30th (Cambridgeshire) Regiment and the 95th (Derbyshire) Regiment went to the left of the village under the command of Pennefather while the 41st (Welsh) Regiment and the 49th (Hertfordshire) Regiment went to the right under the command of Adams. The regiments on the left were so crammed that the 95th advanced behind the 55th. The 47th had to squeeze to the right after passing Bouliouk.

The painting by artist Louis Johns entitled _Fording the Alma, September 1854_. The picture depicts skirmishers of the 2nd Battalion of the Rifle Brigade leading the Light Division across the River Alma. (Courtesy of the Green Jackets (Rifles) Museum, Winchester, Hampshire).

Pennefather's regiments, moving roughly parallel to the Post Road and towards the river bridge, faced the sixteen guns on the ridge south of the river plus the flanking fire from the left shoulder of the Great Redoubt. In reply, Captain Edwin Wodehouse with H Field Battery and Captain Anderson with E Battery formed to the east of Captain Charles Franklin with B Battery in Pennefather's sector. The latter battery was positioned west of the Post Road behind Bourliouk. A total of eighteen British guns had come forward and were firing on the Russians over the heads of Pennefather's men.

At the entrance to the Pass opposite the 2nd Division, Menshikov had placed four battalions of the Borodinsky Chasseur Regiment plus one battalion of Riflemen. Three of the five battalions in this force were involved in skirmishing in the riverside vineyards and the other two stood massed in column. In addition, a battalion of sappers and miners were positioned near the bridge.

The ground over which Pennefather's brigade advanced was perilous. Progress was slow and piecemeal with shelter being taken behind walls and enclosures in between dashes forward when the opportunity allowed. The wooden bridge was on fire and the river could not be crossed under the fierce bombardment. One quarter of the brigade's strength, men either killed or wounded, was lost in the conflict. Adams's brigade further west on the far side of Bourliouk was not under such a devastating fire, but was extremely disorganised and stalled at the River Alma. Kinglake recalled the scene:

> At times, when the balls were falling thickly, the men would shelter themselves as well as they could behind what little cover as the ground afforded; and when there

Looking west down the now deeply-channelled course of the River Alma showing the flood plain to the north and its steep bank to the south. This bank, which was a few yards from the river in 1854, provided shelter from Russian fire for advancing British troops. During the first phase of the battle, the 33rd Regiment would have crossed from right to left in the foreground with the 7th Regiment crossing further downstream. During the second phase, the Scots Fusilier Guards would have been in the immediate foreground with the Grenadier Guards further away. The escarpment attacked by General Prince Napoleon's 3rd division is on the skyline to the right of centre. The Telegraph Height is on the skyline left of centre. The white buildings below the plateau-like summit of Telegraph Height form a winery complex on the spur where Raglan watched much of the battle from behind Russian lines.

Looking approximately east up the now deeply-channelled course of the River Alma showing the flood plain on the left and steep bank to the right. The 19th Regiment would have crossed from left to right in the foreground with the 88th Regiment crossing further upstream during the first phase of the battle. During the second phase, the Coldstream Guards would have crossed this area with the 42nd Regiment further along. In 1854, many gardens and vineyards protected by stone walls lay on the flood plain. Advancing British troops quenched their thirsts by helping themselves to grapes.

came a lull, they would spring forward and find shelter more in advance. There were some buildings that afforded good cover against grape and musketry; and some men who had gained this shelter by a swift rush across the open ground under very heavy fire, were slow to move out again into a storm of grape, canister and musket balls. At a later stage, the enemy shattered the walls of these buildings with round-shot, and some of our men were suffocated by the ruins; but those who died that poor death were men hanging back.

The Light Division under Lieutenant General Sir George Brown, which was to the east and overlapping the left wing of the 2nd Division, also advanced to walled-vineyards and gardens on the north side of the river. Major General William Codrington led the brigade on the right and Brigadier General Sir George Buller the brigade on the left. The Russians were not making a determined attempt to hold the ground on the right bank in this locality and the way was clear to the river. However, formation was lost as there were several cottages and farm buildings in the vineyards before the river that broke the line. Where the 2nd and Light Divisions overlapped, Codrington's 7th Regiment pushed through Pennefather's 95th Regiment. The 95th then veered to its left behind the 7th Fusiliers and 33rd (Duke of Wellington's) Regiment, which was next in line to the east. The regiment then moved forward to the rear of the 23rd (Royal Welch Fusiliers) Regiment on the left of Codrington's brigade.

The attack was supported by Brandling's C Troop, who fired at the Great Redoubt until advancing troops masked its fire. Moving more to the left, fire was continued until the infantry again blocked the target. C Troop then retired to replace ammunition.

Success at the Great Redoubt

The 2nd Battalion of the Rifle Brigade acting as skirmishers were in advance of the Light Division. However, when the battalion had approached the burning village of Bourliouk, it had swung to the left. While Lieutenant Colonel Arthur Lawrence's wing on the right veered in front of the 19th (1st Yorkshire North Riding) Regiment in Buller's brigade, Major William Norcott's wing on the left was even further to the east. Both wings pushed across the flood plain and forded the river driving Russian skirmishers before them. Unfortunately, because of the eastward swing of the Rifle Brigade, the skirmishers ahead of Codrington's brigade to the west were left unmolested.

On reaching the river, the infantry quickly waded across with Russian skirmishers in front of Codrington's brigade firing into the mass of British troops gathering on the south side of the river from the high bank beyond. In Buller's sector, the Russian skirmishers were not as effective because this was where the Rifle Brigade had pushed them back. Therefore, Buller, unlike Codrington, was able to reform his regiments once over the river. Buller ordered the 77th (East Middlesex) and the 88th (Connaught Rangers) regiments to advance to the steep bank at the edge of the flood plain where they were sheltered from enemy fire. He considered his duty was to protect the left flank of the British army from the Russian cavalry, which was positioned to the east of the plateau of Kourganè Hill to their southeast. However, the 19th Regiment on the right flank of the brigade, like the 95th from the 2nd Division, associated itself with Codrington's brigade for the attack on the Great Redoubt.

Opposite the Light Division, and arranged in the vicinity of Kourganè, Menshikov had deployed sixteen battalions of Russian infantry, two battalions of sailors, who acted as

Kourganè Hill on the left skyline with the site of the Great Redoubt below and to the right of the white monument seen on the far right. The view looks south-southwest from the north bank of the Alma floodplain. During the first phase of the battle, Buller's brigade would have advanced down the slope in the foreground and up the far bank where the 88th and 77th Regiments went on the defensive. The 19th Regiment on the brigade's right joined in the attack on the Great Redoubt. During the second phase, the Highland regiments advanced over the same ground and marched through the ranks of 88th and 77th Regiments, who were still on the defensive.

Kourganè Hill on the left skyline with the site of the Great Redoubt between the two white monuments on the far right. The 33rd, 95th and 23rd Regiments would have attacked the Great Redoubt in this area during the first phase of the battle. In the second phase, the Scots Fusilier Guards would have advanced up the same slope only to be held in check by retreating troops of the Light Division and then the Vladimirsky Regiment after it retook the Great Redoubt. The view is to the southeast from south of the River Alma.

skirmishers, and four batteries of field artillery. The infantry consisted of four battalions each of Kazansky and Uglitsky Chasseur Regiments and four each of the Vladimirsky and Suzdalsky Regiments. The Kazansky and Vladimirsky were positioned east of the Post Road supporting the Great Redoubt and the Suzdalsky were on the slopes of the Kourganè Hill plateau to the east of the Lesser Redoubt. The Uglitsky Chasseurs were held in reserve on the high ground of the Kourganè Hill plateau.

In addition to this great infantry force, there were an extra four battalions of the Volynsky Regiment positioned across the line of the Post Road someway behind the ridge where the Causeway Batteries were located. This was part of Menshikov's 'Great Reserve' but these troops were so close to the front line that they could really be called support troops.

Of the four field batteries, one was at the Lesser Redoubt, another on the high ground southeast of the Great Redoubt, while the remaining two were held in reserve. In addition to the infantry, the Russian cavalry of about 3,000 men with three batteries of horse artillery were positioned in a curve from the right front to the centre rear.

Codrington, who by default now commanded a body of men comprised of five regiments, perceived that to stay cowered for long on the south bank under fire from Russian skirmishers above would soon decimate his men. However, it was 500 yards of open country at the shortest between the relatively safety of the bank and the parapet of the Great Redoubt. On his own initiative, he ordered an attack without waiting to dress the lines. Because of the convolutions of the meandering river and a loss of formation, which could not be corrected because of skirmishers, the troops that emerged onto the smooth gentle upward slope before the Great Redoubt resembled 'an armed and warlike crowd' rather than an organised force.

In response, two columns of the Kazansky Chasseurs, each containing 1,500 men, moved down the slope from either side of the Great Redoubt. The column to the right (east) of the Great Redoubt marched towards the 23rd and the 95th. Skirmishers in Norcott's wing of the 2nd Battalion of Rifle Brigade were now moving southwest into this area and fired at the right flank of the Russian columns, but their endeavours were not enough. It was then left to those in the 23rd and 95th, who by now were mixed together, to pour accurate fire into the tightly-packed Russians, who retreated under the pressure. The descending Russian column to the left (west) of the Great Redoubt was made of sterner stuff and began an obstinate fight with the Lieutenant Colonel Lacy Yea's 7th Fusiliers that was to last until almost the end of the battle. In the centre, the men of the 33rd Regiment moved uphill in determined clusters. The Russian skirmishers had either fallen back or had moved out of the way, which allowed the artillery at the Great Redoubt to fire round shot and canister at the British advancing from the centre and right. The missiles cut through ranks of soldiers in their tight knots causing an immense slaughter

Kinglake recalled:

> First one gun, then another, then more. From east to west the parapet grew white, and henceforth it lay so enfolded in its bank of silvery smoke that no gun could any longer be seen by our men, except at the moment when it was pouring its blaze through the cloud. On what one may call a glacis, at three hundred yards from the mouth of the guns, the lightning, the thunder and the bolt are not far apart. Death loves a crowd; and in some places our soldiery were pressing so close together that when round-shot cut its way into the midst of them, it dealt a sure havoc.

View approximately north-northwest over the site of the Great Redoubt showing its position on a slope and the flat flood plain of the Alma in the middle distance. The River Alma, its course marked by large trees, runs unseen from right to left along the southern edge of the flood plain. The village of Bourliouk was where the buildings are visible beyond the flood plain on the left. The course of the tree-lined Eupatoria-Sevastopol Highway can be seen crossing the flood plain below Bourliouk. During the first phase of the battle, the 55th Regiment would have advanced across the flood plain near the highway with the 7th Regiment further east. During the second phase, the Grenadier Guards crossed the same area.

As well as those advancing up the slope, others, who had just emerged over the flood plain bank, were also struck down. However the assailing regiments all rapidly converged on the Great Redoubt. The Russian guns belched smoke and cut swathes through the British moving ever nearer. In the 95th, almost every ensign in succession, several other officers and five sergeants fell under the Colours. Under this galling fire, the British continued to press home the attack.

The horse carrying Lawrence of the 2nd Battalion of the Rifle Brigade was felled by grape shot and he rolled under the parapet before the artillery. The Russians, being by then very hard pressed, limbered up the guns in the Great Redoubt to eight- and ten-horse teams. When the first soldiers reached the redoubt, the embrasures were virtually empty. Lieutenant Henry Anstruther carrying the colours of the 23rd ran forward and stuck the butt end in the parapet. At that moment, he was shot dead and the colours collapsed on him. Another immediately raised the flag and claimed the redoubt for the 23rd. The 95th reached their objective at the same time. Private James Keenan also planted his regiment's

View west from the lower slopes of Kourganè Hill showing the ground to the south of the Great Redoubt. The hollow below is where the Vladimirsky Regiment stood waiting unseen before advancing to drive the Light Division out of the Great Redoubt. The low mound on the right just beyond the hollow was where the Russian's Causeway Batteries were located. The road on the far right changes direction here as it descends towards the Eupatoria-Sevastopol Highway. The plateau of Telegraph Height is on the left skyline. Winery buildings now stand on the spur where Raglan watched the battle and Turner's guns enfiladed the Causeway Batteries. Raglan's position is believed to have been just to the right of the two long buildings. The Alma flood plain is in the middle distance on the far right.

colour in the earthworks. Simultaneously, the right flank of the redoubt was also invaded by skirmishers of Norcott's wing of 2nd Battalion of the Rifle Brigade, who had moved across the battlefield from the east.

Only one 24-pounder howitzer remained abandoned in the Great Redoubt and this was seized by Captain Alfred Heyland of the 95th. However, Captain Edward Bell of the 23rd overtook a bronze 16-pounder gun being slowly dragged off by only a pair of black horses. Bell pointed his pistol at the head of the driver, who dismounted and fled. The two guns were subsequently absorbed into E Battery. The artillery piece captured by Bell can be seen today at the 23rd Regiment's Museum in Caernarfon Castle in North Wales.

About 2,000 British soldiers of five regiments now occupied the redoubt with two captured pieces of artillery. Codrington, who wanted the redoubt held, showed his men how to lie down under cover of the north side of the parapet and rest their rifles on the top. They now had to hold on and wait for support. However, this was late in coming and the delay was to have serious consequences.

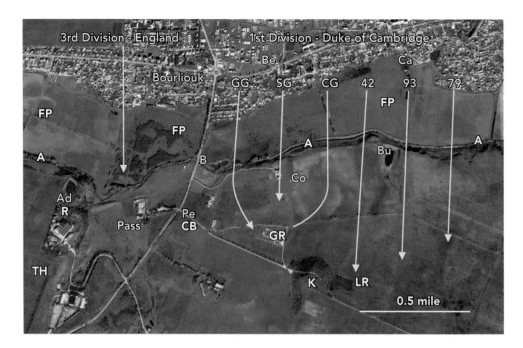

An aerial view of the British sector of the Alma battlefield showing the approximate movements and positions of the British infantry during the second phase of the battle on today's landscape. North is to the top of the image. Regiments are identified by their numbers. Key: A = today's channelled course of the River Alma; Ad = Brigadier General Adams's brigade; B = wooden bridge over the River Alma; Be = Major General H. Bentinck's Guards Brigade; Bu = Brigadier General Buller's brigade: Ca = Major General Sir C. Campbell's Highland Brigade; CG = Coldstream Guards; Co = Major General Codrington's brigade; CB = Causeway Batteries – on a ridge either side of the main road; FP = flood plain of the River Alma; GG = Grenadier Guards; GR = Great Redoubt; K = Kourganè Hill; LR = approximate position of the Lesser Redoubt; Pe = Brigadier General Pennefather's brigade; R = approximate position of Raglan's viewpoint or knoll; SG = Scots Fusilier Guards; TH = Telegraph Height. (Adapted from Google Earth™ image).

The Loss of the Great Redoubt

Raglan had ordered the Duke of Cambridge and the 1st Division to march in support of the Light Division, but on reaching the walled enclosures on the north side of the river, the Duke felt he needed a new instruction before he advanced his men any further. Meanwhile, the Light Division had hurried forward to the river and across to the opposite bank as has been described. When the 1st Division moved again it came under fire from the guns of the Great Redoubt and the Causeway Batteries. The advance of the 1st Division was again stopped for a while for no apparent reason just as the final push to the Great Redoubt by Codrington's men had begun. After hesitating, the Duke of Cambridge eventually ordered his troops forward and they began to negotiate the vineyards. In the 1st Division's Brigade of Guards on the right under Brigadier General Henry Bentinck, the Coldstream Guards Regiment adopted open column of sections on crossing the river and then re-adopted the line of two ranks formation. In contrast, the Grenadier Guards advanced across in a line, which meant some had to wade through shallow water while others had to negotiate deep water.

All regiments reformed under the cover of the high flood plain bank and then moved forward. Because more natural obstacles were encountered by troops the further east they were deployed and the more time needed to overcome these obstacles, the regiments of the 1st Division's Highland Brigade under Major General Sir Colin Campbell found themselves in echelon, with those on the right more advanced than those on the left. The 42nd (Royal Highland) Regiment was the most advanced with the 93rd (Sutherland Highlanders) Regiment to its east further back and the 79th (Cameron Highlanders) Regiment even further to the east the furthest back. While the Highland Brigade faced the ground before and to the east of Kourganè Hill, the Guards Brigade faced the Great Redoubt. The front of the 1st Division stretched for a mile and a half, but was only two ranks deep.

During the period when the Duke of Cambridge had been hesitating, Codrington's men had been waiting for more troops to arrive to help them hold and secure the Great Redoubt so costly captured in terms of human life. Confusion as to how the battle would develop prevented Buller's two remaining regiments from coming to Codrington's aid. Buller, who was with the 77th, did order an advance, but the commanding officer of the 88th on the extreme left of the British line refused to comply because he felt seriously threatened by the Russian infantry and cavalry on his front. His reply was so emphatic that Buller cancelled his order. Because he was short-sighted, Buller may have thought that this officer could judge the situation better than he could.

Time eventually ran out for the relief troops to arrive to help Codrington and his men hold the Great Redoubt. Firstly the Uglitsky Chasseur battalions on the side of Kourganè Hill above and to the left rear surged forward and then inexplicably stopped. The columns of the Vladimirsky Regiment, which consisted of 3,000 men, were then advanced from out of the depression in the landscape behind the Great Redoubt. Just as they were appearing over the crest of the hollow and into view of Codrington's men, disaster struck the defenders of the Great Redoubt. Someone in the British lines shouted that the Russians coming towards them were French and this was followed by a general call to cease fire. The Vladimirsky troops paused, and turned their attention to the 33rd, who with colours flying, were just then firing at some other target. Another mistake was made by the British when the bugler with the 19th was ordered to sound 'retire'. Officers stood to debate this command, as it was unbelievable. Some were shot down where they stood. The bugle call sounded again and the retreat began in earnest as men fell back from the redoubt's parapet. Retreating soldiers, mainly those of the 23rd and 95th, merged into an 'unwieldy crowd'.

Just as this was happening, the Guards regiments rose over the flood plain bank and began the advance up the slope on the south side of the river. The men retreating from the Great Redoubt headed directly downhill for the regiment of the Scots Fusilier Guards. They broke through the left hand side of the line of the regiment, bowling one soldier over and destroying their formation. The Scots Fusiliers tried to steady itself in the confusion, but faced with heavy fire from the Vladimrisky, it was forced back down the slope. The Grenadier Guards on the right faced fewer groups of men retiring from the Great Redoubt. They opened ranks to let them through and then closed ranks 'soon recovering their perfect array'. These troops continued the advance up the slope as did the Coldstream Guards to the right of the Scots Fusilier Guards.

Looking approximately north-northeast from the slopes of the Kourganè plateau over the area where the Highland Brigade advanced during the second phase of the battle. The settlement in the middle distance is on the northern bank of the Alma flood plain about 1½ miles to the east-northeast of the site of Bourliouk. The river lies unseen in its channel close to the steep southern bank just beyond the dam on the left and low ridge rising on the right. The hollow now deepened to hold the waters in the dam may be where the 42nd was attacked with the 93rd coming to its aid over the ridge to the right. The 79th would have in turn aided the 93rd by appearing over the same low ridge further to the right. After defeating the Russians, the brigade would have advanced up the slope in the foreground.

The Vladimirsky seemed content just to hold the Great Redoubt and this resulted in a missed opportunity to inflict serious damage on the disorganised British line. The Russians were without the leadership of Menshikov, who had been positioned on Kourganè Hill, but had ridden off to the west to lead those facing the French. The remaining senior officers, including General Prince Peter Gorchakov who was now in command, were cautious. No attack was ordered. This was a tactical error that may have lost the Russians the battle in the British sector.

Raglan Rides Behind Enemy Lines

Raglan was missing from the scene. After he had given the initial order to advance, he had ridden with his staff officers around Bourliouk to a ford on the west side of the burning village. Crossing over the River Alma and the flood plain, this group then proceeded to ride up a ravine on the boundary between the French and British sectors to gain a view point over the British front from the eastern slopes of Telegraph Height, which overlooked the Pass. This was a brave thing for Raglan to have done, but foolhardy in that it exposed him to serious danger as he was now behind the Russian front line. It also meant he was no longer in effective control of his army. Nevertheless, he had a grandstand view of Codrington's men storming the Great Redoubt to the east from a knoll.

Captain John Turner's G Field Battery, which was attached to Adams's brigade in the 2nd Division, also forded the Alma and made for the same knoll. The first of Turner's guns, which were attached to Adams's brigade, to arrive, opened fire on the left flank of the Russian's Causeway Batteries on the other side of the entrance to the Pass. After helping see off the Russian artillery, Turner then turned his battery's attention to the columns of the Volynsky Regiment, which were positioned further back up the Pass near the Post Road. These columns, as was mentioned earlier, constituted part of Menshikov's 'Great Reserve'. Turner's guns cut lanes through the tight columns of this regiment and after standing firm for a while, it also was forced to retreat. The Vladimirsky Regiment near the Great Redoubt was targeted next, but the range proved too great. Turner's flanking fire had had a disastrous effect on Russian morale.

This artillery action coincided with a push by the 2nd Division against the skirmishers and men of two battalions of the Borodinsky Chasseurs in the Pass. Some units had by then forded the river and others had used the partly destroyed wooden bridge that carried the Post Road. The Russian guns in the Causeway Batteries were now in range of accurate Minié rifle fire. This advance, which coincided with the fire of Turner's guns, helped force

Looking northeast from the edge of the Telegraph Height escarpment over the valley known as the Pass towards the white obelisk on the right that marks the site of the Great Redoubt. A line of trees on the extreme left in the middle distance marks the River Alma's channel today. The mound below these trees and closer to the camera is the ridge where the Causeway Batteries were positioned. The straw coloured field on the slope of Kourganè Hill, which rises on the right, is the hollow where the Vladmirsky Regiment was hidden prior to its advance to retake the Great Redoubt. The Russian reserves, which were fired on by Turner's guns, were believed to have been on the extreme right at the top of today's peach orchard. The knoll where Raglan watched the battle behind enemy lines would have been off the image to the left. A winery complex, whose access road can be seen in the foreground below, occupies this area today.

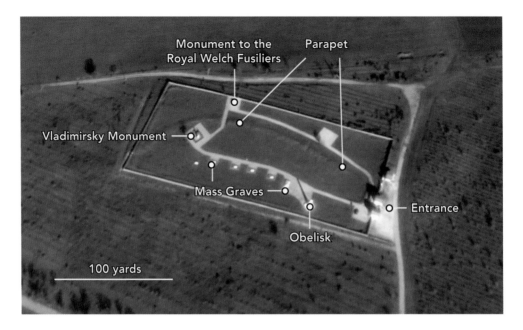

An aerial view of the site of the Great Redoubt on the battlefield of the Alma. North is to the top of the image. (Adapted from a Google Earth™ image).

the Russian artillery to retreat some distance up the Pass, where they again began firing. Lieutenant General Sir Richard England had advanced the 3rd Division to the river and was now crossing in support of the 2nd Division. He also offered De Lacy Evens his field artillery giving the attack in this sector a total of thirty guns.

In the meantime, Lieutenant Colonel Richard Dacres with H Field Battery, which was attached to the 1st Division, moved forward rapidly to the west of the 30th Regiment. As with Turner's G Field Battery, officers had to man the guns until the gunners caught up. Dacres himself fired the first shot at Kourganè Hill. Later E and B Field Batteries, which were attached to the Light and 2nd Divisions respectively, arrived and opened fire on the left followed by the 1st Division's A Field Battery led by Captain David Paynter. These guns were directed at skirmishers and an infantry column advancing towards the British lines from the crest of the hill. After several hits, the Russians in column, who had marched fifty yards down the hill, turned and disappeared back over the crest. It is presumed that this was a battalion of the Uglitsky Chasseurs stationed on Kourganè Hill. All of these British guns were eventually positioned in the Pass close to where the Russian's Causeway Batteries' guns had been sited.

The British position in and to the immediate east of the Pass was dependent on the continued presence of the 7th Fusiliers on the ground to the west-northwest of the Great Redoubt. This regiment, which was still engaging the two right battalions of the Kazansky Chasseurs, was protecting the left flank of the 2nd Division. The fight here had been fierce with exchanges of fire from as close as fifty yards. Gorchakov had become personally involved when he rode down and tried to organise a bayonet charge, but discouraged, he soon made off.

The 1st Division Attacks

The Grenadier Guards had been steadily advancing up the slope to the right of the Scots Fusilier Guards. However, the Scots Fusiliers had suffered from fire from the Vladimirsky in their centre and their left wing had been disorganised by the retreating men of the 23rd Regiment. Nevertheless, the remaining 500-600 Scots Fusiliers pushed toward the 3,000 Russians. Because of the enemy's numbers, the advance soon ground to halt and then the men fell back. The remnants of the Light Division were beginning to rally around Codrington and reorganised to the left of the Scots Fusiliers. However, because the Scots Fusiliers had stalled and were now well to the rear, a significant space had opened between the Grenadier Guards on their right and the Coldstream Guards on their left.

The right wing of the Kazansky Chasseurs fighting the exhausted 7th Fusiliers eventually began to weaken and fell back. At this moment, the Grenadier Guards approached in support and were allowed to pass through the 7th's ranks to pursue the retiring Russians, who regrouped near the left wing of the Vladimirsky.

To the east of the Coldstream Guards, the 42nd, the 93rd and lastly the 79th regiments of the Highland Brigade still moved forward in echelon. Campbell, who commanded this brigade, had seen the 88th Regiment of Buller's brigade ahead formed in a hollow square as though expecting a cavalry charge. He thought this formation most unsuitable and ordered it to form a line. However, the regiment still remained halted and a disgusted Campbell marched his men through its ranks.

The Russians now had 15,000 men, most of which had not yet seen action, in the vicinity of Kourganè Hill. However, most of their artillery had disappeared. Looking down the slope, the right and left wings of the Vladimirsky observed the Grenadier and Coldstream Guards approaching quite a distance apart. The Grenadier Guards were covered on their right by Pennefather's brigade, but by no one on their left where there was a gap.

Gorchakov rode up to the two left battalions of the Vladimirsky and again put himself in personal charge of his troops. He ordered them to charge with the bayonet and, without firing a shot, they moved forward towards the extreme left of the Grenadier Guards. A well-coordinated left wheel of the end of the line of Grenadier Guards showed the encroaching Russians an unbroken face. The fire erupting from this face sent shock waves through the tightly-packed Russians. Gorchakov's horse was killed. The left wing of the Vladimirsky was checked.

Meanwhile, the Coldstream Guards 'in superb array' on the left occupied a position where the regiment was able to pour fire into the right wing of the Valdimirsky at the Great Redoubt. There were no advances or retreats as the two opposing sides directed fire into one another. However, the heavy fire from the extended lines of the British regiments imposed more damage than the restricted fire from the small compact front shown by the Russian columns. When these columns showed signs of wavering, a British advance was ordered. The right wing of the Vladimirsky retreated along the eastern side of the slopes of Kourganè Hill in the direction of the left wing of the Kazansky. The right wing of the Grenadiers took the eastern side of the Great Redoubt and the left wing of the Grenadier Guards occupied the western side. The retreating Vladimirsky Regiment stopped when it reached the Kazansky Chasseurs and turned to face the British. However, the Great Redoubt had been recaptured.

While this was happening, Campbell at the head of the Highland Brigade on the left of the Guards Brigade, had ridden up the slopes ahead and to the west to view the scene. Ahead lay the Vladimirsky and Kazansky Chasseurs with their four depleted battalions.

While Campbell was reconnoitring, his regiments still in echelon had begun advancing towards the Kourganè Hill plateau from the river. Two battalions of the Suzdalsky Regiment stood some way off to their left. Further to the left and unseen because of the terrain, another two battalions of the Suzdalsky waited. In addition, four battalions of the Uglitsky Chasseurs were positioned on the high ground behind the Vladimirsky and Kazansky Chasseurs. The Suzdalsky and Uglitsky Chusseurs were fresh troops who had so far seen no action. In total, the Russians now had about 8,000 men, though only 6,000 were to take part in the next phase of the battle, opposite Campbell's 2,500 troops

The first of the Highland regiments to ascend the flood plain bank was the 42nd. These troops, went down into the slight hollow ahead to confront the four combined Vladimirsky and Kazansky Chasseur battalions. The 42nd advanced firing, but two battalions of the Suzdalsky began to move forward to take them on the left flank. The 42nd was halted and defensive action was about to be taken when the 93rd appeared over the crest of a low ridge behind and to the left. This regiment was heading straight at the right flank of the columns of the Suzdalsky. Campbell stopped the regiment and dressed its ranks before allowing it to move forward. By this time, the 42nd had recommenced its advance and was again firing on the enemy that lay in front. The Russian columns before the 93rd hesitated and were in danger of giving way when the remaining two battalions of the Suzdalsky came down from the high ground on the left and headed for the left flank of the 93rd. Just at this moment, the 79th appeared on the crest of the ridge even further to the left and, after dressing its line, charged the right flank of the Suzdalsky that threatened the 93rd. All along the left front of the British, the Russians broke and were in full retreat. The highlanders continued their advance towards the high ground of the Kourganè Hill plateau. While all this was in progress, the powerful body of cavalry on the Russian right flank did nothing to relieve the pressure on their countrymen.

The four battalions of the Uglitsky Chasseurs advanced and tried to drive their retiring comrades back into the fight. Three guns of Maude's I Troop of Royal Horse Artillery attached to the Light Cavalry Brigade and three guns of Brandling's C Troop of Royal Horse Artillery attached to the Light Division were brought into action against them after crossing the River Alma near Buller's brigade. Having no supporting artillery, the Uglitsky Chasseurs were forced to turn. Maude and Brandling were joined on Kourganè Hill by W Field Battery under Captain George Barker and part of F Field Battery under Captain William Swinton, both of which were attached to the 3rd Division. They opened fire on the retreating Russians to the right of C Troop.

Raglan had ordered up some of Adams's brigade on to the north-eastern edge of the Telegraph Height where he had his viewpoint. When they arrived, they were formed up in a red-coated line to impress upon the Russians that the British were in command of the heights on the west side of the Pass. Raglan then descended from his viewpoint into the Pass and rode over to the Guards on the opposite slope. Turner's G Field Battery advanced south along the eastern edge of Telegraph Height and fired at the retreating Russians at long range. The battle ended at about 17.00 hours.

The men of the Light Cavalry Brigade, who had advanced up to the plateau, were given orders to cover the advance of the field artillery. One half under Cardigan went with the guns on the right and the other half under Lieutenant General Lord Lucan, who was in overall commanded of the cavalry, went with the guns on the left. Lucan's men started to take prisoners, but they were ordered to stop and concern themselves only with the safety

The site of the Great Redoubt in the early twentieth century as taken by Klembovsky with the monument to the Vladimirsky Regiment in the foreground just beyond the remains of part of the earth parapet. Kourganè Hill is on the skyline. The area, as grassland, must have looked similar to this at the time the battle. (Walter Havighurst Special Collections, Miami University Libraries, Oxford, Ohio).

The site of the Great Redoubt today showing the locations of mass graves, which are now identified and commemorated, beyond the Vladimirsky monument. Kourganè Hill is now planted with peach trees, which are struggling to survive. The remains of the earth parapet are just discernible in the foreground.

of the guns. As a result, the prisoners were grudgingly released. Because Raglan did not want to lose any of his scarce cavalry, the Light Brigade had been told not to attack the enemy. It was widely believed that had the cavalry been allowed to pursue the demoralised Russian infantry, it could have caused panic and mayhem. Raglan wanted the French infantry with assistance from the British cavalry and artillery to set off after the retreating Russians. However, when he met St. Arnaud on the battlefield at about 16.30 hours, he was told that the French troops were tired and had to reclaim their knapsacks left north of the river.

During the course of the battle, the French lost 138 killed and 1,199 wounded compared to the British who lost 351 killed and 1,612 wounded with eighteen missing. The official figures for Russian casualties were 1,821 killed and 3,173 wounded. Few prisoners were taken except those left wounded on the battlefield. The British artillery at the Bulganak and at the Alma were reported to have fired 887 rounds of ammunition with British troops expending a total of 90,175 rounds of Minié rifle ammunition during the Battle of the Alma. This was broken down to 38,939 rounds by the Light Division, 36,360 by the 1st Division, 14,829 by the 2nd Division, forty-seven by the 3rd Division and none by the 4th Division.

Raglan established his headquarters, which consisted of a few tents on elevated ground, to the right of the British line and ordered his troops to bivouac on the heights they had won, even though it was some distance back down to the Alma and fresh water. The French did likewise. After this remarkable victory, men were still sickening and dying of cholera, as they had done on previous nights.

The Battle of the Alma was won by the Minié rifle, which had a range and accuracy that far exceeded the muskets carried by most of the Russian soldiers. This advantage meant that telling fire could be concentrated on the Russian infantry before they could reply with any hope of inflicting serious damage on Allied troops. As a result, the Russians became reliant on bayonet charges, which were usually stopped by concentrated rifle fire before they could connect with Allied soldiers. In addition, the 'line of two ranks' tactic enabled British troops to envelop and bring much more firepower to bear on the crowded Russian columns, whose outermost ranks only were capable of returning fire. However, despite these disadvantages and the lack of initiative of their officers, which resulted in successes not being exploited, the Russians fought well.

A Visit to the Battlefield

Driving south from the site of the old village of Bourliouk, a surfaced side-road to the southeast leaves the Eupatoria-Sevastopol Highway 400 yards after it crosses the bridge over the River Alma. The high ground ahead, now cut-through by the main highway, is where the Russian Causeway batteries were located. The side-road leads to the site of the Great Redoubt, which is enclosed within a low wall with monuments, mass graves, the remains of the low earth parapet and a visitor's centre. From the Great Redoubt, the visitor looks north down the glacis and over the river Alma to the flood plain beyond, which is now devoid of stone walls and vineyards A walk down the slope to the bank of the now channelled river would be well worth while to see the protection it afforded to British soldiers sheltering from Russian fire. The view back to the Great Redoubt from here reveals that the slope that attacking British forces had to ascend, although significant in the face of concentrated fire, is not as steep as is depicted in many paintings of the battle. The Battle of the Alma is re-enacted most years on 20 September on the slope below the Great

Redoubt. An unsealed road continues beyond the Great Redoubt up Kourganè Hill, which was Menshikov's initial look-out, and along the top edge of the slope where the Highland brigade fought the Russian columns below.

A private, surfaced side-road, which exits the Eupatoria-Sevastopol Highway to the right just over 600 yards further along the Eupatoria-Sevastopol Highway from the Great Redoubt turn-off, leads to a car park outside a large winery complex. From here, which is on the now levelled spur that led up to Telegraph Height, the visitor has a good view east over the Pass towards the Great Redoubt from a little further south than where Raglan would have watched the battle, Telegraph Height is covered with vineyards, which are patrolled just prior to harvest to deter those that may be tempted to steal grapes. The winery does not encourage tourists on its lands at this time. Parking outside the winery gates will undoubtedly attract the attention of security guards,

A dirt road to the west from where the Eupatoria-Sevastopol Highway reaches the top of the escarpment leads through vineyards to a large earth mound where it is highly likely the unfinished Telegraph Tower, which was attacked by the French, was situated. Again, this is private land.

A road west from the roundabout on the Eupatoria-Sevastopol Highway about 700 yards north of the bridge over the Alma, leads to the site of the village of Almatamack. The escarpment attacked by the French lies to the south of this road, which ends at a car park where there is a short walk to the beach and a view of the sea cliffs scaled by Bouat's men. There is a bridge over the Alma at Almatamack, but it is not easy to find. The track from this bridge leads west and then south up the escarpment through the ravine where Bosquet's and Canrobert's guns, which inflicted significant damage on Russian columns, were hauled onto the plateau.

The March from the Alma to Balaklava
A Rethink of Strategy

The day after the Battle of the Alma, a start was made to attend to the wounded left on the battlefield and the burial of the dead. The battlefield was described by William Russell as in a 'most filthy state':

> The quantity of firelocks, great coats, bearskin caps, shakoes, helmets and flat forage caps, knapsacks (English and Russian), belts, bayonets, cartouch boxes, cartridges, swords, exceeded belief; and round shot, fragments of shell smeared with blood, grape and bullets, were under the foot and eye at every step. Our men broke the enemies' flintlocks and rifles which lay on the ground. As many of them were loaded, the concussion set them off so that dropping shot never ceased for about forty hours.

Russell estimated that 1,200 Russians were interred on the 21 and 22 September. Hundreds of Russians, who lay wounded in the British sector, were brought to a sheltered location near the river. They lay in even parallel ranks and covered an area shaped like an oblong. This ground was located not far from the headquarters camp, but out of general view. This 'isolation' may have been one of the circumstances that led to the Russian wounded and their British guards not being fed for many hours. However, Captain William Sankey, Deputy Assistant Quartermaster General, and his volunteer William Romaine, the Deputy Judge Advocate of the Army in the East, brought them food and drink. They worked from 19.00 hours in the evening until late on this task.

The British loaded their wounded on to ships that would take the men back to Constantinople. The French with fewer wounded and positions closer to the ships had finished this task earlier. St. Arnaud wrote in his private journal that the British, as at the landing grounds, were delaying the allied departure and it was making him angry. According to Alexander Kinglake, his comment was extremely unfair considering it was he who had prevented the pursuit of the Russians immediately after the battle.

When the Allies resumed their march on 23 September 1854, the Russian wounded were left behind under the care of Assistant Surgeon James Thomson of the 44th (East Essex) Regiment and his servant. Relief came three days later when two British ships arrived and the Russian wounded were taken under a flag of truce to Odessa. Of the approximate original 500-750 men, 342 were handed over alive.

Sevastopol was sixteen and three-quarter miles to the south-southwest of the bridge over the River Alma as the crow flies. The headquarter tents were struck at about 08.00 hours and the Allies advanced south along the line of the Post Road. This road was

Looking west-northwest along the Katcha Valley towards the Black Sea from a hill to the southeast of the village of Vyshneve, today's name for the settlement that was known as Eskel. Vyshneve is located just over three-quarters of a mile down a side road that leaves the main Eupatoria to Sevastopol highway after it crosses the Kacha River. Raglan spent the night after the march from the Alma in a vandalised villa in the village. The Allied army bivouacked in the river valley and on the hills to the south.

described as 'a mere beaten track marked with cart wheels, hoofs and the nails of gun-carriage wheels'. The nearby ground was strewn with arms and accoutrements, which testified to the haste in which the Russians had retreated. The land was 'undulating and barren' with some 'steep hillocks covered with thistles' in between which lay patches of steppe. Raglan and his staff rode some distance ahead of the army that day showing complete disdain for the enemy.

Katcha Valley

The course of the Post Road taken by the Allied army marching south from the Alma no longer seems to exist along most of its route. Maps dating from the time of the Crimean War show the Post Road continuing in a south-southwest direction across the plateau south of the Pass and cutting straight across country towards the River Katcha passing close to where today's village of Sonyachnyi now stands. The present main road veers off this line to the southwest when leaving the Pass and continues to change direction west of the line of the old Post Road until linking up with it at the top of the escarpment on the north side

Above and opposite: The south-western bastion and ditch of the Star Fort as it looks today. The fort was octagon-shaped having sides of 190-230 yards in length. At the angles lay small bastions with earthen parapets alternating with barbettes. Each bastion was fourteen feet high and nineteen feet thick while other parts of the fort had a height of four to seven feet with a thickness of three to seven feet. The fort was surrounded by a ditch twelve feet deep and eighteen feet broad. Two lunettes covered the south side. Kinglake stated that the Star Fort, which was constructed to protect the sea forts that line the north shore of Sevastopol's roadstead from being taken from the north, was 'ill-contrived and dilapidated'. It was built in 1818 and in need of improvement by 1854. Between the landing of the Allied army at Kalamita Bay on the 14 September 1854 and the evening of the 24 September 1854, the Russians had toiled day and night with a force at one time of 1,500 workmen to repair and strengthen the fort. An effort was made to increase the height of the parapet using sacks of earth, but the extra weight caused it to give way in one location causing a breach. It was vulnerable to a determined attack.

of the Katcha Valley. The British army advanced at an average speed of two and a quarter miles an hour and the verdant Katcha Valley came in sight at 15.00 hours.

The Post Road descended to the small and rapid River Katcha, the course of which was marked by neat white cottages, vineyards, orchards and gardens. Crossing the bridge, the British army turned east off the Post Road towards the village of Eskel while the French occupied the area around Mamaschal, a village downstream from the bridge. Low walls lined the Eskel road on both sides with apple, pears, peaches and apricots growing beyond.

The first villa seen by Russell was the home of a physician, but had been abandoned. The windows, furniture, crockery and glassware appeared to have been destroyed by Cossacks. The walls and doors were hacked by swords. All houses in Eskel had been similarly vandalised. Nevertheless, the troops found plenty of grapes and fruit to eat in the neighbourhood.

While the French and British armies were establishing themselves in the valley and on the hills south of the Katcha, Lord Lucan and the Light Cavalry Brigade had pushed on to the River Belbek. The village of Duvanköi on the road from Sevastopol to the inland town of Baktishi Serai was occupied after the cavalry descended from the high ground to the north down a steep-sided ravine. Their position in the village would have been untenable if attacked by Russians and, after some hours, they retired to the high ground above Duvanköi where they spent the night.

Meanwhile Prince Menshikov, who believed that another major encounter with the Allies north of Sevastopol's roadstead would be unproductive, was beginning to move his defeated army to the hinterland where it could threaten the Allied rear as it besieged Sevastopol. Frantic efforts were also now beginning to be made by the Russians to fortify Sevastopol, which had not been considered a priority before the Battle of the Alma. The key to the defence of the northern side of the harbour was the Star Fort. It is likely that this could have been easily taken by the Allied army against a disorganised enemy with support from the ships at sea if they had moved quickly, as it was in a bad state of repair and had an inadequate garrison. However, it was about this time that the Allies began to question the feasibility of the original plan of taking Sevastopol from the north and were seriously considering the supposed benefits of assaulting the city from the south.

During the night and the next morning, the French army was augmented by 7,000-8,000 men, who landed at the mouth of the River Katcha. The 2nd Royal North British Dragoons (Scots Greys) of the Heavy Cavalry Brigade also disembarked from HMS *Himalaya*. In addition, the 57th (West Middlesex) Regiment of Foot joined the British army.

When Lucan arose from his bivouac above Duvanköi on 24 September 1854, he saw Russian troops in the direction of Sevastopol. However, he was recalled back to the general line of march before he could ascertain what was happening. The Russians had in fact been heading in his direction and Menshikov spent that night in a village in the neighbourhood.

The Allied army on the Katcha turned out and got ready for the day's march soon after daybreak. However, nothing then happened. The troops standing under arms felt the heat. The delay was the result of a top level discussion of the news that the Russians had scuttled a line of their warships across the entrance of the roadstead thus depriving entry to the Allied navy. A decision had also now to be made by the Commanders-in-Chief as to the next move by the Allies. Lieutenant General Sir John Burgoyne, who commanded the Royal Engineers, argued against attacking the Star Fort in the belief that it was occupied by a whole army. Another problem with the north shore attack plan for the Allies was that there were no harbours suitable on the coast north of Sevastopol from where the army could be conveniently supplied by the fleet. These factors now became part of a compelling argument for by-passing Sevastopol to the east. An attack on the city of Sevastopol from the south had become a much stronger viable alternative. What the Allies didn't know was that a mere 11,350 soldiers and sailors defended the north shore on a front that extended for a mile.

Bourgoyne advocated a march to the east of Sevastopol, followed by a swing around the southern side of the city to seize the Black Sea harbours of Balaklava, Kamiesch and Kazatch. He was so persuasive that his views carried the day. A north shore offensive plan, that may have ended the war quickly, was now dead in the water.

The Allied armies set off at about 10.00 hours according to Kinglake. The day was hot. The land was hilly and barren for a couple of miles and then fresher and more level. The march deviated away from the Post Road, which led to the north shore of Sevastopol. While this road went southwest, the Allies went south. Crowning the ridge of hills overlooking the Belbek Valley, the troops could see Sevastopol in the distance. The armies halted and St. Arnaud, who was feeling unwell, got off his horse and lay on the ground. When the march began again, the men descended to the River Belbek over gently sloping meadows.

Belbek Valley

The Belbek Valley, 'studded with snow-white cottages, with stately villas, with cosy-looking hamlets buried in trees, and fringed with a continuous line of the most gloriously green vineyards and the noblest of orchards' was just as picturesque as the Katcha Valley. The army soon swarmed into the valley's gardens and men clustered around every orchard tree seeking fruit. After a brief halt, the troops forded the river. Some looting occurred as soldiers, who took their cue from one staff-officer, occupied a small chateau.

Lord Cardigan rode on ahead with a section of the Light Cavalry Brigade to reconnoitre the road to Sevastopol. He got as far as gazing down on a causeway that carried the road across a marsh and then on to the Inkerman Bridge, the first crossing over the River Chernaya that ran into the head of the roadstead to the east of Sevastopol. It was guarded by a battery of guns, infantry and some cavalry, Cardigan declared the route unsuitable.

The view south-southeast over the Belbek Valley from the escarpment on its north side. The busy Sevastopol-Simferopol Highway can be seen descending from the high ground on the far side of the valley. The Allied army bivouacked on these slopes above the river. The Mackenzie Heights lie on the right skyline. The Allies marched through the dense bush on these heights on the morning of 25 September 1854.

The allied Commanders-in-Chief decided that the march should continue on the high ground beyond the Belbek towards the southern edge of the Mackenzie Heights, where the land dropped down steeply into the Chernaya Valley, and hence to the second river crossing point higher up the Chernaya at the Tractir Bridge. The undertaking was hazardous because it would physically separate the army from the navy for two days and also opened up a possibility of a surprise attack from the Russian army. The enterprise, which took the armies around Sevastopol, was to become known as the 'flank march'.

The armies bivouacked on the slopes of hills on the south side of the Belbek Valley. The sun had long set before the men lay down around their fires. Lord Raglan occupied one of the plundered villas near the only bridge over the Belbek that the Russians had left serviceable. Cholera was on the increase and many men fell sick and died in the night. The armies had been asleep for only a few hours when they were awoken between 01.30 and 02.00 hours by musket and gun fire. The bugles sounded and men were alerted, but it amounted to nothing. Some found it difficult to sleep afterwards knowing there was to be an early start.

Mackenzie's Farm
At 05.30 hours on the morning of 25 September 1854, the troops were under arms. Those sick with cholera were arranged in ranks parallel to the road prior to transportation back to

the Alma and the ships. At 07.00 hours, Raglan again visited French Headquarters, but St. Arnaud, who by now was extremely ill, was unable to participate in discussions. Nevertheless, it was resolved that the French army should follow the British army on the day's march. The terrain to be covered that morning was rough and forested, but the goal was a clearing called Mackenzie's Farm marked on Russian maps on the 'Great Road' from Sevastopol to Baktishi Serai.

The cavalry supported by the 2nd Battalion of the Rifle Brigade was to lead the advance along a woodland track. The main body of infantry was to navigate through the forest and scrubland using compasses so as to keep the track clear for the cavalry, artillery and wagons. As soon as all these were past, the French army was to follow on behind. The British 4th Division and the 4th Light Dragoons were to remain on the Belbek to help facilitate the evacuation of the sick.

Lucan and his cavalry had had to wait for the appearance of the men of the Rifle Brigade, half of whom were then positioned to the fore and half to the rear of the reconnoitring party. This delay meant that the cavalry was not too far ahead of the rest of the army when the flank march began at 08.30 hours.

About two thirds of the way to Mackenzie's Farm, Captain Edward Wetherall, an officer of the Quartermaster General's Department, who was guiding Lucan's column, took a wrong turn. The track now being followed by Lucan and most of the cavalry degenerated to a path and then disappeared. This slowed the advance of the reconnoitring group that was supposedly leading the army and took it in a different direction.

Moving independently, the infantry pushed on through the forest, which was so thick in places that men had to march in single file. The ground was also steep and rough making it very laborious for the soldiers, who became thirsty. However, there were no natural water sources in the dry forest, which led to the men becoming irritable and impatient. Nevertheless, by means of the compass, the soldiers continued to move in the right direction.

On the top of the heights, Raglan rode off to the left with his personal cavalry escort until he came to a view point over the head of the Sevastopol Roadstead. He saw Sevastopol and the docks, the Star Fort on the north shore, ships in the bay and casemated batteries on the water's edge. This was the prize! Raglan then turned his horse back to the line of march of the rest of the army.

Meanwhile, Captain Maude's I Troop of Royal Horse Artillery, assigned to Lucan's cavalry, had taken the correct turn at the fork in the track where Lucan had deviated. As a consequence, this group moved steadily towards Mackenzie's Farm and unknowingly overtook Lucan's cavalry struggling through the bush to the west. Raglan and his escort coming from the west missed Lucan's men and intercepted I Troop. Thinking himself behind the main body of the cavalry, Raglan and his escort joined Maude. The track was just broad enough for one gun and the advance was virtually in single file. Raglan was blissfully unaware that he was now leading the vanguard of the Allied army.

Raglan was expecting a report back from Lucan, who he presumed was some way up ahead. However, at length, his group reached a point where the light was increasing as they neared a clearing in the forest. Brigadier General Airey, who was on Raglan's staff, went on alone to reconnoitre. He had not gone too far when he held up his hand in a gesture that meant for the others to stop and not make any noise. Airey had seen a Russian wagon-train halted on the Great Road from Sevastopol to Baktishi Serai at a point very

A clearing in the heavily forested country of the Mackenzie Heights where Mackenzie's Farm was located. It was here where Raglan's party leading the 'flank march' around Sevastopol ran into the rear-guard of Prince Menshikov's army as it made its way to the hinterland from the vicinity of Sevastopol.

The Chernaya Valley viewed from the northeast. The Allies on their flank march crossed the valley from the left heading for the Tractir Bridge, which was in the wooded area at the base of the low-lying Fedioukine Hills seen to the right of centre. The valley that ran into the hills from the bridge, which was the route taken by the army the next day, appears as a wooded cleft. The dome-shaped hill seen to the left at the end of the valley is Mt Hasfort, which was held by the Sardinians at the Battle of the Chernaya in August 1855.

close to Mackenzie's Farm. This was later identified as the tail end of Menshikov's army, which was on its way to the hinterland from Sevastopol.

The Russian force saw Airey at about the same time as they heard the rumble of the wheels of Maude's gun carriages coming up behind. Raglan, who was alarmed, immediately gave orders for someone to bring up his personal cavalry escort. However, although the British contingent was very vulnerable, the Russians did not take advantage of the opportunity presented to them and remained stationary. Captain George Chetwode and the escort troop of the 8th Hussars came forward in single file.

Fifteen minutes after Airey had seen the Russians, the cavalry under Lucan and the Rifle Brigade, alerted as to what was happening by Major Wetherall scouting on their left, arrived on the scene. Raglan angrily informed Lucan as he went by that he was late. Maude's I Troop of horse artillery had by now unlimbered and opened fire. In addition, the Rifle Brigade discharged a volley. This show of strength caused the Russians to abandon all their wagons and flee from the scene in the direction of Baktishi Serai.

The 2nd Dragoons dismounted and began skirmishing in the woods either side of the road. Moving along the road in pursuit, I Troop found the enemy drawn up ready to receive cavalry about thirty yards away. On seeing the British guns, the Russian defence line broke. Some ran into the woods and opened an ineffectual fire on the gun teams, some were pursued and cut down by the cavalry; some were hit by case shot from the guns and others were shot by the dragoons. Kinglake reported that a group of twenty Russian infantrymen turned and fired a volley at Lucan and Cardigan riding ahead of their troops, but the shots were high and they were soon cut down by sabres as they tried to escape in the forest. The pursuit was stopped at a point where the Great Road descended from the Mackenzie Heights into a plain to the northeast. From here, Russian infantry in Menshikov's army could be seen marching away along the road with some cavalry and a field battery.

When the rest of the British field artillery arrived at Mackenzie's Farm, it was deployed in the clearing so as to confront any other enemy force passing along the Great Road. There was a building at Mackenzie's Farm, which most likely served as a temporary barrack for Russian troops on the march. Two wells nearby quenched the thirst of those marching. An immense quantity of clothing, such as boots, coats, furs and shirts, was found in the captured Russian wagons together with valuables, ornaments and a military chest containing money. Plenty of champagne was also liberated. A Russian captain of artillery occupied one of the carriages, but he was so drunk as not to be useful for intelligence purposes. It was not until later that it was discovered that the leading units of the British army had run into the rear of Menshikov's army on its way inland from Sevastopol.

Tractir Bridge

It was now about mid-day and the troops marched on in jovial mood. They very quickly reached the southern edge of the Mackenzie Heights and took the steep road down into the Chernaya Valley. After descending the escarpment of the Mackenzie Heights, the army marched into the Chernaya Valley and then across its floor on the track to the Tractir Bridge. The leading British troops, which included the 2nd Battalion of the Rifle Brigade crossed over the River Chernaya on the stone Tractir Bridge and bivouacked on the Fedioukine Hills beyond. It was dark when the bulk of the British army arrived and many slept on the banks of the river. Raglan spent the night in 'a miserable lodge' that stood near the bridge. Most of his staff slept in a ditch outside.

View to the Chernaya Valley looking south from the escarpment of the Mackenzie Heights near the site of Mackenzie's Farm. The straw-coloured Fedioukine Hills rise from the valley floor in the distance on the right.

The road from the Mackenzie Heights was full of British wagons, which prevented the French following on from Mackenzie's Farm that day. Indeed, the French rear-guard did not arrive at Mackenzie Farm until 03.00 hours. The scant supply of water in the wells ran out and many remained thirsty. Meanwhile Cathcart and the 4th Division were still back in the Belbek Valley and vulnerable to attack had the Russian army still remained in the vicinity. The sick from the night before were sent back to the Katcha in exposed wagon trains and taken on board ships for Constantinople. Raglan sent a message back to Rear Admiral Sir Edmund Lyons via the Belbek to the effect that he was going to advance on Balaklava the next day and he hoped that the fleet would be there to meet him.

Balaklava
The march resumed on the morning of 26 September along a road in a valley through the Fedioukine Hills that later climbed over a low ridge to emerge in the North Valley of Balaklava The soldiers continued to follow the road as it obliquely crossed the North Valley and up onto what would be called the Causeway Heights. On the crest of the heights, the men had a view over the South Valley of Balaklava towards the village of Kadikoi. From this angle of view, it was difficult to see the narrow pass between the towering hills beyond Kadikoi that led to Balaklava and the sea.

The valley through the Fedioukine Hills taken by the British army on the morning of 26 September 1854 on its way to capture Balaklava. The view is southwest from near the entrance to the Chernaya Valley. Fierce fighting took place between the French and Russians here at the Battle of the Chernaya in August 1855.

Once in Kadikoi, the local inhabitants seemed friendly and informed the British that Balaklava was undefended. However, when Raglan and his advanced party arrived at a spot where a small stream flowed into Balaklava harbour, a shot rang out from a mortar positioned near an ancient castle on a hill that commanded the harbour entrance. The first shot fell to the ground near Raglan and his staff without exploding. The next shot fell in the harbour. Raglan prudently retreated a little to shelter behind a rock. More shots were fired and exploded in the air and in a nearby vineyard.

The guns of Captain Brandling's C Troop could not be elevated enough to return fire so the 1st Brigade of the Light Division was ordered to climb the heights to the west of the harbour while the 2nd Brigade with half of C Troop under Lieutenant Shadwell Grylls was told to scale the heights to the east that looked down on the castle. The 2nd Battalion of the Rifle Brigade supported by the 1st Division were positioned so as to prevent the enemy from moving out of the area. The sound of a booming gun of 'majestic calibre' signalled the arrival of Lyons and the fleet outside the harbour. The 77th (East Middlesex) Regiment plus the artillery had by this time reached the eastern heights and could look into the interior of the castle. Colonel Monto, who commanded a small group of Greek militiamen, realised his position was hopeless and surrendered.

After the garrison had capitulated, Raglan rode along a little street into Balaklava. Because they were afraid of retribution, the local inhabitants went down on their knees and offered bread. Raglan made his way down to the water's edge, but still couldn't see the sea because of the twists of the harbour. Just then, a British vessel came gliding into view between the enfolding hills. Raglan knew then that Lyon's flagship the HMS *Agamemnon* wasn't far away. The vessel that was the first to enter the port took soundings and it was soon discovered that the water was deep enough 'to float a ship of the line'. In a short space of time, the town was crowded with British soldiers and the harbour full of British ships.

In the meantime, Lieutenant General Cathcart with the 4th Division and the French had reached the Tractir Bridge. That evening, the very seriously ill St Arnaud finally handed over his command of the French Army to Canrobert. He died on 29 September 1854 on board the French ship *Berthollet* that had just left Balaklava en route to Constantinople.

The occupation of Balaklava by the British army and its reunion with the Royal Navy meant that the gamble of the 'flank march' had succeeded. The expeditionary force was no longer in danger of being attacked and defeated piecemeal by the Russians as its strung out forces marched around Sevastopol. However, the Russian army was still in the field and Balaklava was in danger. The besiegers of Sevastopol later found themselves in a situation whereby they were virtually besieged by this enemy force.

Ships continued to crowd into the harbour from the sea and the French marched into the valleys before Balaklava. There was an inclination by the French to remonstrate about the town being totally occupied by the British. They believed on the terms of the 'flank march' that the port was for all of the Allies. However, the smallness of the harbour and the narrowness of the surrounding flat land under the hills, soon led to the recognition that it could not be divided between the two major Allies. Canrobert could see the problems if the British were asked to leave, so he wisely asked Raglan to decide if he wanted to stay. The decision would in effect also decide the section of the siege lines the British and French would subsequently be obliged to man. Because Balaklava was seen at this stage as a prize and the potential of Kamiesch and Kazatch as supply ports had not yet been ascertained, Raglan elected to keep Balaklava after consulting Lyons.

The French marched on westwards to occupy the ground around the bays of Kamiesch and Kazatch, which were found to be excellent places to land supplies and provide for the French troops. On the other hand, Balaklava turned out to be a huge disappointment, as it soon became overcrowded with ships and soldiers, and became renowned for its unsanitary conditions.

Believing that Sevastopol had first to be 'softened-up' by a bombardment, an opportunity to overcome the defenders by an infantry assault before they became organised was again lost. Work on preparing gun batteries along the siege lines began. The supply ports chosen by the British and French dictated the areas of responsibility of the two armies in the siege lines around Sevastopol. It made sense for the French to besiege the western approaches to the city closest to Kamiesch and Kazatch while the British would man the trenches in the eastern sector. The Great Ravine, which ran towards Sevastopol from the high ground to the south, separated the sectors under siege by the two allies. The disadvantage of this choice for the British was that the eastern end of the siege lines at Inkerman and the port of Balaklava were more open to a Russian attack by Menshikov's troops, who now occupied the hinterland, than were the French positions.

Balaklava
The British Army's Supply Port in the Crimea

John Nicolas Laverty, who was a naval Instructor on HMS *Queen,* was responsible for the first surviving photograph taken of Balaklava harbour after its occupation by the British army and navy on 26 September 1854. The ship prominent in his image is HMS *Agamemnon,* which was completed in 1852. She served in the Crimean War as flagship of Rear-Admiral Sir Edmund Lyons and participated in the bombardments of Sevastopol on 17 October 1854 and Fort Kinburn on 17 October 1855. HMS *Agamemnon* was the first British battleship to be designed and built to be powered by steam. However, because of the inefficiency of steam power at the time, she carried a full square rig on three masts in common with large sailing warships of the period. Ninety–one, muzzle-loading, smooth-bore cannon were found on two decks.

The picture is of interest because it is of the original town. It shows how picturesque Balaklava appeared before the buildings along the waterfront were levelled to provide space for warehouses, sheds and railway workshops. What is noticeable when this image is compared to photographs taken later in the war is the absence of rows of tents on the slopes of Guards' Hill seen beyond the head of the harbour, camps in the valley leading towards Kadikoi and huts below the hospital buildings on the far right on the slopes of Mt Hiblak. The village of Kadikoi can be seen in the distance on the right above the lower slopes of Guards' Hill and Mt Hiblak. Its white church, which was a local landmark during the Crimean War, is clearly visible. The Sapoune Ridge at the edge of the Chersonese Plateau is on the skyline.

Laverty took his photograph from the hillside behind the town. This area is accessible today by ascending the balustrade steps at the southern end of the town and then climbing the slope to the left of the path as it begins to enter the ravine that runs upwards towards the col east of Castle Hill.

Today's view was taken close to where Laverty must have positioned his camera. It shows the results of the quarrying on the hillside at the left of the harbour and the expansion of Balaklava into the valley at the northern end of the harbour and up the lower slopes of Guards' Hill. A huge apartment building now occupies the area of Kadikoi to the east of where the church once stood.

Balaklava from Castle Hill

The Genoese fortress on Castle Hill offers a magnificent viewpoint. From here, the observer looks down on the harbour of Balaklava and up the valley at its far end to Kadikoi and beyond. The James Robertson/Felice Beato team took two images from the slopes leading

Laverty's image entitled *HMS Agamemnon in the harbour of Balaklava.* (© Victoria and Albert Museum, London).

The identical view today taken from the slope of the hill behind Balaklava.

The Robertson/Beato image entitled *Harbour of Balaklava.* (©National Army Museum, London)

The same view of Balaklava harbour today from the slopes of Castle Hill.

up to the hilltop fortress from the harbour in the summer of 1855, but only one has survived that is of sufficient quality to reproduce here. This photograph, which is entitled *Harbour of Balaklava*, shows the harbour full of ships from a lofty vantage point. The top of a ruined tower is in the left foreground. The Cattle Pier is at lower left between where two ships with disembarking ramps are moored. The cottages that feature later in the chapter in Roger Fenton's images of the Cattle Pier area are in the centre foreground. Timber lies piled on the wharf beyond the cottages and also further along the shore to the right.

The hillside to the right of the cottages is where Fenton took his images of the Cattle Pier area. The building with the white walls at the base of this slope and near the timber wharf was the Commissariat Office with the Commissary General's house, which was built in the same style, further to the right.

The town hospital nestles in the slope leading up to Mt Hiblak at upper right. Light-coloured hospital huts lie below with a long dark-coloured hut above. Most ships in the harbour have awnings stretched across their decks to act as sun shades. Long lines of tents run up the slope of Guards' Hill in the left background. Mule sheds lie in a recess of the hillside below these tents and above the eastern end of the harbour. The South Valley of Balaklava can be seen between the slope of Guards' Hill on the left and Mt Hiblak on the right with the Sapoune Ridge on the edge of the Chersonese Plateau on the skyline to left of centre.

The comparable view today shows the ruined tower on the slope in the foreground left of centre as on the contemporary image. A sunbathing and swimming platform now occupies the shoreline to the north of the site of the Cattle Pier. The cottages in the Cattle Pier area photographed by Fenton have disappeared and the walls of a partially demolished building now occupies the site. The lower section of the hillside where Fenton took his images of the Cattle Pier area has been excavated to make a level base for the large multi-storey building that extends to the right over the sites of the Commissariat Office and Commissary General's house. Steps now zig-zag up the side of the slope that appears on the lower right of the Robertson/Beato image.

On the right of the modern view, the wharf along the foreshore in Balaklava where ships once unloaded their cargoes, is now a promenade for tourists lined with shops and restaurants. High-rise buildings and trees occupy the site of the hospital on the slope of Mt Hiblak at upper right. A naval base is now located at the end of the harbour and buildings associated with the local quarrying industry lie near to where the mule sheds once stood on the left. Dachas and apartments dot the treed lower slopes of Guards' Hill and a road constructed for rock-hauling trucks disappears round a bend under a wooded area on the upper slope.

A large white apartment building is visible at Kadikoi, now known as Kadykovka, seen beyond and between the slopes of Guards' Hill and Mt Hiblak. Behind Kadikoi, the South Valley of Balaklava, which is covered with vineyards, rises to the ridge that was known as the Causeway Heights. The British Heavy Cavalry Brigade charged uphill to turn the Russian cavalry at the Battle of Balaklava on the slope of this ridge directly above the white apartments. This gives the reader an idea as to just how close the Russians came to the British supply port during the battle. The Sapoune Ridge is on the left and centre skyline.

Castle Hospital

The Castle Hospital or Castle Sanatorium was located on a shoulder of land that joined Castle Hill, which was above and to the east of the entrance to Balaklava's harbour, It was

The Robertson/Beato image entitled *Sanatorium, Balaklava.* (Royal Collection Trust © Her Majesty Queen Elizabeth II, 2016).

The same view today looking down towards Castle Hill from the lower slopes of Mt Asketi.

The Robertson/Beato image entitled **Entrance to Balaklava Harbour.** (Royal Collection Trust/© Her Majesty Queen Elizabeth II, 2016).

The view from the headland on the west side of the harbour entrance today.

Shaw-Lefevre's photograph of HMS *Leander* anchored at the harbour entrance close to Castle Point. (©Manuscripts and Special Collections, University of Nottingham).

The entrance to Balaklava harbour today with Castle Hill on the right.

Fenton's image entitled *The old Genoese Castle at Balaklava, from above the Cattle Pier.*
(Library of Congress, Washington).

Today's view of the lower slopes of Castle Hill from above the site of the Cattle Pier

regarded as better than the town hospital in Balakalva because of its situation overlooking the sea and breezes that aided recuperation. Florence Nightingale visited the Crimea in May 1855 and when she became sick with 'Crimean fever', which is today known as brucellosis, she was admitted to the Castle Hospital. For twenty-four hours she was in great danger and the doctors were anxious, but she recovered.

The Robertson/Beato team took two almost identical pictures looking down on the Castle Hospital from the slope leading up towards the top of Mt Asketi. They were entitled *Balaklava, with the Hospital Huts* and *Sanatorium, Balaklava*. The latter is reproduced here. This image, which looks west, shows the hospital huts arranged in a row along the crest of the shoulder of land or col between Castle Hill and the slope up to Mt Asketi from where the photograph was taken. A ravine to the right of the hospital leads down towards Balaklava's harbour, where an arc of ships can be seen moored in Cossack Bay. Rows of cultivated plants are visible in a garden below the closest huts. It is known that grapes grew at the hospital.

The same view today shows apartments and other tourism developments on the slopes of the ravine in the foreground where trees now grow. A track that enables vehicles to be driven to the area from Kadikoi follows the ravine floor on the right. The castle perches on Castle Hill with other towers seen on the slope down to Balaklava harbour on the right to the right. The indent on the far shore of the harbour is Cossack Bay. The road skirting Cossack Bay ascends a valley between hills from the site of Lavender Bay. The hillside at upper right is scarred as a result of quarrying.

Entrance to Balaklava Harbour

The image entitled *Entrance to Balaklava Harbour* was photographed by the Robertson/Beato team in the summer of 1855. Their image shows the harbour crowded with ships and the town beyond clinging to the lower slopes of Mt Hiblak. The first ship in Castle Bay around Castle Point, which is the east side of the harbour and is seen on the right, is HMS *Leander*. Ships line the eastern side of the harbour behind HMS *Leander* with the Cattle Pier area being a little way along from where the shoreline changes direction on the far right. The church at Balaklava is visible on the slope beyond. Cossack Bay, where other ships are moored stern to the shore, is on the left. This image was taken from the elevated headland on the west side of the harbour entrance.

Today's view shows that topographical features near the harbour entrance have not changed significantly since 1855. A road now skirts the shore along Cossack Bay on the left and allows access to the site of Lavender Bay, where there is a swimming beach. The building with the green roof seen on the right over Castle Point is an exclusive yacht club. The area of the Cattle Pier was where the low building to the left of the yacht club is now located.

The next contemporary mage was taken by George Shaw-Lefevre and shows HMS *Leander* at the entrance of the harbour in the same position close to Castle Point as in the Robertson/Beato image. This 1,987-ton warship, which was 181ft 6in long, 51ft wide with fifty guns, was built at Portsmouth and launched on 8th March 1848. HMS *Leander* was commissioned by Captain Sidney Dacres on 1st October 1849. Converted to screw propulsion in 1861, the *Leander* was sold in 1867. Seamen from the ship served on land as part of the Naval Brigade. Some are buried on the hill above Cossack Bay.

The photograph below, which was taken from above the shoreline on the western side of the harbour south of Lavender Bay, shows the same view today. The site of the lower defence tower of the Genoese castle, which was built on the pinnacle on the far right, is now occupied by a maritime look-out station. Green-roofed apartment buildings associated with the yacht club are visible on the shore of Castle Bay to the left of centre and boats occupy berths at the wharf. The slopes of Mt Asketi are on the skyline in the centre. It was along this ridge that the inner defences to Balaklava known as 'Marine Heights' were constructed and armed in places with naval guns.

Cattle Pier at Balaklava

On 5 March 1855, the photographer Roger Fenton departed Constantinople, which he described as the 'worst villainous hole' he had been in, on board the *Hecla*, which had a cargo of railway building materials. Two days later on 7 March 1855, he arrived in the port of Balaklava. Because of difficulties in landing his equipment and getting established after arrival, Fenton didn't start to take photographs until 15 March 1855.

Fenton initially concentrated on documenting the sights of Balaklava, which he called a 'great pigsty' even though the port was reportedly much better looked after than on 3 December 1854, when it was colourfully described by Mrs Fanny Duberly, the wife of the paymaster of the 8th Hussars, as a 'swamp of filth'. At night, Fenton returned to the *Hecla* to sleep.

Some of Fenton's most reproduced images in the Crimea were taken in the vicinity of the Cattle Wharf at the southern end of Balaklava's harbour. His first image to be presented here, which is entitled *The old Genoese Castle at Balaklava from above the Castle Pier*, looks south towards the ruined towers associated with the outer defences of the Genoese Castle on Castle Hill. The Genoese Castle was and still is on the summit, which is off the picture at top left. Fenton took this image on the lower slope of the high ground to the east of the Cattle Wharf. It was higher up and to the north on this hill where Laverty took his picture of HMS *Agamemnon* looking north-northwest.

In the foreground, a man leads a horse down a path towards a small ridge tent. A clothes line hangs from two posts. Two cottages joined by a makeshift wooden extension to the one on the left can be seen behind the bell tents. Smoke issues from the chimney of the cottage on the left. These cottages were probably used as storehouses or accommodation. The ships on the right are moored to the south of the Cattle Wharf in Castle Bay.

Below Fenton's image is its modern equivalent. The nearest tower on the castle wall on the left is easily recognisable today. A second tower seen on the skyline above and to the right of the first tower has disappeared with the crag now occupied by a coastal lookout station. Similarly, the remains of a tower seen further down the slope from the high tower is absent today.

Where sailing ships were moored on the right in Fenton's image, luxury pleasure boats and yachts now line the quay next to expensive apartments. The old castle wall seen on the hillside above the ships has been superseded by a new wall that keeps intruders out of the gated-community below. The two cottages have disappeared.

The second of Fenton's photographs presented is entitled *Cossack Bay, Balaklava*. It shows the view to the west or right of his first image. The end of the cottage seen on the far left is the same end of the cottage seen on the extreme right of the Genoese castle picture. However, the orientation of the cottage end wall is different in the two photographs suggesting that Fenton was a little more to the southeast and slightly higher than where he was when he took the castle image. His position could have been where the slope seen

Fenton's image entitled **Cossack Bay, Balaklava.** (Library of Congress, Washington).

Today's view looking over the site of the Cattle Pier with Cossack Bay the indent in the steep slope to the right of centre.

Fenton's image entitled **The Harbour at Balaklava, the Cattle Pier.** (Library of Congress, Washington).

Today's view showing that area of the wharf where the **St Hilda** was moored.

The Robertson/Beato image entitled **Genoese Castle, Balaklava.** (Royal Collection Trust/© Her Majesty Queen Elizabeth II, 2016).

The same view today taken from the hillside to the east of the Cattle Pier area.

Fenton's image entitled *The Ordnance Wharf at Balaklava.* (Royal Collection Trust/© Her Majesty Queen Elizabeth II, 2016).

Looking north-northeast along the Balaklava quayside at the site of the Ordnance Wharf today

in the left foreground of the castle photograph exits the frame. Horses, presumably recently off-loaded from a ship, are confined in an enclosure in the foreground below.

The steam ship in the centre of the picture at the Cattle Pier has the number '69'. This number identifies it as the *Albatross*, which was engaged as a Crimean War transport at the time of the photograph. It was built on the Clyde in 1850 as a passenger and cargo screw steamer for a shipping company in Cork, Ireland.

One of the passengers on board the *Albatross* on its second voyage to Balaklava in March 1855 was Mrs Mary Seacole, who went on to build the 'British Hotel', which was a sutlers' store and eating establishment, with her business partner. In her autobiography, Mrs Seacole described the cargo on the *Albatross* as cattle, which fits with the official data and its position at the Cattle Wharf in Fenton's photograph. Sailing ships, some moored at the bottom of a steep slope, can be seen in Cossack Bay across the harbour beyond the *Albatross*

Sailing ships can be seen across the harbour beyond the *Albatross*. Cossack Bay was where ships are moored around the headland on the opposite shore seen at centre.

The modern equivalent of Fenton's photograph of Cossack Bay shows more of the view to the left so that most of the end of the headland to the west of the harbour entrance can be seen. This same headland is seen on the right of the modern equivalent of Fenton's first image and should help the reader gain more of an insight into how the two Fenton images relate to each other.

The absence of moored ships on the opposite side of the harbour when today's image was taken means that the indent that was Cossack Bay can be seen more clearly. A road around the case of the steep slope here makes the small beach at Lavender Bay accessible by car. The building at centre now occupies the ground just in front of the site of the Cattle Wharf. The red, crenelated wall on the right stands where timber was stacked on Fenton's image.

The third of Fenton's images taken in the same vicinity is entitled *The Harbour at Balaklava, the Cattle Pier*. It shows the sailing ship seen on the right of his image entitled *Cossack Bay, Balaklava* in more detail. Timber has been off-loaded here.

The cottage in the foreground is the same one as seen in the foreground of *Cossack Bay, Balaklava*. Baskets stacked along its end wall are now more clearly seen. The horses in the enclosure are also at a different angle indicating that Fenton was lower and more to the east when he took this image. The shadow of the end wall of the cottage on the left in Cossack Bay can be seen on the ground on the extreme left of Cattle Pier. Its angle and direction suggests both images were taken in the morning.

The number '11' on the sailing ship's bows and also quarter (to the immediate left of the large stack of timber) identifies her as the *St Hilda* built in Quebec in 1849. The *St Hilda's* lower yards, which would normally have been horizontal if ready for sea, are titled diagonally or 'cockbilled'. This may have been so they could be used as derricks to unload the cargo, but more likely to stop them becoming entangled with those of other vessels within the confines of the anchorage. The topgallant mast and any higher masts have been removed to make her more stable after unloading. The sails visible on the *St Hilda* may have been in the process of being dried before being stowed.

Like the *Albatross*, the *St Hilda* was engaged as a Crimean War transport. In January 1855, she had conveyed those in need of care from the Crimea to hospital at Scutari, which was across the Bosphorus from Constantinople, with twenty-three dying on board during the voyage. The *St Hilda* took part in the Kertch expedition of May and June 1855. She transported troops, guns and horses to the area and in early August 1855 anchored three miles off Kertch serving as a hospital ship. In early November 1855, the *St Hilda* was recorded as being in Constantinople and in early December 1855 as passing through Gibraltar en route for Portsmouth.

Fenton took this photograph lower down the slope from where his two previous images of the area were taken. Today's equivalent of Fenton's image of the *St Hilda* could not be taken from where he stood because of the removal of the slope to create a level platform for of a large building that now stands just to the right of the image. The wharf where the ship was berthed lies just beyond the red, crenelated wall, which is now a public sunbathing and swimming platform. The cottage at the centre of Fenton's image was probably located where the car can be seen near a sun umbrella in today's view.

Buildings and a road are now found on the far side of the harbour where the hillside dropped precipitously into the water in 1855. Immediately above the curved right end of the building with the red roof at centre, two exposed, circular-shaped rocks are visible, one larger than the other, with a diagonal scar running across both of their faces. These same two rocks and scar can also be seen to the left of the mast of a ship on the far side of the harbour located just above *St Hilda*'s bows in Fenton's photograph. Many distinctive rocks seen on contemporary photographs can still be identified today and help confirm locations.

The final image in this section is by the Robertson/Beato team and is entitled *Genoese Castle, Balaklava*. It was taken from higher up the slope than where Fenton took his images of the Cattle Pier area and looks southeast at the ruins of the castle's lower fortifications spread out on the side of Castle Hill and the headland at the west side of the harbour entrance. The ruined tower at lower left is the same as the one at upper right in Fenton's image entitled *The old Genoese Castle at Balaklava, from above the castle pier*. The higher tower further to the right in Fenton's image is the same as the one at upper left in *Genoese Castle, Balaklava*. The ships in Castle Bay below on the right have awnings stretched across their decks to provide shade as in *Harbour of Balaklava*, another image by Robertson/Beato that was probably taken the same day.

The modern view shows the same ruins of the Genoese Castle on the slopes of Castle Hill. However, the tower seen on a crag at upper left of the contemporary image has now been replaced by a maritime look-out station. In addition, the ruined castle wall of 1855 on the slope above and to the left of the lower tower appears to have been incorporated into a new wall that prevents trespass into the area of luxury apartments on the shores of Castle Bay below. *Entrance to Balaklava Harbour* and today's equivalent were taken from the treeless area above the cliff edge on the headland at the entrance to the harbour above Powell Point at left of centre.

Waterfront at Balaklava

Roger Fenton also took photographs of the other wharves at Balaklava soon after his arrival in the Crimea in March 1855. His first image shown entitled *The Ordnance Wharf at Baklaklava* was taken close to the Ordnance Office seen in the next contemporary image. The wharf at this location is crowded. Shells and round shot are neatly stacked in the foreground. An artillery gun is just visible over tree trunks with another to its left glimpsed over large calibre shell casings. A group of Turkish or Croat labourers face the camera on the left. Beyond them to the right are the ends of two of the sheds at the Railway Depot.

Fenton's image entitled *Landing Place, Ordnance Wharf, Balaklava; Genoese Castle in the Distance.* (Library of Congress, Washington).

Today's view looking south-southeast from the bend in Balaklava's quayside towards the site of the Ordnance Wharf

Fenton's image entitled *Landing Place, Railway Stores, Balaklava, looking up the Harbour.* (Library of Congress, Washington]).

The scene today looking north-northwest along Balaklava's quayside from adjacent to site of the Railway Stores.

Fenton's image entitled **HMS** Diamond *and HMS* Wasp *anchored in the harbour at Balaklava.* (Royal Collection Trust/© Her Majesty Queen Elizabeth II 2016).

The view of the harbour today from a two-storey restaurant that now occupies Balaklava's quayside in this vicinity.

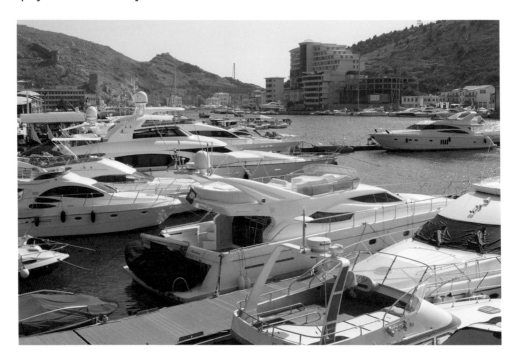

Above their heads, the white hospital buildings can again be seen on the hillside. Transports lie in the harbour, the waters of which are unseen.

Today, the promenade that follows the east side of the harbour through the town extends past the site of the Ordnance Wharf, which is in the foreground. The three-storey building with the red roof at centre is where the Railway Yard was located. The Railway Stables would have been near where the old cinema to its right with the red security fence is now found. The Ordnance Office building would have been to the right of the camera. Instead of transport ships, small boats that take tourists to around the harbour now occupy the mooring positions.

Fenton's next image entitled *Landing Place, Ordnance Wharf, Balaklava; Genoese Castle in the Distance* was taken looking south-southeast towards the Ordnance Wharf from a position close to the Railway Depot. At this location, the direction of the quay is bending from the south-southeast to the south-southwest. The Ordnance Office is the building closest to the camera. The cottage seen on the hillside behind the tree branches on the far left is likely the one featured in the right foreground of *The Town of Balaklava*, another of Fenton's images shown later in this chapter. The area with stacked round shot and parked artillery pieces in front of the Ordnance Office was the Ordnance Store Yard, which was adjacent the Fuel Store Yard. The Railway Stables would have been just off the image to the left.

The view today was taken close to where Fenton stood with his camera. The curve in the harbour side is comparable to the curve caught in Fenton's image. The Ordnance Office would have been where the furthest tree seen behind the row of stalls is found. The end wall of the Railway Stables would have occupied a site just a few yards to the left of the face of the old cinema building under repair on the far left.

The third of Fenton's images taken near the bend in the waterfront is entitled *Landing Place, Railway Stores, Balaklava, looking up the Harbour*. It shows the view along the quay at Balaklava to the north from very close to where his previous image was taken. It is likely that he just swivelled his camera around on its tripod between photographs. The end of the most northerly shed at the Railway Depot seen in the background of his first image is on the right. Split logs that served as railway sleepers are piled in the left foreground. Some rails have been laid on a few sleepers along the wharf. This may have been arranged for the photograph as no railway was built here at this time.

The buildings in the background were later demolished to make way for warehouses and storage yards. They are not seen in *Balaklava*, which is shown later, taken in the summer of 1855. Two large stacks of bags what are likely to have contained flour partially protected by waterproof covers lie on quay just left of centre.

The modern view looks north along the promenade that now runs along the harbourside. Holiday makers now stroll where labourers worked to off-load cargoes. Restaurants and shops now line an attractive waterfront. A large floating restaurant is on the left.

Fenton took an image looking out across the harbour from the northern entrance to Balaklava entitled *HMS* Diamond *and HMS* Wasp *anchored in the harbour at Balaklava*. The sailing ship on the right was HMS *Diamond* and the steamship on the left was HMS *Wasp*. These warships, which were positioned to deliver a broadside up the valley to the north if needs be, were the last line of defence for Balaklava at the time of the photograph, which was March 1855. Some of the crew of HMS *Diamond* served under Captain William Peel in the Diamond Battery in the siege lines as part of the Naval Brigade. The double-

The Robertson/Beato image entitled *Balaklava.* (Royal Collection Trust/© Her Majesty Queen Elizabeth II 2016).

The same view of Balaklava today from the hillside south of the Orthodox Church.

Fenton's image entitled *Balaklava from the Russian Church, Upper Harbour, and Church of Kadikoi in the distance.* (Royal Collection Trust/© Her Majesty Queen Elizabeth II 2016).

The Orthodox Church in Balaklava as it looks today.

Fenton's image entitled **The Town of Balaklava.** (Library of Congress, Washington).

Today's view north-northeast over Balaklava showing the same track in the foreground.

tracked military railway is in the foreground with freight waiting to be loaded on wagons stacked on the quay. Horses with carts wait on the right. The photograph gives the impression of much activity on the waterfront.

Today, the shoreline where Fenton took his image is a private marina for pleasure craft with controlled access. The view from a two-storey restaurant adjacent to the marina shows the harbour at this point today. Castle Hill is on the left with tourist developments evident over the water on the west side of the harbour. Jetties now act as moorings for boats where once the low pier on the left of the contemporary image once stood.

Balaklava Town

The first photograph was taken by the Robertson/Beato team from the hillside behind the southern end of the town and is entitled simply *Balaklava*. They would have reached the viewpoint by walking northeast from where they took their image entitled *Genoese Castle, Balaklava* shown earlier. It was very close to where John Laverty took his view of Balaklava's harbour, which is the first image presented in this chapter, in 1854.

Balaklava town in the summer of 1855 is seen in exceptional detail. Ships lie anchored or moored off the general landing area on the left. Again awnings stretch across decks suggesting hot, sunny weather. The cleared area at lower left with a single tree and what looks like a sentry box was the Fuel Store Yard with the Fuel Wharf to its left. This open space was just northeast of the Ordnance Wharf. The building beyond the empty Fuel Store area was the Railway Stables. Horses are visible outside in the yard. The curve in the shoreline here is where Roger Fenton took images of the Landing Place shown earlier. The long sheds beyond the stables were the Railway Depot and Saw Mill. The tracks of the military railway can be seen forking to their right as they swing around a street corner. The uncompleted, new church is at lower right. The two-storey building a little further away to its left was the Commandants House. Above the onion dome of the church there is a row of five huts. The last hut was the new Post Office with the Police Station in the building just beyond.

The cottage at lower centre to the right of the Fuel Store Yard with a single window visible on its end wall may have been where William Russell lived for a while. The railway runs to the left of this building. In the first week of March 1855, he humorously wrote:

> I left (Balaklava) on one post-day and arrived on another and it was with difficulty that I recognised the spot. A railway was running right across my courtyard, the walls were demolished, a severance existed between the mansion and its dependencies, and just as my friends and myself entered the "saloon and bedchamber" – a private apartment, through the floor of which I could investigate the quadrupeds below – the navvies gave us a startling welcome by pulling a poplar down on the roof, which had the effect of carrying away a portion of the balcony, and pent-tiles (pantiles), and smashing in my two windows elegantly 'glazed' with boards.

The road and railway into Balaklava can be seen rounding the bottom of Mt Hiblak next to the head of the harbour. The hospital with the hospital huts below are on the slope to the right. The row of huts seen high on the slope on the far right served as accommodation for the railway navvies. The three attached warehouses seen end-on near the waterfront comprised the Rum Store. Further away, two lines of tents rise up the lower slopes of

Fenton's image entitled **Balaklava looking Seaward, the Commandant's House in the Foreground.** (Library of Congress, Washington).

The same street today with the building on the left being where the Commandant's House would have stood.

Fenton's image entitled *View of Balaklava looking Seaward, with Ruined Shed in the Foreground.* (Royal Collection Trust/© Her Majesty Queen Elizabeth II 2016).

Fenton's image entitled *View of Balaklava looking Seaward, Russian Cottages in the Foreground.* (Royal Collection Trust/© Her Majesty Queen Elizabeth II 2016).

Guards' Hill from the valley floor, where the broad road to Kadikoi extends into the distance. The Sapoune Ridge is on the left skyline.

The same view today records the changes. The dome of the church tower, no longer onion-shaped, is at lower left amongst trees. All other buildings present in 1855 have disappeared and been replaced. Apartment buildings cover the hillside. A broad promenade lined with shops and restaurants extends along the waterfront where boats and a large floating restaurant are moored. A naval base lies at the end of the harbour with industrial buildings associated with the hillside quarries beyond. The large white apartment building at Kadykovka is visible between the slopes of Guards' Hill on the right and Mt Hiblak on the left. The Sapoune Ridge runs along the skyline left of centre.

The next contemporary image shown was taken by Roger Fenton in March 1855 and is entitled *Balaklava from the Russian Church, Upper Harbour, and Church of Kadikoi in the distance*. The dome and roof of the church remain unfinished with the windows and a side door blocked by stones. Tents are pitched in the church grounds. The white-washed cottage where Russell may have stayed is below on the left. The Fuel Store Yard beyond has a pile of wood. Horses on the far side of this yard stand outside the Railway Stables. The Railway Depot is behind the stables at the bend in the waterfront. The wharf that extends away from the camera appears congested with small boats near the shore while larger ships are moored further out in the harbour. The extensive hospital buildings are in a hollow above the town. Two rows of tents are again visible on the slopes of Guards' Hill beyond the harbour. The blurred white building in the cleft formed by the slope of Guards' Hill on the left and Mt Hiblak on the right is the church at Kadikoi.

In the modern view, the church at Balaklava can be recognised from Fenton's contemporary image even though the dome is no longer onion-shaped. The side door with steps seen in Fenton's photograph has been converted to a window. Trees obscure the view of the harbour-side to the left. The angle is different from the original because of trees and a wall at the top of the slope of the church yard made it impossible to take a photograph with exactly the same perspective.

Fenton's image entitled *The Town of Balaklava* is presented next. There are two images by this name taken from the same position with the same cottage with its roof being repaired on the right. Both feature the same tethered horse on the right and the same man sitting on the edge of the veranda. Differences include the number of horses on the track with the man standing on the left of the veranda in the shown image leading a horse in the other image. The baggage outside the door of the cottage also changes. Both photographs were taken further to the south-southwest and higher up the track that ran in front of the church. The cottage was lower down the same hillside from where *Balaklava* was photographed.

The end wall and veranda of the cottage and where Russell may have stayed is visible directly above the blurred man walking up the track to the right of the last horse. The railway passes in front of this cottage. The furthest of the two white-walled houses seen close together immediately above the cottage is likely to have been the old Post Office, which was the subject of Fenton's first photograph in the Crimea. The large building below on the left was being used as the Ordnance Office. Between this building and the Railway Stables were the Ordnance Store Yard and the Fuel Store Yard. The dark-roofed accommodation huts for the railway navvies are the highest structures seen on the slope behind Balaklava at centre. To their left and partly obscured by ships masts are the hospital buildings.

Fenton's image entitled *General View of Balaklava, the Hospital on the Right.* (Library of Congress, Washington).

Today's view over the same area from close to where Fenton took his image.

Fenton's image entitled **Railway Sheds and Workshops at Balaklava.** (Royal Collection Trust/© Her Majesty Queen Elizabeth II 2016).

The view over the same area today looking across Balaklava's harbour towards the entrance to the Cold War submarine base.

Fenton's image entitled **Railway Yard at Balaklava.** (Royal Collection Trust/© Her Majesty Queen Elizabeth II 2016).

Fenton's Image entitled **The Old Post Office, Balaklava.** (Royal Collection Trust/© Her Majesty Queen Elizabeth II 2016).

Simpson's watercolour entitled *Balaklava – looking towards the Sea.* (Library of Congress, Washington).

Today's view over Balaklava looking south from the hillside above where the hospital was located.

Simpson's watercolour entitled **The Railway at Balaklava.** (Library of Congress, Washington).

The same view today looking south from the car park at the entrance to 'old' Balaklava.

Fenton's image entitled **Cattle and Carts leaving Balaklava.** (Royal Collection Trust/© Her Majesty Queen Elizabeth II 2016).

Looking north from the northern entrance to Balaklava today.

The modern view was taken from a position further south-southwest along the track that passes in front of the church. Dachas with established trees, bushes and shrubs in gardens now line the track making it impossible to exactly reproduce the image from the same location. The hospital was located in the trees a little further down the slope to the left of the red-roofed apartment building seen in the middle distance just to the left of centre.

The Commandant's house, which was identified in the image entitled *Balaklava*, also appears in Fenton's photograph entitled *Balaklava looking Seaward, the Commandant's House in the Foreground*. The commandant from January 1855 onwards was Lieutenant Colonel Francis Pym Harding, whose portrait was also taken by Fenton. Russell believed that Harding partly closed down 'Vanity Fair', a collection of sutlers' stores and drinking establishments at Kadikoi, at the end of the summer of 1855 because he 'got angry at the evil habits of the people, who permitted dirt, offal, bones, bottles, and nasty things of all kinds, to accumulate, and would not clear then away when ordered to do so'.

The photograph of the Commandant's house is interesting because it shows the area when buildings were being knocked down to clear the way for new less picturesque, but more practical structures needed for the war effort. For instance, the cottages on the right are not seen in *Balaklava* taken later in the year. The building in the left foreground belonged to the Main Guard. The church was just beyond this building, but is unseen. The Ordnance Office is next to the wharf beyond and to the right of the Commandant's House. Further along the harbour side beyond the Ordnance Office, timber can be seen stacked on the Rough Timber Wharf. Castle Hill rises on the left in the middle distance. The lower tower that featured in *The old Genoese Castle at Balaklava, from above the castle pier* is visible above the slope. The white-walled cottage with the veranda seen immediately below and slightly to the right of the tower is in the right foreground of *The Town of Balaklava*. The modern view shows the street that ran in front of the Commandant's House with another house of a similar style in approximately the same position.

Fenton took two images of the cottage on the extreme right of *Balaklava looking Seaward, the Commandant's House in the Foreground* showing its attached 'shed' in the process of being demolished. These he called *View of Balaklava looking Seaward, with Ruined Shed in the Foreground* and *View of Balaklava looking Seaward, Russian Cottages in the Foreground*. They are really before and after shots of the same scene with exactly the same background. The only real difference is that the shed is partially destroyed in the first image and totally destroyed in the second. Fenton may even have waited with his camera on its tripod between photographs while navvies went to work to finish the job.

Fenton's image entitled *General View of Balaklava, the Hospital on the Right* shows the same cottage that featured in the previous images before any demolition work had started. This photograph was taken from further south looking back to the north. Just right of centre, the railway can be seen curving as it follows a bend in the main street. Piles of goods with waterproof covers are visible on the wharf behind the long shed of the Railway Depot. Above the poplar on the right, the town hospital can again be seen on the slopes of Mt Hiblak. Guards' Hill is across the harbour on the left and the three rows of mule sheds can be seen on lower slopes of the valley below. The scene today has dramatically changed with many holiday apartments now on the slopes above of the old town.

The Fenton image *Railway Sheds and Workshops at Balaklava* was taken further north than *General View of Balaklava, the Hospital on the Right* and looks to the northwest The railway yard is in the foreground with what is likely to be the corner of the old Post Office at lower left. Wagons loaded with sleepers wait to be transported to where the line was still under construction on the Chersonese Plateau. The Saw Mill is the shed on the left with a pile of cut sleepers outside. The long shed beyond is the Railway Workshop. Landed goods lie stacked on the wharf to the left of original white-walled building. These buildings had disappeared by the time *Balaklava* was taken by the Robertson/Beato team a few months later. The same view today extends over the harbour to the northern entrance of the Cold War era underground submarine pen, which is now a major tourist attraction.

Fenton positioned himself in the centre foreground of *Railway Sheds and Workshops at Balaklava* when he took *Railway Yard at Balaklava*. The view is to the northeast with the end of the long railway workshop shed on the left. A winding drum, which may have been too small for use at the stationary winding engine at the top of the slope out of Kadikoi, is behind the man on the left. The railway track on the far right went in front of the old Post Office and on to the Ordnance Wharf. All three tracks seen in the picture joined before running north-northwest as a single track along the main street of Balaklava. The row of huts furthest up the slope in the background served as accommodation for the railway navvies. Fenton took another similar image from exactly the same position, but without the wagon containing sacks and with more people in the foreground.

Fenton took his first image after arriving at Balaklava, which was entitled, *The Old Post Office, Balaklava*, looking east-southeast from the railway yard. The roof of the same house, which was commandeered for use as a military post office, is seen between the cottages and long railway shed in *General View of Balaklava, the Hospital on the Right*. The building has been damaged most likely as a result of navvies constructing the railway through its front garden. How long it served as the post office is not clear, but 'old' in the photograph's title suggest it was no longer in use as such. Discarded bottles are visible to the left of the door and individuals pose for the camera on the balcony and steps. A winding drum for cables is on the left. The building seems to have survived at least until the time when Robertson/Beato team took *Balaklava* a few months later.

William Simpson drew and later painted a watercolour entitled *Balaklava - looking towards the Sea* which shows the view south from the slopes of Mt Hiblak on the north side of the town at an early stage of the war. Tents are prominent in the foreground in front of buildings on the right that could be part of the hospital. The church, which is described as incomplete in the painting's description, stands on the hillside in the left middle distance. A track passes the church and runs in front of several houses. It was here that Fenton took his images entitled *The Town of Balaklava*. The large building further down the slope from the church behind a single poplar was where the Ordnance Office was located and is the same one as seen on the lower left of Fenton's image. A transport ship is in the harbour to the right of the Ordnance Office. The small boat moored alongside is Lord Cardigan's yacht. HMS *Agamemnon* is the large warship to the right of the transport. The town is depicted as it looked before much was destroyed to make way for railway workshops, warehouses and the rum store.

The modern view from what is believed be the same location as where Simpson drew his picture shows the castle towers much as the artist portrayed them. Again the exception is the tower on the crag over the harbour entrance which has been replaced by a maritime look-out station. The dome of the church is just visible above a tree on the left where Simpson placed it. The west side of the harbour was unspoilt in 1854, but now boasts a waterfront road and a large hotel, apartments and a wharf for pleasure boats.

Fenton's image entitled *Balaklava from the camp of the Scots Fusilier Guards.* (Library of Congress, Washington).

The view today showing the changes to the terrain that have occurred as a result of quarrying operations and the activities of associated industries.

The Robertson/Beato image entitled *Balaklava: Huts of the Guards.* (Royal Collection Trust/© Her Majesty Queen Elizabeth II 2016).

The modern view today from the much disturbed slope of Guards' Hill.

A later watercolour by Simpson entitled *The Railway and Balaklava* depicts the military railway entering the town from the north. Croats, who worked as labourers, are shown on the left and local Tartars on the right. The church is glimpsed at the end of the road. Ships line the wharf on the right with goods covering the quay. Castle Hill is prominent in the distance.

The area today is still the gateway to the old town. It is where visitors park their cars and where the buses turn around. The street that disappears just left of centre leads to the church. Restaurants are now found on the waterfront at right. The fortress on Castle Hill still looms over the town.

Fenton took a photograph at the entrance to Balaklava looking in the opposite direction to the depiction by Simpson of the railway entering the town. Fenton called his image *Cattle and Carts leaving Balaklava*, when the direction they were pointing would suggest that they were heading into the town. The steep, rocky slope descending from the right is that of Mt. Hiblak. The distant hillside on the far left is Guards' Hill with the Sapoune Ridge just visible beyond. The image looks north with Balaklava behind the camera. The edge of the military railway that ran parallel to the road along the narrow strip of flat land between Mt Hiblak and the harbour is at lower left.

The modern equivalent image shows today's main road leaving Balaklava with the rocky slope of Mt Hiblak on the right. To accommodate the buildings, the lower slope of the hill was removed. The view behind the camera is as shown in the previous colour photograph.

Balaklava from Guards' Hill

The Guards Brigade had suffered significant losses at the Battle of Inkerman. The troops were excused trench duty and were sent to Balaklava to recuperate and help defend the port on 22 February 1855. The Coldstream Guards, the Grenadier Guards and the Scots Fusilier Guards camped on the slopes of the hill that rose on the western side of the valley that ran from Kadikoi to Balaklava.

Roger Fenton visited the Guards' camp at the end of March and took a number of images from the slopes of Guards' Hill, as it was called locally by the occupying British force. Fenton recalled in a letter home that a hot wind was blowing and the thermometer reached 82°F in the shade. He complained that the dry heat warped and split his camera slides. As a consequence, several of his pictures were spoilt.

Fenton took three similar images looking south-southeast from Guards' Hill. They all show the harbour of Balaklava full of ships in the distance, but he moved his camera to get different views of the Guards' camp in the foreground. The image presented here is entitled *Balaklava from the camp of the Scots Fusilier Guards*. The others are called *Guards' Hill, Church Parade, Balaklava in Distance* and *View of Balaklava from camp of Fusilier Guards*.

In the image shown, timber for hut construction can be seen strewn on the ground to the extreme right. Horses graze between the bell tents in the foreground. More tents can be seen further down the slope on the left below a hut. These may have belonged to another regiment. Horizontal smoke emanating from piles of burning rubbish in the foreground and valley floor indicates that a strong wind was blowing from the south, which was the sirocco described by Fenton. The broad road in the valley below leaving Balaklava went to Kadikoi and then on to the Col de Balaklava and the infantry camps of the Chersonese Plateau. To the left of the road and on the other side of the tents on the valley floor on the far left can be seen the straight line of the military railway, which also ran to the camps on the Chersonese Plateau via the Col de Balaklava. Castle Hill with the Genoese castle on its summit is on the right skyline. The faint shape of the high, steep cliffs at Cape Aya further east along the Black Sea coast are just visible at centre left over the slope of the hill behind the port of Balaklava.

The modern photograph, which was taken from a relatively flat area where rows of garages have been constructed, shows how the contours on the hillside have been altered today by quarrying operations. The hillside is now terraced with another level platform below for industry. Dirt roads to carry quarry trucks have been cut into the hill side. The large expanse of exposed rock on the right of the contemporary images has disappeared. A rock crushing plant with a conveyer now stands at the base of its old location. The valley floor is today an urban extension of Balaklava with a naval base at the near end of the harbour.

James Robertson and Felice Beato visited Guards' Hill in the summer of 1855 to take photographs of not only the spectacular view to the south-southeast over Balaklava, but also the equally impressive views in other directions shown later. Their image of the Guards' camp, which was taken from higher up the slope than Fenton's picture, is entitled *Balaklava: Huts of the Guards*. It shows three rows of wooden cabins with a sentry box beyond. The road on the valley floor after leaving Balaklava is on the far left. It is crossed at right angles by a branch of the military railway that serviced the Diamond Wharf on the west side of the harbour. In the background, huts that provided accommodation at the Castle Hospital can be seen on the shoulder of land to the left of Castle Hill. In this image, the cliffs at Cape Aya in the distance are more visible than in Fenton's photograph. When the Robertson/Beato photograph was taken is not precisely known, but it was probably before the Guards returned to frontline duties in the middle of June 1855.

The view today from higher up Guards' Hill shows trees, probably planted to minimise erosion, in the foreground on the once grassy slopes. One thing that has not changed in the last 160 years is the magnificent view over Balaklava harbour to Castle Hill and Cape Aya.

The Battle of Balaklava
The Russians go on the Offensive

Soon after Balaklava's occupation, work began on constructing defences to deter attacks by the Russian army at large in the hinterland. Three British gun batteries were established in redoubts on the high ground known as the 'Marine Heights' which lay to the east of the port. These gun positions faced north and looked out over the South Valley of Balaklava. Battery No.1 was the highest and located on the ridge that led up to the summit of Mt Asketi with Battery No. 2 lower down and 470 yards to the west-northwest. Battery No. 3 was positioned about 800 yards to the north-west-northwest of Battery No. 2 on the top of a hillock that was attached to Mt Hiblak by a col. In addition to the guns on the Marine Heights, artillery was deployed in Battery No. 4 within Campbell's Redoubt, which was on a knoll near the settlement of Kadikoi, and at Battery No. 5 on the eastern slope of Frenchman's Hill, which was also known as or Vinoy's Hill, to the west of Kadikoi. These last two batteries covered the immediate northern approaches to the valley that led down to Balaklava from Kadikoi.

As further protection, an outer defence perimeter consisting of four earthwork redoubts was hurriedly constructed by the Turks on the summit of what became known as Canrobert's Hill, at the eastern end of the South Valley of Balaklava, and on three hillocks on the eastern Causeway Heights, a ridge which separated the North and South Valleys of Balaklava. These were known as Nos. 1, 2, 3 and 4 Redoubts respectively, but consisted of little more than a ditch and parapet. A further two unoccupied redoubts, known as Nos. 5 and 6 Redoubts, were under construction on the western end of the Causeway Heights.

Major General Sir Colin Campbell with about 4,000 men and a total of thirty-five naval and field guns was responsible for the defence of Balaklava in October 1854. The force on the Marine Heights consisted of a garrison of 1,200 Royal Marines (two battalions) with artillery plus 200 men (two companies) of the 93rd (Sutherland Highlanders) Regiment. Another 550 men (six companies) of the 93rd and 600 Turks (one battalion) were stationed near Campbell's Redoubt at Kadikoi together with about 200 men in Captain Barker's W Field Battery. The outer redoubts on Canrobert's Hill and the Causeway Heights were manned by 1,500 Turkish soldiers (two-and-a-half battalions) with three British 12-pounder position guns at No.1 Redoubt and two at each of Nos. 2-4 Redoubts. To supervise gun operations, two British artillerymen were stationed at No.1 Redoubt and one at each of the other redoubts.

In addition to the above, approximately 1,500 men of the British Heavy Cavalry and Light Cavalry Brigades under the command of Lord Lucan with another 200 men of Captain Maude's I Troop of Royal Horse Artillery were camped near a vineyard on the

Klembovsky's image of the knoll, which is seen on the left, that carried Campbell's Redoubt as it looked in the early 1900s from the southern slopes of Sutherland Hillock. A house has been built on its summit since the Crimean War. Kadikoi church stands in front of a line of trees on the extreme right. Guards' Hill is in the middle distance on the right, and a castle tower on Castle Hill in Balaklava is visible on the skyline on the extreme left. (Walter Havighurst Special Collections, Miami University Libraries, Oxford, Ohio).

western slopes of the Causeway Heights near the unfinished No. 6 Redoubt and available for defence duty.

In total, almost 6,000 men could be immediately called upon to defend Balaklava. However, as the capture of Sevastopol took precedence over everything else, most allied troops were camped several miles away on the Chersonese Plateau closer to the siege lines. When Balaklava was threatened, it took some time for these men to march to the aid of those under attack outside Balaklava.

The Fall of the Redoubts
The attack by the Russian army, which had been moving freely in the countryside to the rear of the allied siege lines, had been planned as a way of alleviating the pressure on Sevastopol by taking the thinly held defences around Balaklava and cutting the British lines of communication. The Russian force approaching Balaklava early on the morning of 25 October 1854 were under the overall command of Prince Menshikov, who had led the Russians at the Battle of the Alma, with Lieutenant General Liprandi as local commander. Under these men were the cavalry led by Lieutenant General Ryzhov and infantry columns led by Colonel Skyuderi, Major General Levutsky, Major General Semyakin and Major General Gribbe. In addition, there was follow-up support led by Major General Zhabokritsky

The same view today looking south from Sutherland Hillock to the knoll, again seen on the left, that carried Campbell's Redoubt. The summit, which is lined by trees, is now occupied by a school and its recreation area. The tower on Castle Hill is again visible on the extreme left skyline. During the Battle of Balaklava, the 93rd Highlanders advanced from behind Campbell's Redoubt to Sutherland Hillock to face the Russian cavalry as 'the thin red line'.

and reserves. It has been estimated that 25,000 Russians with seventy-eight guns were available for action at Balaklava on that day.

The opening move before dawn was the seizure of the village of Kamara by Gribbe's column and the establishment of gun positions on the high ground that overlooks the South Valley of Balaklava from the east. These guns opened fire on No.1 Redoubt on Canrobert's Hill. At first light, Semyakin's column, which had entered and crossed the eastern end of the North Valley of Balaklava from the Chernaya Valley attacked the strongpoint. Soon afterwards, No. 2 Redoubt on the Causeway Heights was attacked by Levutsky's column, which also entered the North Valley through the gap from the Chernaya Valley. In addition, Nos. 3 and 4 Redoubts came under attack by Skyuderi's men, who had marched along the track through the Fedioukine Hills from the Tractir Bridge before descending into the North Valley.

Soon afterwards, No. 2 Redoubt on the Causeway Heights was attacked by Levutski's column, which also entered the North Valley through the gap from the Chernaya Valley. In addition, Nos. 3 and 4 Redoubts came under attack by Skiuderi's men, who had marched along the track through the Fedioukine Hills from the Tractir Bridge before descending into the North Valley.

As an initial response, the British cavalry was moved forward into the eastern part of the

An aerial view of the battlefield of Balaklava showing the principal cavalry movements of 25 October 1854. The yellow line follows approximately the route taken by the Russian Cavalry from just after it crossed the Tractir Bridge at the upper right to its encounter with the 93rd Highlanders on Sutherland Hillock (SH) and its repulse on the southern slopes of the Causeway Heights. The route taken by the Heavy Brigade (HB) up until its engagement with the Russian cavalry is in red as is the route taken later by the Light Brigade (LB) from its starting point in the North Valley of Balaklava through the Don Cossack gun battery (G) and on towards the aqueduct where the valley narrows between Mt Hasfort and the Fedioukine Hills. The movement of the French Chasseurs d'Afrique (CA) from the North Valley onto the Fedioukine Hills, where Russian guns that had fired on the Light Brigade, is shown in light blue. North is at the top. Key: R1, R2, R3, R4, R5 and R6 indicate the positions of Nos. 1-6 Redoubts. (Adapted from a Goggle Earth™ image).

South Valley and Maude's I Troop of Royal Horse Artillery was sent to the high ground to the right of No. 3 Redoubt in support of the Turks.

After a courageous defence and a fierce struggle, No. 1 Redoubt was captured from its Turkish garrison. Meanwhile, the Turkish troops in Nos. 2-4 Redoubts and Maude's artillery on the Causeway Heights had been coming under fire from Russians under advancing across the North Valley. After Maude was seriously wounded, many gunners killed and with the ammunition almost exhausted, I Troop was withdrawn under the protection of the cavalry and replaced by two guns in the right division of Barker's W Field Battery under Lieutenant Dickson. However, this section of W Battery was also forced to retreat when no infantry support for the Turks was in the offering and its position became untenable. Faced with a determined and well supported foe, the Turkish defenders in Nos. 2-4 Redoubts abandoned their positions. Retreating Turks were pursued either along the Causeway Heights or across the South Valley by mounted Cossacks and lancers. Many were overtaken and killed. Survivors reaching British lines regrouped near the men of the 93rd Regiment, who had been brought forward to a low hillock 500 yards to the north of Campbell's Redoubt.

Nos. 1-4 Redoubts were in Russian hands by at least 08.00 hours. The British cavalry was forced to retreat west along the South Valley because of cannon fire from Canrobert's Hill and the Causeway Heights. However, the Russian infantry did not advance any further than No. 4 Redoubt. One saving grace was that most, if not all, of the guns left behind had been spiked by British gunners. The Russians continued to occupy Nos. 1-3 Redoubts throughout the battle, but quickly withdrew from No. 4 Redoubt after the wooden gun platforms here were dismantled and their broken parts scattered. The two guns were later recovered.

By 08.30 hours, the British Heavy and Light Cavalry Brigades were hidden from Russian gun fire and the Russian view behind the most westerly hillock in the Causeway Heights chain that carried the unfinished No. 6 Redoubt.

At about this time, Fanny Duberly, who had been instructed by her husband Captain Henry Duberly, the paymaster of the 8th Hussars, to ride to the Light Cavalry Brigade camp as soon as possible, arrived on the scene from Balaklava. She helped her husband strike his tent and pack up his belongings before they retreated on horseback over a ditch and into a vineyard. She witnessed the next stage of the battle from a safer position further to the west.

The Thin Red Line
The next significance event was the advance of the Russian cavalry comprising of about 2,000 horsemen into the North Valley of Balaklava. This force is believed to have used the track through the Fedioukine Hills from the Tractir Bridge that the British army had used a month before when approaching Balaklava at the end of the 'flank march'. Ryzhov had received vague orders to take action against what the Russians perceived to be an artillery park near Kadikoi. The main body of the Russian cavalry moved diagonally across the North Valley in a west-southwest direction and up onto the Causeway Heights after passing the ridge carrying No. 4 Redoubt. Some outriders may have ascended this ridge. The Russians crested the Causeway Heights at No. 5 Redoubt close to 09.00 hours. Four squadrons of hussars consisting of approximately 400 men then detached themselves from the main force and turned towards the low hillock before Kadikoi now defended by the 93rd Highlanders.

This knoll was a natural barrier protecting the approach to the village of Kadikoi from the South Valley and lay to the north of the hillock where Campbell's Redoubt was sited. It had a steep slope on its western edge and gentler declines to the north, east and south. Today, 'Sutherland Hillock', as it came to be known, runs for about 530 yards from the bottom of its western slope to where it merges with vineyards in the east. On the morning of the battle, it was occupied by 550 men the 93rd Highlanders and 100 or so miscellaneous invalid soldiers under the command of Sir Colin Campbell. These troops were supported by a battery of four pieces of Barker's W Field Battery on their left flank and on both flanks by a total of about 1,000 Turkish soldiers that had regrouped after retreating from the Causeway Height redoubts.

To avoid casualties from Russian field guns now firing from the Causeway Heights, the 93rd Highlanders lay down on the reverse slope of Sutherland Hillock out of the line of fire. The Russian cavalry cresting the Causeway Heights may have seen only a Turkish force and some cannon before deciding to attack. Most Turks broke ranks and fled towards Kadikoi

Klembovsky's image of Canrobert's Hill, which carried No.1 Redoubt, in the South Valley of Balaklava in the early 1900s. The view is west from the high ground near the village of Kamara. The hillock on the Causeway Heights that carried No. 2 Redoubt is on the far right. The Sapouné Ridge is on the right and centre skyline with the Col de Balaklava the low point on the left skyline. (Walter Havighurst Special Collections, Miami University Libraries, Oxford, Ohio).

Canrobert's Hill from just west of Kamara as it looks today. A Russian column under Major General Semyakin attacked the hill from the right after it was bombarded by Major General Grippe's guns positioned on the high ground near where this photograph was taken.

as the Russians approached. However, two lines of British soldiers appearing to William Russell observing the battle on the Sapoune Ridge as a 'thin red streak tipped with a line of steel' rose on the approach of the Russian cavalry. It seems likely that the 93rd Highlanders fired a volley into the midst of the charging Russian cavalry at about 600 yards, which then veered to the southeast, and another volley at about 250 yards, which turned the charge to the east. Campbell wrote later that only 100 soldiers, who were wheeled into line to face the northeast as the Russians passed, fired the second volley. Repulsed without any obvious casualties, the Russians rode back to the Causeway Heights. The engagement was all over in five minutes with the gateway to the port of Balaklava remaining in British hands.

The Charge of the Heavy Brigade

At the time the Russian cavalry was approaching the crest of the Causeway Heights, most of the Heavy Brigade was advancing into the South Valley from the north-northwest having orders from Lord Raglan to make for Kadikoi in support of the defenders of Balaklava. This redeployment from behind the hillock carrying No. 6 Redoubt had been ordered before the Russian cavalry had entered the North Valley. Only the 1st (Royal) Dragoons were instructed to remain behind under the Sapoune Ridge.

After the separation of the detachment that attacked the 93rd Highlanders, the main Russian force consisted of approximately 1,600 horsemen. Although unclear from contemporary accounts, the Russian cavalry must have ridden roughly west from No.5 Redoubt along the southern edge of the plateau that constitutes the Causeway Heights in this area. The ends of the lances of the Russian cavalry moving along the skyline must have been seen by the Heavy Brigade on its way to Kadikoi just before the leading Russians saw the first squadrons of the Heavy Brigade in the South Valley. Gone were any thoughts in the minds of the British cavalry commanders of riding to the support the Turks and the 93rd Highlanders. The main threat was now from the enemy on the high ground to the north and the Russians here had to be faced.

It seems likely that the Russians turned to the south and realigned on the top of the slope of the Causeway Heights when they saw the Heavy Brigade. After dressing their lines and extending to their left, they then advanced down the slope until nearly level with the top of a vineyard to their right. When the Heavy Brigade was about 400 yards away and 100 feet below, the Russians hesitated on the slope long enough for the leading three squadrons of the British cavalry to face north and dress their lines. The Russian cavalry had missed a narrow window of opportunity to charge the flank of the Heavy Brigade, which they outnumbered two to one from a height advantage.

At about 09.10 hours, initially with only 300 men of the first squadron of the 6th (Inniskilling) Dragoons and the two squadrons of the 2nd (Scots Greys) Dragoons, Brigadier General James Scarlett led the attack into the centre of the startled Russian horsemen. Initially, the Scots Greys had to traverse the abandoned and partially struck camp of the Light Brigade. It was only when clear of this obstruction could it align with the first squadron of the Iniskilling, which had been restrained, and gather speed. Shots were fired by the Russians as this first wave of the Heavy Brigade approached at little more than an uphill trot. Led by Scarlett, the British troopers then disappeared into the enemy column, which began to close around them from the flanks.

Almost immediately afterwards, the second squadron of the Iniskilling engaged the Russian left flank, which was turning inwards, followed by the whole of the 5th (Princess

The knoll on the Causeway Heights that carried No. 2 Redoubt looking west from the Sevastopol-Yalta Highway. This strongpoint on Sevastopol's outer line of defences was attacked and captured by Major General Levutsky's column. The Sapoune Ridge is on the right skyline.

The hillock on the Causeway Heights that carried No. 3 Redoubt looking south over the North Valley of Balaklava from the Fedioukine Hills. This strategic position was attacked and captured by Major General Skyuderi's column and Russian guns positioned at this location later fired on the Light Brigade as it advanced from right to left down the 'Valley of Death' in the foreground. The Don Cossack battery was probably about a further 1,000 yards to the left. Marine Heights is the hill on the skyline on the right.

Klembovsky's image of the hillock on the Causeway Heights that carried No. 4 Redoubt as seen looking southwest from the North Valley of Balaklava in the early 1900s. Major General Skyuderi's men held this ridge for a short time during the battle before retreating. (Walter Havighurst Special Collections, Miami University Libraries, Oxford, Ohio).

The same view today showing the hillock that carried No. 4 Redoubt from the North Valley of Balaklava. The monument on the summit marks the location of the redoubt. Lieutenant General Ryzhov's cavalry moved from left to right up the valley before ascending the Causeway Heights on the far right skyline. Later the same morning, the Light Brigade advanced from right to left at the beginning of its ride down the valley.

Looking north from the knoll that was the site of Campbell's Redoubt in Kadikoi towards the straw-coloured eastern end of Sutherland Hillock in the South Valley of Balaklava. The men of the 93rd Highlanders lay down behind this low ridge as protection from Russian gun fire, but rose when the Russian cavalry charged down the now vineyard-covered slope of the Causeway Heights seen on the centre skyline. The ridge on the Causeway Heights where No. 4 Redoubt was located is on the extreme right skyline.

The view to the north-northeast over the South Valley of Balaklava from the high point on Sutherland Hillock with the ridge on the Causeway Heights that carried No. 4 Redoubt on the right. The Russian cavalry would have charged down the slope seen on the left and then veered off to the right as a result of fire from the 93rd Highlanders.

Charlotte of Wales's) Dragoon Guards in the centre. After crossing the bottom of a nearby vineyard, the two squadrons of the 4th (Royal Irish) Dragoon Guards rode up its eastern side, turned and penetrated the Russian right flank. Although ordered to remain behind near No. 6 Redoubt, the men of the 1st (Royal) Dragoons came to the assistance of their comrades on the initiative of their commanding officer. This regiment followed the Royal Irish and fell on the Russian right front. This brought the total attacking force to 750-800 men. Observers on the Sapoune Ridge saw British formations emerging from the mêlée after cutting their way through the Russians. The staggered frontal and flanking attacks broke the Russians, who turned and fled after only five to eight minutes fighting.

After the engagement, the disorganised Russian cavalry tried to regroup, but were subject to artillery fire from W Field Battery positioned west of Sutherland Hillock and I Troop just in advance of the Light Brigade's position near No. 6 Redoubt. In addition, Captain Brandling's C Troop of Royal Horse Artillery, having quickly redeployed from the Chersonese Plateau to the South Valley, was in action behind the Heavy Brigade. The discouraged Russian cavalry retreated back over the crest of the Causeway Heights and rode east down the North Valley to take up positions behind eight guns of the Don Cossack field battery. This was the high point of the day for the Allies. A large force of Russian cavalry had been defeated by the 93rd Highlanders and half its number of British cavalry.

Despite the fierce clash of the opposing cavalries, relatively few fatal casualties were recorded. It has been suggested that the blunt swords of the Heavy Brigade and the even blunter swords and thick coats of the Russian cavalry were the reason. About nine were killed and ninety-six wounded in the Heavy Brigade while forty to fifty Russians were reported to have been killed and about 200 wounded. The Russian cavalry now had a healthy respect for the British cavalry.

During the fight, officers of the Light Brigade had been watching from the high ground close to No. 6 Redoubt. Eager to engage the flank of the enemy cavalry as it moved off in disarray about 500 yards away, Captain William Morris of the 17th Lancers is reputed to have tried to persuade Lord Cardigan to initiate an attack. However, this attack, which may well have resulted in the rout of a disordered force, did not happen. Cardigan afterwards insisted that he had been ordered by his superior Lord Lucan to hold his ground, but Lucan's version of the orders he gave differ in that he was sure that he told Cardigan to attack all that came within reach. An opportunity for a crushing blow on the Russian cavalry had been lost.

Moves to Recover the Captured Guns on the Causeway Heights

After the successful charge by the Heavy Brigade and the retreat of the Russian cavalry, the attention of Raglan positioned on the elevated Sapoune Ridge was turned towards the recovery of Nos. 1-3 Redoubts that had been lost to the enemy. Raglan's intention was for the Heavy and Light Brigades to move against the Russians on the Causeway Heights immediately with later support from advancing infantry, which was descending into the South Valley from the Chersonese Plateau via the Col de Balaklava. Raglan sent an order to this effect to Lucan down below on the battlefield which reached him at about 09.50 hours. However, the message about recovering the Causeway Heights was ambiguous and Lucan decided that it meant he had to wait for infantry support. As a result, Raglan became more and more exasperated about the lack of action, especially as he believed the captured British guns were being withdrawn from the occupied redoubts as trophies. At

The first image of Fenton's 1855 panorama looking out over a hazy battlefield of Balaklava from the edge of the Sapoune Ridge near where Raglan would have watched the action. The view is east down the North Valley of Balaklava with the line of the Vorontsov Road clearly visible on the right. The southern edge of the Fedioukine Hills is on the left. The Light Brigade would have begun its advance down the valley on the right to the left of the road. (Royal Collection Trust/© Her Majesty Queen Elizabeth II, 2016).

The same view looking east over today's vineyards in the North Valley of Balaklava from the Sapoune Ridge. The Sevastopol-Yalta Highway, which roughly follows the line of the old Vorontsov Road, disappears into the distance along the Causeway Heights on the right. The modern road below at centre not seen in 1855 intersects the Sevastopol-Yalta Highway at a large roundabout.

The second image of Fenton's 1855 panorama of the battlefield of Balaklava from the Sapoune Ridge looks over the most westerly hillock in the Causeway Heights chain towards the South Valley of Balaklava. The light-coloured marks on a ridge of this hillock in the centre are works associated with the construction of the unfinished No. 6 Redoubt. The Vorontsov Road is now on the far left. The light-coloured patch to the right of the bend in the road is the site of the unfinished No. 5 Redoubt. The conical-shaped Canrobert's Hill, which carried No. 1 Redoubt, rises from the valley floor in the distance beyond the same bend. (Royal Collection Trust/© Her Majesty Queen Elizabeth II, 2016).

The same view today looking over the most westerly hillock in the Causeway Heights chain from the Sapoune Ridge. The Russian cavalry crossed the ground from left to right beyond this hillock before being attacked by the Heavy Brigade. The Sevastopol-Yalta Highway can be seen on the far left as it swings on to the Causeway Heights. Canrobert's Hill is at the end of the South Valley above the curve in the road.

The third image in Fenton's 1855 panorama of the battlefield of Balaklava from the Sapoune Ridge. The undulations at the western end of the South Valley of Balaklava are in the foreground with the valley itself below and before the tents seen in and around Kadikoi in the left middle distance. Mt Hiblak with the higher Marine Heights beyond are in the distance on the left with the cliffs at Cape Aya above on the skyline. Castle Hill in Balaklava is on the skyline just left of centre. The low elongated ridge seen at centre is Frenchman's or Vinoy's Hill. The tents seen beyond where this ridge drops on the right are those of the cavalry. (Royal Collection Trust/© Her Majesty Queen Elizabeth II, 2016).

10.55 hours, with growing impatience, Raglan selected Captain Louis Nolan to carry another written command to Lucan.

Nolan rode down the steep escarpment of the Sapoune Ridge below Raglan's viewpoint and at 11.00 hours delivered the infamous 'Fourth Order to the Cavalry' to Lucan, who has been reported as watching the approach of the British infantry from a knoll on the Causeway Heights between Nos. 4 and 5 Redoubts. Unfortunately, the dictated message from Raglan handwritten by Brigadier General Airey was again ambiguous when it needed to be precise. The order was for the cavalry to advance rapidly to the front and try and prevent the enemy carrying away the guns. In Raglan's mind, it was linked to the previous order which stated that the redoubts on the heights were the objective, but it was not interpreted as such by Lucan.

Nolan, who disliked Lucan strongly for his perceived dithering, did not fully explain the action required of the cavalry. When Lucan asked about the position of the guns referred to in Raglan's order, an exasperated Nolan was reported to have pointed down the North Valley. However, from where they were positioned, the angle between the guns in the North Valley and the guns on the Causeway Heights at No. 3 Redoubt was a mere twenty degrees. Lucan later recounted in a letter to Raglan dated 30 November 1855:

The same view today looking south-southeast over the South Valley towards Balaklava from the Sapoune Ridge. The most westerly hillock in the Causeway Heights chain is now on the extreme left. It is believed that the Light Brigade would have been positioned on its slopes near the pylon with the Heavy Brigade to its right at around 08.30 hours on 25 October 1854. Most of the Heavy Brigade later moved off in the direction of Kadikoi and attacked the Russian cavalry where a settlement is now found on the far side of the hillock. The large apartments in the middle distance to the left of centre now occupy the site of Kadikoi. The ridge to their right was known as Frenchman's or Vinoy's Hill. The valley where the cavalry camped in 1855 can be glimpsed beyond and to the right of Frenchman's Hill.

> After carefully reading of the order, I hesitated, and urged the uselessness of such an attack, and the dangers attending it; the aide-de-camp, in a most authoritative tone, stated that they were Lord Raglan's orders that the cavalry should attack immediately. I asked him where? and what to do? as neither enemy nor guns were in sight. He replied in a most disrespectful but significant manner, pointing to the further end of the valley, 'There, my lord, is your enemy, there are your 'guns'.

Lucan claims that he could see neither the guns in the North Valley nor the guns in the captured redoubts on the Causeway Heights from his position. In Lucan's defence, there is an area around his location between Nos. 4 and 5 Redoubts where the views of both are obstructed by the lie of the land. Lucan's restricted view may not have been fully appreciated by Raglan and even by Nolan. Nevertheless, Lucan if confused, should have questioned Nolan further until he was sure he understood the order. This didn't happen. Lucan perceived the need for action without waiting for the support of infantry, which by now was just arriving.

Cardigan, as commander of the Light Brigade, was instructed by Lucan to advance on the Russian guns stretched partly across the eastern half of the North Valley and not the

captured British guns on the Causeway Heights as Raglan intended. Both men knew that it was foolhardy for cavalry to attack field batteries, but as Cardigan and his brother-in-law Lucan were hardly on speaking terms, there was little discussion between the two men on the seemingly military inappropriateness of the order. In addition, speed was essential as Raglan had also demanded immediate action from Lucan, which Nolan had been eager to emphasize. The frosty relationship between the Nolan and Lucan and Lucan and Cardigan, and the imprecise order sent by Raglan, all contributed to the disaster that was to follow.

The Charge of the Light Brigade
At 11.10 hours, the Light Brigade moved from its start position northeast of No. 5 Redoubt down the North Valley towards the eight guns of the 3rd Field Battery of the Don Cossacks. Cardigan was out in front followed by his brigade staff and trumpeter. The front line consisted of the 17th Lancers on the right and the 13th Light Dragoons on the left. On the orders of Lucan, the 11th Hussars were dropped back to make up a second line at left rear. The 4th Light Dragoons and the 8th Hussars were a supporting third line, which almost caught up with the 11th Hussars during the final stages of the charge. The Heavy Brigade under Scarlett was ordered by Lucan to follow in the rear as support.

During the long delay in implementing Raglan's orders, Russian infantry and guns under Major General Zhabokritsky had occupied the low plateau of the Fedioukine Hills. From here, the Russians looked across the North Valley towards the British cavalry. Guns fired on the left flank of Cardigan's men almost as soon as they began to trot east. There is much evidence that Nolan, who had permission to ride with the 11th Hussars, realised the serious error about to be made concerning the objective. However, he was killed by the first Russian

Opposite top: Simpson's watercolour entitled *Charge of the Heavy Cavalry Brigade, 25th October 1854.* The picture shows the Heavy Brigade attacking the Russian cavalry uphill from the right. In the foreground, Turkish soldiers are depicted looting the campsite of the Light Brigade and retreating downhill. Sutherland Hillock is seen in the centre middle distance across the South Valley of Balaklava with a double line of soldiers extending up its steep western slope and down its gentler eastern slope. The detachment of Russian cavalry that attacked the 93rd Regiment on this hillock is moving off to the left. The hillock that carries Campbell's Redoubt is to the right of Sutherland Hillock with Balaklava in the far distance beyond and further to the right. On Marine Heights in the centre background, smoke issues from guns firing from Battery No. 1, which is the highest and furthest to the left on the slope of Mt Asketi, Battery No. 2, which is lower down and to its right, and Battery No. 3, which is lower and even further to the right on the summit of a small hillock on the side of Mt Hiblak. (Library of Congress, Washington).

Opposite bottom: The same view today looking south-southeast from the slopes of the most westerly hillock on the Causeway Heights over the settlement of Zolataya Balka in the South Valley of Balaklava where the camp of the Light Brigade is likely to have been located. Sutherland Hillock is in the middle distance to the left of centre with the knoll that carried Campbell's Redoubt and Battery No. 4 to its right. Castle Hill in Balaklava is on the right in the cleft between Mt Hiblak and Guards' Hill.

The South Valley of Balaklava and the western Causeway Heights from the summit of Mt Asketi showing the likely movements of the Russian cavalry in yellow and the Heavy Brigade in red on 25 October 1854. The Heavy Brigade had been ordered to help defend Balaklava and had just skirted a vineyard when the Russian cavalry was observed on the Causeway Heights. A detachment of Russian cavalry attacked the 93rd Regiment on Sutherland Hillock and was repulsed. The remaining Russian cavalry moved down the slope into the South Valley only to be charged uphill by the Heavy Brigade. This action is believed to have occurred where the modern settlement of Zolataya Balka now stands.

shell just as he seemed to be attempting to change the direction of the advance. After the battle, he was most likely buried in the defensive ditch at No. 5 Redoubt together with others who had suffered a similar fate in this vicinity.

A few minutes further down the valley, eight Russian guns near the captured No. 3 Redoubt began firing at the right flank of the Light Brigade. Russian infantry in the vicinity formed squares on the Causeway Heights thinking they could be attacked. Rifles and muskets were fired by these troops as the cavalry passed. The Light Brigade found itself moving quicker in the extremely dangerous environment in which it found itself than it would have in normal circumstances. Because of their speed, a number of Russian shells are believed by some to have exploded harmlessly overhead after the cavalrymen had passed by underneath. Nevertheless, casualties were still high.

The Heavy Brigade following behind the Light Brigade also began to suffer serious casualties and Lucan, who was riding with them, ordered a turn-around. He is reported to have said 'They have sacrificed the Light Brigade. They shall not have the Heavy, if I can help it'. The Light Brigade continued to proceed down the valley without its crucial support.

The exact position of the Don Cossack field battery on an approximately 150-yard front across the North Valley varies on maps describing the Battle of Balaklava. Information sources at the time suggest that the distance from the start position of the Light Brigade to the Don Cossack field battery could have been anything between 0.75 and 1.50 miles.

A scaled plan of the charge, which was approved by participants Lieutenant Colonel George Mayow and Lieutenant Daniel Clutterbuck for a 1860s legal case involving Lord Cardigan, shows the Russian battery to be roughly 1.53 miles from its start position. On maps today, the same distance measures 1.56 miles.

The guns of the Don Cossack field battery, which were the target of the attack, fired directly ahead from the time the Light Brigade came into range until the artillerymen were overrun. It has been estimated that the Light Brigade reached the guns, on the slight downhill slope of the valley floor, about seven and a half minutes after starting to advance. Grape and canister shot would have caused havoc on the final approach.

After the Don Cossack field battery had been overrun and its artillerymen scattered or killed, Cossacks clashed with the remnants of first line of the 13th Light Dragoons and the 17th Lancers. The second line of the 11th Hussars, who were on the far left, brushed the northern end of the Russian battery. The 4th Light Dragoons in the third line charged through the northern half of the Russian gun line just after the 11th Hussars had passed to the left and joined the mêlée beyond. Senior officers in each regiment were seeking orders from Cardigan as to what to do next. However, after being poked in the ribs and prodded in the thigh by Russian lances in addition to almost being captured, Cardigan had abandoned his men and was on his way back up the valley to British lines. He possibly believed that he had led the charge up to its objective and his duties to his men were now over.

Cossacks and other sections of Ryzhov's cavalry were chased through the relatively narrow passage between hills that led out of the North Valley into the Chernaya Valley. Masses of retreating Russian horsemen were reported converging at the two bridges over the aqueduct beyond the defile. The Chernaya River was now in sight of those of the Light Brigade who had ventured the farthest. Far to the right, the 8th Hussars in the third line completely missed the southern end of the Don Cossack gun line and turned back after riding on for about another 500 yards.

As the anticipated support from the Heavy Brigade did not materialise, those who had attempted to secure the guns were unable to hold them against an increasingly aggressive Russian cavalry. Many of the scattered surviving horsemen joined larger groups and began to retire.

When retreating back up the North Valley, the mounted survivors of the charge had to fight their way through four squadrons of Russian Uhlans armed with lances. It soon became everyman for himself. The Light Brigade again experienced cannon and rifle fire from the Causeway Heights though four squadrons of the French 4th Chasseurs d'Afrique had silenced the Russian guns on the Fedioukine Hills by forcing the gunners to retreat. Some stragglers, such as the walking or crawling wounded, were either captured or killed by Uhlans and Cossacks. Others, whose horses had been killed early in the advance, managed to walk back with their saddles. The 'Valley of Death', as the North Valley was to become known, was left strewn with dead men and horses.

Out of a total of 664 in the Light Brigade, 110 died (including seven later from wounds), 130 were wounded and fifty-eight taken prisoner. The casualty rate was forty-five per cent. Horses lost amounted to 362 or fifty-four per cent. After the charge, the Light Brigade was no longer an effective fighting unit. However, the damage could have been much worse had the Russians taken full advantage of the situation and prevented any of the Light Brigade from retreating to British lines.

Looking west along the Causeway Heights from the western end of the ridge that carried No. 4 Redoubt. The Sevastopol-Yalta Highway is on the far right. The side-road to Balaklava, which follows the course of the old Vorontsov Road at this location, is on the left. The fold of land in the vineyard just beyond the side-road may be the 'knoll' where Lucan received Raglan's fateful 'Fourth Order to the Cavalry' from Nolan. Beyond this fold and just to the left of a track through the vineyards, a monument marks the site of No. 5 Redoubt. The land rises in the right middle distance to the straw-coloured hillock that is the most westerly on the Causeway Heights and the site of the unfinished No. 6 Redoubt. The Sapoune Ridge is on the skyline with the low point on the far left being the Col de Balaklava.

Closing Events

At the time the Light Brigade began to move down the North Valley, infantry units of the 1st Division under the Duke of Cambridge were deploying in the South Valley having been the first of the relief force to descend from camps on the Chersonese Plateau via the Col de Balaklava. In addition, the 4th Division, which had followed the 1st Division down into the South Valley from the Col, had reached the Causeway Heights.

The 4th Division had been late in starting out for the conflict because previous false alarms of a Russian attack at Balaklava had made its disgruntled commanding officer, Sir George Cathcart, incredulous. After receiving his orders to proceed to the South Valley on 25 October 1854, Cathcart procrastinated and, as a result, his troops were slow to begin their march and consequently slow to arrive. This was unfortunate because they had been desperately needed when the redoubts had been taken and a quicker response may have saved the Light Brigade.

By 11.30 hours, when the mounted remnants of the Light Brigade had returned to British lines, Cathcart's infantry was occupying the area around Nos. 4 and 5 Redoubts. An advance by the 4th Division supported by artillery was anticipated with the intention of taking No. 3

Looking east-southeast along the Causeway Heights from a location to the north of the settlement of Zolataya Balka. The white monument on the left commemorates the Battle of Balaklava and stands on the site of No. 5 Redoubt. The Russian cavalry moved from left to right across the Causeway Heights near No. 5 Redoubt before its encounter with the Heavy Brigade on the slope down into the South Valley. The low hillock seen beyond the monument carried No. 4 Redoubt. The dome-shaped Mt Hasfort lies much further away behind this hillock. To the immediate right of the hillock that carried No. 4 Redoubt, the straw-coloured hillock that carried No. 3 Redoubt can just be seen with a foothill to the right of Mt Hasfort visible to its rear.

Redoubt. However, after some exchanges of fire, the action was called off. It has been suggested that the reason was because Cathcart thought losses would be unacceptably high and, in any case, troops could not be spared from the siege of Sevastopol to adequately defend all the extended perimeter redoubts around Balaklava even if recaptured. The Russians towed away seven captured British guns and displayed them later in Sevastopol's Theatre Square claiming victory.

Aftermath
At the end of 25 October 1854, the Russians had control of the three most easterly redoubts in Balaklava's outer defence line, but had a healthy respect for the British cavalry. The day's events were interpreted by Russia as a victory, but they had failed to isolate Balaklava from the besieging forces and, apart from the virtual destruction of the Light Brigade, had not resulted in a shift in the balance of military power.

Although the Russians failed to breakthrough to Kadikoi during the Battle of Balaklava, they did capture the eastern section of the all-weather Vorontsov Road on the Causeway Heights. This limited the extent to which this road could be used by the British to move

Simpson's watercolour entitled *Charge of the Light Cavalry Brigade, 25th October 1854.* This elevated view looking over the North Valley of Balaklava from above the Fedioukine Hills shows the final stages of the charge just before the Don Cossack battery is overrun. The image depicts the Light Brigade in better order than they were in reality. While the 17th Lancers and 13th Light Dragoons in the first line of the Light Brigade went through the guns, the 11th Hussars following behind passed the guns to the north and the 8th Hussars, who were last and on the far side of the valley, bypassed the guns to the south. The key that accompanies this image does not identify the redoubts in the background, which are on hillocks exaggerated in height. However, it is believed that the one on the left with gun smoke was Canrobert's Hill as the village of Kamara is on the shoulder of land to its left. The hillock on the right where troops are seen in a square was most likely where No. 3 Redoubt was located. (Library of Congress, Washington).

troops, supplies and ammunition up to the siege lines. The alternative route from Kadikoi was on a dirt track along the South Valley of Balaklava and then up to the Chersonese Plateau via the Col de Balaklava. However, it became almost impassable during the wet winter weather, which further compounded the problems associated with the choice of Balaklava as a supply port. In 1855, a military railway followed by a well-constructed military road had to be built to ease the situation.

The Russians never capitalised on their territorial gains. They maintained a presence on the eastern Causeway Heights until December 1854 when they abandoned their positions and retreated across the Chernaya River. The area then became a no-man's land until occupied by Allied forces the following year.

A Visit to the Battlefield
The ground fought over at the Battle of Balaklava is probably best appreciated from the edge of the Sapoune Ridge. There are look-outs at a museum with a diorama

commemorating the storming of the Sapoune Ridge by Russian troops during the Second World War on 7 May 1944 to the south-southwest of the Sevastopol-Yalta Highway just before it begins its descent to the Plain of Balaklava. However, by walking for three quarters of a mile from the highway through the museum complex and out along the ridge line on a well-worn path, the actual area near where Raglan most likely viewed the battle is reached. From here, the low ridge of the Causeway Heights stretches at almost right angles across the Plain of Balaklava dividing it into the North Valley on the left and the South Valley on the right. The view is directly down the 'Valley of Death'. The positions where all the Turkish-held redoubts were located can be identified by those who know where to look. The low Fedioukine Hills lie to the north of the North Valley with Kadykovka at the entrance to the valley leading down to Balaklava beyond the South Valley. The keen observer can also find Sutherland Hillock across the vineyards. Over the edge of the ridge, the ground falls steeply and it was down this slope that Nolan rode with his fateful order for the Light Brigade to attack.

After descending the Sapoune Ridge, the Sevastopol-Yalta Highway meets a large roundabout. Going straight ahead for 1,000 yards, the highway passes an intersection coming in from the right near a petrol station. The North Valley to the left at this point is where the Light Brigade began its advance. Parking near the petrol station, one can cross over the nearby railway track, taking care to look out for freight trains, and ascend the low ridge of the Causeway Heights on a track between vineyards that leads after 350 yards to the British monument to the battle at the site of No. 5 Redoubt. The vineyards stand on

This modern view, which was taken from the Fedioukine Hills and looks southwest across the North Valley of Balaklava, shows an area of newly planted vines where the Don Cossack Battery was likely to have been situated. The Light Brigade would have advanced down the valley from the right. The low ridge of the Causeway Heights lies on the other side of the valley with the hillock that carried No. 3 Redoubt the high point on the far right. The treed summit of Canrobert's Hill, which carried No. 1 Redoubt, can be seen over the Causeway Heights in the distance on the left.

Klembovsky's image looking east down the North Valley of Balaklava in the early 1900s. The Causeway Heights are on the right with the village of Kamara on the distant hillside on the extreme right. Mt Hasfort lies on the left at the end of the valley. The distant defile to the Chernaya Valley is off the picture to the left. (Walter Havighurst Special Collections, Miami University Libraries, Oxford, Ohio).

The same view showing the 'Valley of Death' as it looks today. The Causeway Heights are on the right and Mt Hasfort is at the end of the valley. When they reached the line of poplars ahead, which now lies approximately one mile from its start position, the Light Brigade still had about another half a mile further to ride before reaching the Don Cossack Battery.

private land and, as on the Alma, growers are extremely sensitive about trespassers when grapes are being harvested. The Charge of the Heavy Brigade took place 550 yards to the south-southwest where the agricultural settlement of Zolataya Balka now stands.

The Russian obelisk commemorating the battle is at the site of No.4 Redoubt, which can be reached by driving along the side-road that leaves the highway at the petrol station for about 450 yards. This road goes to Balaklava, but follows the course of the old Vorontsov Road on this stretch next to the ridge. The redoubt is reached by ascending a step flight of steps. The view to the north from the redoubt is over the Sevastopol-Yalta Highway and across the Valley of Death at a location near where Nolan must have been killed.

Further east, the Sevastopol-Yalta Highway crosses over the railway and passes a side-road on the left to an agricultural settlement that now straddles the North Valley. The higher ground seen ahead to the left is where No 3 Redoubt was located. The summit offers a magnificent view of the North Valley across to the Fedioukine Hills. To the east lies Mt Hasfort and to the east-northeast is the North Valley's entrance to the Chernaya Valley. It was on the valley floor now covered with vineyards that the Light Brigade swept through the Russian guns and chased the Russian cavalry. To the south-southeast, the hillock that carried No.2 Redoubt is visible. Going even further along the highway, a turn-off to the right leads to the village of Kamara. Canroberts' Hill can be seen to the south-west from this road.

Kadykovka, which is at the end of the urban sprawl north of Balaklava, is the starting point when visiting Sutherland Hillock where the 93rd Regiment as the 'thin red line' held the Russian cavalry. Coming from Balaklava, take the road obliquely to the left after passing over the level-crossing. This leads past Kadykovka's market and then through a dacha suburb before passing an area of light industry and emerging into the South Valley with its vineyards as the road to Zolataya Balka. At this point park your car. The track up the low rise to the right leads to the top of Sutherland Hillock. Looking north over the vineyards from here, it is easy to image the Russian cavalry charging down the slope. Unfortunately, rows of ugly garages now occupy the area just to the south of the crest where the 93rd lay down to avoid Russian cannon-fire. However, by walking further east along the crest, the hillock where Campbell's Redoubt was situated, now occupied by a school and its recreation area, can be seen 600 yards away to the south.

Kadíkoi
The Inner Line of Defence Before Balaklava

Kadikoi was small settlement of scattered houses at the head of the valley that ran through hills to Balaklava, about one and a quarter miles to the south. It was located to the east of high ground known to the British as Frenchman's or Vinoy's Hill, the latter because General Joseph Vinoy's brigade was camped on its western end. Sutlers' stores and canteens lined the road to Balaklava on Kadikoi's southern fringe with an associated trader's camp on the slope behind that led up to Guards' Hill. From Guards' Hill, there were views south down the valley to Balaklava and northwest across the South Valley of Balaklava to the Causeway Heights. Mt Hiblak was to the southeast across the valley entrance.

The principal building in Kadikoi was the Orthodox Church just to the west of the old road from Balaklava to the Col de Balaklava. This road, which turned west near Sutherland Hillock and ran through the South Valley of Balaklava, became an almost impassable muddy track in the winter of 1854-55 and seriously affected the movement of munitions, building materials and essential goods to the infantry camps on the Chersonese Plateau. This promoted the construction of a military railway, the first section of which opened between Balaklava and Kadkoi on 23 February 1855, and later a new, all-weather road that eventually ran parallel to the railway.

A low hillock to the east of the church became a strongpoint known as Campbell's Redoubt named after Sir Colin Campbell, who commanded the Highland Brigade and was in charge of the defence of Balaklava. After the Battle of Balaklava, the redoubt was joined to others by a line of 'intrenchments' that ran from near the Col de Balaklava, to Campbell's Redoubt, across the plain to the lower slopes of Mt Hiblak and beyond up to the Marine Heights. It terminated at the Crow's Nest Redoubt on the top of what is now Mt Asketi. This barrier constituted the inner defence line protecting Balaklava.

The area in and around Kadikoi was much photographed and painted as it was an important location on the supply route to the British siege lines around Sevastopol.

Vanity Fair
'Vanity Fair' and 'Buffalo-town' were two of the colourful names names given to the Kadikoi Bazaar, an area of sutlers' establishments situated about 500 yards to the south of Kadikoi Church. It was where all manner of items required by soldiers away from home could be obtained. A lively and occasionally raucous place, it was a favourite location for buying and comnsuming food and drink often at exhorbitant prices. It was a place of disrepute and a pain in the side of the authotities. William Russel reported on 1 September 1855:

The sutlers' camp and bazaar on the lower northern slope of Guards' Hill as captured by the James Robertson/Felice Beato photographic team in an image entitled *Kadikoi*. (Royal Collection Trust/© Her Majesty Queen Elizabeth II 2016).

The same view today looking towards the site of the sutlers' camp and bazaar from Frenchman's Hill.

The Robertson/Beato image entitled **Huts of the Royal Artillery** showing the camp of W Field Battery. (Royal Collection Trust/© Her Majesty Queen Elizabeth II, 2016).

Today's view of the entrance to the valley that leads west to the site of the cavalry camp from the eastern end of Frenchman's Hill.

The Robertson/Beato image entitled **Russian Church, Kadikoi.** (Royal Collection Trust/© Her Majesty Queen Elizabeth II, 2016).

The same view today looking towards the site of the church from the eastern end of Frenchman's Hill.

'Vanity Fair' has ben partly closed; many of the booths have been shut up for the time, and the proprietors worned off for the present, and Kadikoi now presents a desolute and neglected aspect. The cause of this abrupt proceeding is not exactly known – some say, 'spies', others 'dirt', but in all events, the Crimean Donnybrook, - where luxuries were so bad and so abundant, and where comforts were not unknown – where the poor Provost Marshal underwent daily attacks of despiar and frenzy – where Midas lived in every booth, thievish avarice haunted every turning, and the scum of Europe bubbled up and boiled over – has been sadly curtailed in its fair proportions.

An image of Vanity Fair and the sutlers' camp entitled *Kadikoi* was taken by the James Robertson/Felice Beato photographic team in the summer of 1855. The photograph looks southeast from near Battery No. 5 on the eastern end of Frenchman's or Vinoy's Hill. It shows the huts that served as accommodation for the sutlers stretching up the slopes of Guards' Hill with the stores, shops and booths of the bazaar lining the road below. Barrels can be seen stacked between drinking establishments and the railway on the left. When the image was taken in the summer of 1855, the seven mile-long railway was double-tracked out of Balaklava and had reached the Vorontsov Road between the camps of the Light and 2nd Divisions. Railway wagons were pulled by horses and up a steep slope outside Kadikoi by a stationary steam engine. Steam locomotives, which were used only on the line from Balaklava to Kadikoi, first ran in November 1855.

The hill in the left background was Mt. Hiblak. The inner line of defence for Balaklava extended up its slopes out of the picture on the left. The castle above Balaklava on Castle Hill is visible on the right skyline over the tents on the slope of Guards' Hill. The depression in the foreground was the entrance to the valley off to the right where the British cavalry camped in 1855. The main road from Balaklava to Kadikoi church and beyond turns sharply at Vanity Fair with the road to the cavalry camp continuing straight ahead.

In today's picture, the valley that runs from Balaklava to Kadikoi on the left and the lower slopes of Guards' Hill on the right are covered with apartment buildings and dachas. Trees line streets and walkways, and are common in gardens. Mt Hiblak is beyond the valley on the left with the summit of Mt Asketi behind on the skyline as in the contemporay picture.

Opposite: Two of Simpson's watercolours that show Kadikoi Church. The first, which looks south, is entitled *Commissariat Difficulties*. Guards' Hill rises to the right behind the church with Balaklava in the distance on the left. The lower slopes of the eastern end of Frenchman's or Vinoy's Hill are on the far right. The second watercolour, which looks north from near where the sutlers' camp was established, is entitled *Huts and Warm Clothing for the Army*. Simpson has depicted two cavalrymen as members of the weary procession carrying supplies. Guards' Hill is on the left with the Sapoune Ridge in the distance on the centre skyline. The western end of the Causeway Heights is closer on the right. Both images depict traffic on the old road from Balaklava to the front as it passes through Kadikoi during the severe winter of 1854-55. Movement was much slower on the wet, muddy surface, when wagons and guns became bogged down, than on the frozen ground. (Library of Congress, Washington).

Simpson's watercolour entitled **Highland Brigade Camp** also showing part of Battery No. 4 in Campbell's Redoubt. (Library of Congress, Washington).

Today's view towards Mt Asketi and Mt Hiblak from the high ground where Campbell's Redoubt was situated.

The Robertson/Beato image entitled *Huts of the Sutlers, Kadikoi.* (Royal Collection Trust/© Her Majesty Queen Elizabeth II, 2016).

The same view today looking towards the site of Campbell's Redoubt from the slopes of Guards' Hill.

Fenton's image entitled *View of the lines of Balaklava, Canrobert's Hill in the Distance.* (Library of Congress, Washington).

The view to the east from Guard's Hill today with the conical St Elias Hill on the right.

The top of the cliff at Cape Aya is also visible on the skyline just right of centre above the slope of Mt Asketi.

Possibly by swivelling their camera to the right, Robertson/Beato also photographed the area to the immediate northwest of the sutlers' camp where W Field Battery of the Royal Artillery was situated. This image, which is entitled *Huts of the Royal Artillery*, shows the view to the south over accommodation cabins and stables. Gun carriages are neatly parked in front of the line of huts on the left. Tracks run from left to right along the side of Guards' Hill towards the cavalry camp, which was in the valley off to the right. The lower road is the one seen in *Kadikoi* that went off to the right. This was French-built and went on to the Col de Balaklava via a gorge at the western end of Frenchman's Hill. The tents and huts visible on the top of the slope of Guards' Hill are those of one of the Guard regiments.

The modern equivalent was taken higher up the slope of Frenchman's Hill and more to the west than where Robertson/Beato took their image and is angled so that the summit of Mt Asketi and the high ground that leads to the cliffs at Cape Aya can be seen on the left skyline. The side of Guards' Hill now has trees on its upper slopes with dachas on its lower slopes. Apartment buildings are found closer to the valley floor, which is now devoted to industry. The road in the foreground, which turns sharply to the right after crossing over a railway that was built to service quarry workings, leads west up the valley where the British cavalry camped in 1855.

Kadikoi Church

The Russian Orthodox Church at Kadikoi was photographed by the Robertson/Beato team in the summer of 1855 in an image entitled *Russian Church, Kadikoi*. It was taken on the eastern slope of Frenchman's Hill from close to where they took their picture of the sutlers' camp. However, the view is now east over Kadikoi and towards the eastern section of the South Valley of Balaklava.

The few buildings that made up Kadikoi can be seen next to the church and on the slope behind. The track just beyond the church and churchyard that ascends the slope from right to left was the main supply route from Balaklava to the siege lines before the French built a road through the valley to the south of Frenchman's Hill and the military railway was opened. A team of horses at the head of two wagons is visible at lower right on the far line of the double-tracked railway. This area would have been at the bottom of the steep gradient that required a stationary steam engine to pull trucks up to the top. The building identified as a corn depot on a contemporary map can be seen on the left before the church.

Huts occupy the south side of the summit of the hillock behind the church. It was from the site of this camp that the men of the 93rd Regiment marched the short distance north to Sutherland Hillock, which is off the picture on the left, to make their courageous and successful stand against elements of the Russian cavalry at the Battle of Balaklava. The hillock is also where Campbell's Redoubt with Battery No. 4 was constructed to protect the entrance to the valley that led to Balaklava. 'Intrenchments' that were built to defend Balaklava ran either side of the strongpoint, which is the square-shaped walled area beyond the two distinct rows of huts. The line of intrenchments is evident beyond the house above and to the left of the church as a scar on the landscape. The intrenchments can also be seen on the valley floor to the right of the bottom of the hillock. They consisted of a ditch with an earth bank behind for the protection of troops.

The conical-shaped Canrobert's Hill, where No.1 Redoubt on Balaklava's outer defences was located before its capture by the Russians at the Battle of Balaklava, rises from the plain in the left background. The village of Kamara, which was occupied by the Russians in their opening moves on 25 October 1854, was on the high ground beyond and to the right of Canrobert's Hill. The hills on the left rise towards the Black Sea where they form spectacular cliffs at Cape Aya.

Today, a large apartment building blocks the view of the hillock carrying Campbell's Redoubt from where the image of the church was taken by Robertson/Beato. The unseen knoll is today occupied by a secondary school and a recreation area. The site of the church was just beyond and to the left of the poplar tree seen over the red roof in the foreground. The road that passed to the left of the church and continued on to the hillock in the contemporary image has a modern equivalent today as does the old supply road that passed behind the church. The slope to the right of the church has been excavated to make a flatter area for the market at today's Kadykovka.

Canrobert's Hill is again visible in the distance with today's village of Kamara occupying the slopes of a shoulder of land to its right. The main road from Balaklava to the Col de Balaklava and on to Sevastopol now lies unseen in the valley below the camera where the railway once ran. This modern road follows the route of a new road built from Balaklava via Kadikoi to the Col de Balaklava and beyond by the Army Works Corp under William Doyne in the autumn and winter of 1855. If Robertson/Beato had taken their image *Kadikoi* after this road had been constructed instead of before, it would be seen running between the railway and the drinking establishments lining the old road through Vanity Fair.

The contemporary photographs described above were three of a panorama of five taken from the eastern end of Frenchman's Hill by the Robertson/Beato team. The two not shown are not readily available for reproduction. William Simpson used Kadikoi as a location to depict in watercolours the hardships associated with transporting goods from Balaklava to the infantry camps on the old road during the 1854-55 winter.

Campbell's Redoubt

Campbell's Redoubt on the inner defence line of Balaklava at Kadikoi was the subject of a watercolour by William Simpson entitled *Highland Brigade Camp*, which shows the view over the redoubt to the south-southeast. Two guns of Battery No. 4 at the redoubt are positioned at embrasures in the earth wall behind the defensive ditch. The accommodation huts and tents of the 93rd Highlanders lie on the downward slope beyond the level area of the redoubt.

The line of intrenchments can be seen extending across the valley beyond at centre and skirting the summit of the hillock where Battery No. 3 was located. Turks manned the defences in this area. The lower hillock to the right of the hillock carrying Battery No. 3 was known as St Elias Hill where there was a chapel. Just left of centre, the intrenchments can be seen climbing up into the hills that were known as the Marine Heights. The camp of the 42nd (Royal Highland) Regiment was to the left of the hillock with Battery No. 3 with the camp of 79th (Cameron Highlanders) Regiment further along under the crag. The peak on the skyline at centre, which is now known as Mt Asketi, is where the Crow's Nest Redoubt, the last on the defence line, was located. The Marines and the 2nd Battalion of the Rifle Brigade were camped here.

Fenton's image entitled *Encampment of the 71st Regiment.* [Library of Congress, Washington]

The view over the valley that runs from Kadikoi to Balaklava from the site of Battery No. 3.

The view southeast from Guards' Hill looking towards Mt Hiblak.

The peak to the right of Mt Asketi, which is lower and closer, is Mt Hiblak. Castle Hill with the harbour at Balaklava below is on the far right. The military railway on the extreme right approaches the valley that led to Balaklava. The three lines on the slope beyond the wagons on the railway were the huts of Croat labourers.

Today, the knoll in Kadykovka where Campbell's Redoubt was located is, as mentioned before, occupied by a secondary school and its recreation area. The modern photograph looks to the south-southeast and shows the view over a row of garages where once the accommodation huts for the Highlanders stood. Mt Hiblak is at centre with Mt Asketi further in the distance to its immediate left. The ridge seen on Mt Asketi is where the defence line of the Marine Heights ran in 1855. The two hillocks in front of Mt Hiblak are recognisable from Simpson's watercolour. The one on the right was St Elias Hill and the higher one on the left was the location of Battery No. 3. The Genoese fortress on Castle Hill is visible on the skyline on the extreme right.

Today's view north from Campbell's Redoubt towards Sutherland Hillock and the Causeway Heights is shown in Chapter 4.

Kadikoi from Guards' Hill
The Robertson/Beato image entitled *Huts of the Sutlers, Kadikoi* shows the view northeast from Guards' Hill. The tents and huts in the foreground below form part of the sutlers' camp

also shown in the image *Kadikoi*. However, the road from Balaklava lined by stores and canteens in *Kadikoi* is obscured by the line of the slope, though some of the bazaar's establishments can be seen on the valley floor on the left. Just beyond the camp in the lower part of the picture, the course of the military railway that carried supplies and munitions from Balaklava to the camps on the Chersonese Plateau via the Col de Balaklava can be seen as a straight line running from just right of centre to the left. Neat rows of tents are visible on the valley floor at centre and to the right. On one contemporary map, dated April 1855, these tents are marked as belonging to the Turks.

The hillock in the middle distance with the large, light-coloured huts carried Campbell's Redoubt with its Battery No. 4 on the defence line that protected the approaches to Balaklava. The location of the battery was in the walled area between the two concentrations of huts, which served as accommodation for the defending 93rd Highlanders. The battery was 900 yards away from the camera. The South Valley of Balaklava lies beyond Campbell's Redoubt.

The eastern end of the low ridge known as Sutherland Hillock, where the 93rd Highlanders stood against units of the Russian cavalry as 'the thin red line' during the battle of Balaklava, would have been on the far left about 600 yards further on from the battery. A faint white scar indicates its likely location.

The far ridge, which appears on the skyline on the extreme left and runs to the right, is the Causeway Heights. All of this ridge in view was occupied at some time by Russian infantry during the Battle of Balaklava, though the western section seen on the left, which carried No. 4 Redoubt, was abandoned soon after it was captured. The tops of the mountains that make up the Mackenzie Heights can be seen above the Causeway Heights on the skyline at centre.

Today, the slope where the sutlers' camp was situated is covered with dachas and gardens. The apartment building seen on the right in the modern view is also on the slope down to the valley floor where low rise flats visible on the left have been built. A sports field occupies the valley floor further to the northwest with dachas beyond almost to the summit of the hillock that carried Campbell's Redoubt. The military railway on the valley floor would have run between the low-rise apartment block and the sports field beyond.

The secondary school that is now found on the western section of the flat top of the hillock that carried Campbell's Redoubt is the long building with a light blue roof to the right of the tall smoke stack. To the right of the school building is its recreation area. The straw-coloured area beyond and to the left of the school is the eastern end of Sutherland Hillock. Vineyards now cover the South Valley of Balaklava beyond the urban area of Kadykovka. The Causeway Heights are seen with more clarity than in the contemporary image. The ridge on the skyline at left carries No. 4 Redoubt. No. 3 Redoubt, where Russian guns did much damage to the Light Brigade as it advanced down the 'Valley of Death' to the north, was on the summit of the low, straw-coloured knoll on the Causeway Heights just to the right of centre. No. 2 Redoubt was on the larger straw-coloured knoll on the right. As in the contemporary image, the tops of the Mackenzie Heights can be seen above the Causeway Heights on the centre skyline.

View East from Guard's Hill

Roger Fenton took this image entitled *View of the Lines of Balaklava, Canrobert's Hill in the Distance* looking east from Guards' Hill in late March 1855. In the foreground, huts are being erected for the Scots Fusilier Guards, who were recuperating here at the time after suffering heavy losses at the Battle of Inkerman.

The valley below on the right leads down towards Balaklava and this was the most obvious route that any Russian attack on the supply port would be directed. The conical hillock on the right beyond this valley was St Elias Hill and it lay just to the north of Mt Hiblak, which is unseen off to the right. Mt Hiblak dominated the east side of the valley into Balaklava.

The hillock behind St Elias Hill was joined to Mt Hiblak by a shoulder of land or col seen on the extreme right. Battery No. 3 of Balaklava's inner defences was positioned on its summit. A line of intrenchments stretched from here to Campbell's Redoubt. The intrenchments can be seen as a dark line running around the slope and down the side of the hillock and across the valley floor parallel to the rows of tents below Mt Elias. It then changes direction as it extends across the plain and disappears behind the hut on the far left. The tents belonged to the Turks, who manned the defence line at this location.

At the bottom of the slope in the foreground, the light-coloured band, which is obscured by the lie of the land in places, marks the course of the road from Balaklava to Kadikoi. The line beyond that runs parallel to the road was the military railway.

Canrobert's Hill, which carried No. 1 Redoubt of Balaklava's outer defences at the time of the Battle of Balaklava, can be seen on the left across the South Valley of Balaklava. The village of Kamara would have been situated on the shoulder of land that rises to its right. At the time of the photograph, this was virtually no man's land. The Russians abandoned the redoubts captured on the Causeway Heights and Canrobert's Hill during the Battle of Balaklava on 6 December 1854 and they retired beyond the River Chernaya, but any Allied troops venturing out in the area ran the risk of interception by Cossack patrols. It wasn't until 19 April 1855 that the Allies undertook a reconnaissance in strength and established a tenuous presence as far as the pass through the hills to the Baidar Valley and the west bank of the River Chernaya.

Today, apartments and dachas, which extend from Balaklava to Kadykovka, fill the valley and spread outwards into the South Valley of Balaklava. The course of the line of intrenchments across the plain has disappeared under urban development. Trees, dachas and light industrial premises are located on the slopes in the foreground where once huts for the British army were being constructed. The hut seen on the extreme left of Fenton's image may have been occupying the platform of ground on the lower left of the modern image. The hillock that carried Battery No. 3 can still be seen behind the conical and easily recognisable St Elias Hill. Canrobert's Hill is in the left distance with the hillock that carried No. 2 Redoubt further to the left.

Camp of the Highland Light Infantry

Fenton's image entitled *Encampment of the 71st Regiment* was most likely taken on 4 April 1855 when a letter he sent home indicates he visited the location. The view is to the southwest and looks over the Kadikoi-Balaklava valley, which is below on the right. The slope of Mt Hiblak is seen on the left. Huts appear to have largely replaced tents as accommodation when this image was taken. St Elias Hill is off the picture on the right.

The three rows of sheds on the opposite side of the valley were where mules were stabled. The huts behind and to the right may have housed the mule handlers. The road and railway from Balaklava to the infantry camps run from right to left on the valley floor.

Kadykovka and the South Valley of Balaklava from the summit of Mt Hiblak.

The line of the railway is identified by what appears after magnification to be an iron crane mounted on a four-wheeled, flat-bed wagon. This railway crane is on the far right. The road lies beyond.

The slope where the 71st (Highland Light Infantry) Regiment, which was defending Balaklava, was camped is now covered with dachas and gardens. Today, this area is serviced by a road that climbs steeply from the valley floor and passes close to the site of the Battery No. 3. This road continues as a rough track around the east side of Mt Hiblak and then down towards the ravine that is found to the north of the site of the Castle Hospital. The houses and trees now found where the 71st Regiment were once camped make an exact reproduction of the scene impossible, so the modern view was taken looking southwest from the summit of the hillock that carried Battery No. 3. The site of the battery is now a look-out with a car park.

Today, the skyline on the other side of the valley is just recognisable despite the extensive quarrying operations that have drastically altered the landscape. The slope of Mt Hiblak that was prominent on the left of the contemporary photograph is just visible below on the far left near apartment buildings. The large industrial buildings associated with the quarrying operations on the left above the slope of Mt Hiblak are near the head of the harbour. Mt Elias Hill is again off the picture on the right.

The location of the camp of the 71st Regiment today is shown on the next photograph, which looks to the southeast from Guards' Hill across the valley between Kadikoi and Balaklava towards Mt Hiblak. St Elias Hill is on the far left with the higher hillock that carried Battery No. 4 beyond. The saddle of land between these knolls and Mt Hiblak, which slopes towards the camera and where dachas are now found, is where the 71st Regiment camped.

The camp of C Troop of the Royal Horse Artillery was near the bottom of this slope just to the left of St Elias Hill. C Troop was later joined by A Troop sometime after the latter's arrival in the Crimea in June 1855 The summit of Mt Asketi, which was the end of the defensive line of intrenchments, is visible on the skyline to the right of Mt Hiblak.

The last image shows the view north from the summit of Mt Hiblak with Kadykovka below. The top of conical St Elias Hill is at lower left. The summit of the hillock that carried Battery No. 3, but which now has a circular car park, is at lower right. Kadikoi Church was situated just to the left of the line of four tall white apartment buildings seen in Kadykovka on the far left. Campbell's Redoubt was situated in the small open area surrounded by trees seen at centre with vineyards above to its right. Sutherland Hillock extends to the left from the bare area within the vineyards at centre to its high point seen with buildings. The vineyards in the South Valley of Balaklava rise up to a low ridge that is the Causeway Heights. The Heavy Brigade charged uphill to meet the Russian cavalry at the Battle of Balaklava on the slope at centre where the settlement of Zolataya Balka now stands. The uncultivated area beyond Zolataya Balka is the most westerly hillock on the Causeway Heights and was where No. 6 Redoubt was situated. The Sapoune Ridge is on skyline. The course of the Sevastopol-Yalta Highway cuts through the trees on the ridge's slope at centre as it descends from the Chersonese Plateau. Raglan's look-out at the Battle of Balaklava was on the edge of this escarpment to the left of centre.

The Battle of Inkerman
Carnage on the Heights Above the Chernaya

Initially, the British army had the responsibility of manning the siege lines east of the Great Ravine, a steep sided valley that ran towards Sevastopol from the south. Most activity in the British sector was to the south-southeast of the city where guns were positioned so as to direct fire on the bastions of the Redan and Malakhov, which were the major Russian strongpoints in the area. The British constructed their first batteries on the Green Hill Ridge, immediately east of the Great Ravine, and on the Vorontsov Ridge, which was further to the east over the Vorontsov Ravine. There was also a battery constructed on Victoria Ridge, which ran parallel and to the east of the Vorontsov Ridge. However, a large area of high ground even further east was either unoccupied or lightly defended because of a lack of troops. The Russians decided that this weak point, known as Mount Inkerman or the Inkerman Ridge, was where they would strike in an attempt to dislodge their enemies and lift the siege.

Little Inkerman

On 26 October 1854, the day after the Battle of Balaklava, the Russians made a sortie out of besieged Sevastopol to test the strength of British defences to the southeast and to divert the attention of the Allies. Under the command of Colonel Dimitry Federov, six battalions of the Borodinsky and Bourtirsky regiments, which amounted to 4,3000 men and four light guns, left the city, crossed the Careenage Ravine and ascended the high ground at the northern end of the Inkerman Ridge. At the same time, a column of 700 sailors moved southeast up the deep Careenage Ravine to protect the right flank of the main attack and penetrate behind British lines.

At 13.00 hours, the Russians reached Shell Hill, which was the high point on the Inkerman Ridge, and ran into a line of British pickets stationed at intervals from east to west just south of the summit. Each picket consisted of around sixty to seventy men, which included pairs of troops positioned someway in advance of the main body as observers. These outlying men first raised the alarm, which galvanised the others into immediate action. Although the job of pickets in case of attack was to delay the enemy's advance and then to fall back, this did not happen. The pickets decided to stand and fight. Their determination held up the Russian attack.

The Inkerman Ridge was defended by the 2nd Division commanded by Lieutenant General Sir De Lacy Evans. His regiments were camped about 1,400 yards south-southeast of Shell Hill behind a feature known as Home Ridge. Men of 49th (Hertfordshire) Regiment acting as pickets that day were the first to encounter the Russian sortie. Pickets formed

Aerial view of the Inkerman Ridge area today identifying most of the battlefield locations mentioned in the text. North is to the top. The Careenage Ravine (C) cuts through the landscape in a south-easterly direction from the upper left and passes the site of the Right Lancaster Battery (RL) on Victoria Ridge. A trench (T) across the floor of the ravine here served as a defensive line at the Battle of Little Inkerman. The ravine continues until it forms the Wellway (W) where the Russians were stopped at the Battle of Inkerman. The site of the Victoria Redoubt (VR) is indicated on the left of the ravine although it wasn't completed until 1855. Mikriakov Glen (MG) is the side-ravine that leaves Careenage Ravine east of the Right Lancaster Battery and runs towards where Saddle-top Reach (STR) is indicated. The Russian gun line at the Battle of Inkerman ran from East Jut (EJ) to West Jut (WJ) through Shell Hill (SH). The Gap (G) was the ground between the top of the Kitspur (K) and the Barrier (B). At the Barrier, two roads run into Quarry Ravine (QR). The highest on the left follows the course of the old Post Road around East Jut. This road now carries heavy traffic from Sevastopol to Simferopol. The Inkerman Tusk (IT) is the ridge between Quarry Ravine (QR) and St Clement's Ravine (CR). Fierce fighting occurred at the Sandbag Battery (SB), which changed hands many times. The top of the Kitspur (K) merged into Mount Head (MH) at the northern end of the Fore Ridge (FR). The final Allied defence line was along Home Ridge (HR) that joined the Fore Ridge (FR) and Hill Bend (HB). South of Home Ridge (HR), the ground falls away as it passes through the site of the 2nd Division camp (2DC). The River Chernaya (RC) flows in the Chernaya Valley (CV) on the far right. (Adapted from Google Earth™ image)

from the 95th (Derbyshire) Regiment also moved forward from positions further to the right to join in the fray.

De Lacy Evans wanted to bring eighteen guns positioned on Home Ridge into action, but this couldn't be done because of the risk of hitting his own men, who were stubbornly and courageous resisting the Russians. As a result, he initially denied reinforcements to move forward. However, the weight of the Russian attack eventually forced the pickets to retreat down the southern slopes of Shell Hill to where a Post Road from the Chernaya Valley gained the heights from the Quarry Ravine. Here a wall made of stones and earth had been built across the road at a location known as the Barrier. Russians moving up the Post Road after descending into the Quarry Ravine on the British right flank were held here. The guns from Home Ridge could now fire over the heads of the defenders and began to inflict serious damage on the Russian columns on and around Shell Hill. De Lacy Evans ordered a company of the 41st (Welch) Regiment to reinforce the British line on the left and a company of the 30th (Cambridgeshire) Regiment to advance to the Barrier on the right.

While this had been going on, the Russian sailors down in the Careenage Ravine had advanced to a location just southwest of Shell Hill where they ran into a roving picket of sharpshooters from the Guards' regiments which made a stand at a shallow trench dug across the valley. Accurate rifle fire stopped the Russian column who could not now make a surprise appearance behind the camp of the 2nd Division. The Guards were reinforced by men of the 2nd Battalion of the Rifle Brigade of the Light Division camped nearby on Victoria Ridge. The Russians eventually broke off the attack and retreated back down the ravine.

Above the site of the conflict on the west side of the Careenage Ravine stood the Right Lancaster Battery, which had been positioned on Victoria Ridge to fire on the Malakhov Bastion and ships in the harbour. The approach of the Russians below led to calls to spike the Lancaster gun in case of capture, but an enterprising seaman in command instead broke down the parapet so that the gun could be turned at right angles to fire on the enemy near Shell Hill.

More guns had arrived on Home Ridge and the Guards had been moved up in support from its camp further to the south-southwest. De Lacy Evans now decided to send more troops forward. The remaining four companies of the 41st and four companies of the 30th were ordered to support their comrades together with seven companies of the 95th Regiment. The tide was now turning. The Russians began to fall back on the summit of Shell Hill. They removed their guns and a wounded Federov was carried away on a stretcher. Some companies of the 95th were allowed to harry this retreat.

The Russians lost 270 men killed and wounded with eighty taken as prisoners. The British had twelve killed and seventy-five wounded with no prisoners being taken. However, the Russians had discovered that the Inkerman Ridge was only lightly held and that a determined push might result in a crucial victory. If the British learnt anything, little was done to improve defences in the area despite the weaknesses of the position being highlighted. This lack of action has been attributed to Lord Raglan's need to pursue the siege with vigour and the extra resources required to secure the right flank of the army could not be spared. The stage was now set for a much bloodier conflict ten days later.

The Plan

The Russian plan for the next attack, which was earmarked for 5th November 1854, was for men from within the garrison in Sevastopol to join forces with Prince Menshikov's field army to push the British off the Inkerman Ridge. To delay or prevent the French coming to the aid of the British, a diversionary sortie was to be made out of Sevastopol in the French sector and a considerable force under General Prince Gorchakov was to display in the

A poor quality Robertson/Beato image entitled *The Inkerman Ravine* shows the Careenage Ravine from just east of the Right Lancaster Battery. It was on the floor of the ravine just right of centre that Captain Goodlake and his roving picket of sharpshooting guardsmen stopped the Russian advance towards the rear of British lines at the Battle of Little Inkerman. (Royal Collection Trust/© Her Majesty Queen Elizabeth II, 2016).

The scene today from a little further to the northwest and slightly further down the side of the ravine. The floor of the ravine where the column of Russian sailors was prevented from going any further is now full of garden allotments, but the track along the lower slope of the far side still follows the same route as in 1850s. The Careenage Ravine continues to climb upwards on the right while the side-ravine known as the Mikriakov Glen turns off at centre and then bends to the right in front of the sheer rock face seen in the middle distance. Shell Hill is on the skyline beyond.

Chernaya Valley in front of the French defending the Sapoune Ridge. Once the British were in retreat, Gorchakov's men were to storm the ridge and take the Chersonese Plateau by driving all before them. In addition, another attempt would be made to flank the British by sending another body of men up the Careenage Ravine. However, the plan did not work as expected and the British were supported by units of the French army at a crucial stage of the battle. As a consequence, the Allies held their ground, there was no general retreat and Gorchakov and his men did not move against the Sapoune Ridge, although his support may have won the day. The Battle of Inkerman was fought in much of the same area as the Little Inkerman engagement except that it extended further south and up to the British defence line on Home Ridge.

Instead of being bright and sunny, as it was on 26 October, the hills were shrouded in fog on 5 November. With visibility being poor and the terrain covered with thick brush, units of the opposing forces often passed within yards of each other without being seen. The fighting also ebbed to and fro across the battlefield with one side having the advantage at one time and the other the next. It was also a conflict of attrition with terrible losses suffered on the Russian side and a considerable number killed and wounded on the Allied side, especially within the British army. The outcome of the battle set the scene for the future conduct of the siege.

The First Russian Offensive, 05.45 – 07.30 hours

The vanguard of the Russian army was led by Lieutenant General Soimonov. He marched his men out of Sevastopol not long after 05.00 hours and they were soon scaling the northern end of the Inkerman Ridge. Here he was to join General Paulov and his massive contingent coming from the hinterland via the Inkerman Bridge. Together they were to assault British positions under the general command of General Dannenburg with a total of just over 40,000 men. However, General Paulov's men were delayed, as it took longer than expected to repair the Inkerman Bridge over the Chernaya River, which his forces had to cross. Soimonov decided not to wait and began the offensive on his own.

The British pickets on the Inkerman Ridge on and around Shell Hill were soaked after spending a miserable night in drizzle. The relief pickets arrived an hour before dawn. Pickets from the 55th (Westmoreland) Regiment now occupied positions to the east, including the Barrier, while men of the 41st Regiment, 47th (Lancashire) Regiment and 49th Regiment were to the west. In addition, the Guards' sharpshooters were in the area. These men were the first to encounter the advancing Russians columns and could hold them off for only a short while before having to retreat down the southern slopes of the hill. Soimonov soon had his guns lined along the crest of Shell Hill and began firing over Home Ridge and into the 2nd Division's camp, which lay just beyond.

De Lacy Evans had been injured from a fall from his horse and Brigadier General John Pennefather was now in charge of the almost 3,000 men of the 2nd Division. His first orders were for small bodies of men from the 30th, 41st, 47th, 55th and 95th Regiments to be pushed forward to 'feed the pickets'. As a result, groups of soldiers consisting of fragments of regiments encountered advancing Russians in the mist and fought fiercely under the command of junior officers. On one occasion, a major of the 49th saw a Russian column emerge from the mist and shouted the famous command 'Give them a volley and charge', which was to be repeated during the day. His men pushed the enemy back further than its gun line on Shell Hill. Soimonov decided to mount a more determined attack.

Meanwhile, the first of Paulov's troops had begun to arrive on the battlefield by way of the East Sapper's Road and Volovia Ravine. Crossing the Quarry Ravine on the British right, they then ascended the Inkerman Tusk spur and descended into St Clement's Ravine before climbing onto the Kitspur to attack a position known as the 'Sandbag Battery'. This battery had contained two guns, but they had been withdrawn and all that was left was a high parapet with two embrasures. The Russians drove out a sergeant and six men to take possession.

Battalions of the Ekaterinburgsky, Tomsky and Kolyvansky regiments under Siomonov were now on the east side of the battlefield with a combination of Soimonov's and Paulov's men in battalions of the Borodinsky, Ekaterinburgsky and Tarutinsky regiments on the west side. In between and to their rear was a line of thirty-eight guns on Shell Hill. A total of twenty battalions consisting of 15,000 infantrymen now moved forward, but were fragmented because of the undergrowth. Alexander Kinglake described the formation as akin to 'a huge number of skirmishers unaccountably thronging together'. In addition to the attacking force, there were sixteen battalions or 10,000 men in reserve. Facing the Russians, Pennefather now had, after the arrival of 649 men of the Light Division, a total of 3,600 infantry and eighteen guns.

To the left of Home Ridge, 349 men of the newly arrived 88th (Connaught Rangers) Regiment and six guns moved forward to be confronted by the 2nd and 3rd battalions of the Ekaterinburgsky Regiment near the head of the Mikriakov Glen. The British withdrew and three unlimbered guns were captured despite a valiant effort by the artillerymen to fight off approaching Russian infantry. The 1st Ekaterinburgsky battalion then chanced upon Major Samuel Fordyce and 300 men of the 47th Regiment, who were also positioned near the Mikriakov Glen and to the left of the 88th. Accurate rifle fire sent the Russians into retreat. This reverse for the 1st Ekaterinburgsky became known to the regiment's 2nd and 3rd battalions and they stopped their advance on the 88th.

It was at about this time that the Russian column marching up the Careenage Ravine reached the Wellway, which was a valley that ran up behind the 2nd Division camp. Major General Buller had just arrived at the rear of the camp with 259 men of the Light Division's 77th (East Middlesex) Regiment under Lieutenant Colonel Thomas Egerton. The enemy were noticed on the left and charged. This had the result of decapitating the head of the Russian column from its trunk. Fire was also now being directed into the column from the opposite bank of the Wellway by a picket of Grenadier Guards. The Russians turned and retreated down the valley with many prisoners being taken.

Afterwards, Buller and Egerton pressed on with their advance towards the main fight with the 77th soon moving past the 88th, which was to its left. In front of the 77th were 8,000 Russian soldiers led by Soimonov in person. Egerton's 259 men were on collision course with its right flank, which consisted of two battalions of the Tomsky Regiment amounting to about 1,500 troops. Because of the mist, the Russians were unsure of the strength of the small force they had encountered and stopped. Buller instructed Egerton to fire a volley and charge. The Russians broke when the 77th surged forward. The British pursued the enemy back up the slopes of Shell Hill and then lay down in the brush to avoid shell fire. The two Ekaterinburgsky battalions before the 88th also fell back in sympathy leaving behind the three guns they had captured earlier. The 88th also pursued their enemy to within canister range of its guns on West Jut.

To the east of these events, two battalions of the Tomsky and four battalions of the Kolyvansky regiments were advancing across Saddle-top Reach with impunity, as the

Klembovsky's image of the Inkerman Bridge over the River Chernaya in the early years of the twentieth century. A church that stood within the walls of Kalamita Castle can be seen on an escarpment in the middle distance to the right of a pole on the western approach to the bridge. The Mackenzie Heights lie on the skyline. (Walter Havighurst Special Collections, Miami University Libraries, Oxford, Ohio).

The River Chernaya today has been widened and deepened to accommodate ships and is no longer crossed by a bridge at this location. The church seen in the grounds of Kalamita Castle in the early 1900s has disappeared. St Clement's Monastery is now found at the base of the cliffs below the castle. The remains of an old cave church is a tourist attraction.

Klembovsky's image taken in the early 1900s of the view southwest over the upper reaches of the Quarry Ravine from the line of the Post Road as it climbs around the southeast face of East Jut. The steep northwest-facing slope of the Inkerman Tusk is on the left. Saddle-top Reach is on the far skyline with the land rising up to Shell Hill to its right. Russian battalions descended from the high ground in the right middle distance before crossing the ravine and ascending the slopes on the left on their way to attack the right flank of the Allies. (Walter Havighurst Special Collections, Miami University Libraries, Oxford, Ohio).

The same view today from the side of the main highway that follows the line of the old Post Road as it climbs around East Jut and up to the Inkerman Ridge. The lower road in the bottom of Quarry Ravine follows the line of the track that diverged from the Post Road at the Barrier. Russians retreated down the ravine by both routes following the failure of their third offensive.

Klembovsky took this view of Home Ridge, which is on the centre to right skyline, looking south from Shell Hill in the early 1900s. Mount Head with the Fore Ridge beyond is on the left skyline. The Kitspur begins on the extreme left skyline. Below Mount Head was the area known as the Gap. The highway, which follows the line of the old Post Road, can be seen winding through trees in the centre middle distance as it climbs out of Quarry Ravine to the site of the Barrier before continuing across more open country to Home Ridge. (Walter Havighurst Special Collections, Miami University Libraries, Oxford, Ohio).

Today's view from near the monument on Shell Hill looking towards Home Ridge, which is in the middle distance in the centre and right of centre. The knoll in the left middle distance is an artificial mound that now stands on Mount Head. The Kitspur begins to fall away to the left of Mount Head. The low ground seen between the camera and Home Ridge is Saddle-top Reach.

Klembovsky's view north from Home Ridge towards Shell Hill from west of the line of the Post Road in the early 1900s. The white British monument commemorating the battle seen in the middle distance to the right of centre is on Saddle-top Reach. Shell Hill slopes down into the head of Quarry Ravine on the far right with East Jut beyond. (Walter Havighurst Special Collections, Miami University Libraries, Oxford, Ohio).

The view north-northwest towards Shell Hill, which has a Russian monument to the battle on its summit, taken from the artificial mound at Mount Head on the northern end of the Fore Ridge. The head of Quarry Ravine is the depression in the foreground. The main highway from Sevastopol to Simferapol, which follows the line of the old Post Road, can be seen running along the slopes of Quarry Ravine on the right. The high ground rising to the right of Shell Hill on the far right is the beginning of East Jut. Russian guns were positioned along Shell Hill and East Jut during the battle. The north shore of Sevastopol's roadstead is in the distance on the right. The Black Sea is on the horizon.

pickets, who had virtually expended their ammunition and were being driven before them, were masking the fire of British guns on Home Ridge. One battalion of the Kolvansky made for Hill Bend while the others moved in echelon towards the part of Home Ridge that was on the western side of the Post Road. Here they were confronted by three guns of Turner's G Battery, Royal Artillery. After ordering the retreating pickets to lie down, two rounds of case shot were fired into the advancing Russians. This caused slaughter in the first column and all following battalions retreated pursued by the pickets, who had jumped to their feet. At the top of Hill Bend, Captain William Bellairs and 183 men of the 49th were waiting behind a low parapet and to the right of guns that were in danger of being overrun by the battalion of Kolvansky which was only eighty yards away. Bellairs gave the order to fix bayonets and advance. His men rushed forward and the Russians turned and fled.

Even further east, 6,600 men of the Borodinsky, Tarutinsky regiments and one battalion of the Ekaterinburgsky were arranged on a front that extended from the Post Road at the head of the Quarry Ravine to beyond the Sandbag Battery. On the right flank of this body were 200 men of the 30th Regiment under Lieutenant Colonel James Mauleverer. They were having troubles firing their damp rifles, but Mauleverer ordered them to the Barrier. As the enemy approached, they mounted the wall and then bayonet charged. Again the Russians turned and collided with their support columns causing confusion. Four battalions of the Borodinsky were put to flight back up the slopes of Shell Hill. Another remarkable victory had been achieved by the few over the many.

Brigadier General Henry Adams led 500 men of the 41st Regiment along the Fore Ridge to Mount Head and then down the Kitspur towards the Sandbag Battery. Here they engaged the 4,000 men in the four battalions of the Tarutinsky and one battalion of the Ekaterinburgsky regiments. Rifle fire cut through the Russian ranks and they turned. Adams pressed forward and retook the Sandbag Battery, but forbade his men to go any further down the slopes.

The Borodinsky and Tarutinsky regiments retreated off the high ground and did not see action again. All in all, twenty battalions of Russians had been defeated by significantly inferior numbers of British soldiers. The sixteen Russian battalions in support did nothing to intervene. Soimonov was killed along with large numbers of his officers and men. Round one went to the vastly outnumbered British defenders.

The Second Russian Offensive, 07.30 – 08.30 hours
To replace the 15,000 troops now leaving the battlefield, Paulov brought forward 10,000 untried soldiers with an additional ninety-seven guns. This force, which was tired after marching to Sevastopol from the hinterland, had crossed the Inkerman Bridge and made its way to St George's Ravine via the East Sapper's Road. Ascending the ravine, it reached the rear of the Russian position on Shell Hill. Dannenberg then took command of the Russian force as was intended in the Russian plan.

The extra guns were deployed along the crest from Shell Hill to East Jut and the Russian artillery line now extended for a whole mile on a commanding position. Dannenberg decided to launch fresh attacks using his march-weary soldiers rather than the reserves that had stood waiting in support. He resolved to move against the British centre and right. The Okhotsky Regiment was the first to move and its four battalions made their way down into the Quarry Ravine, up onto the Inkerman Tusk and down again into St Clement's

Fenton's image entitled **The site of the Guards' Battery during the Battle of Inkerman** looks southeast from the beginning of the Inkerman Tusk over an unseen St Clement's Ravine towards the Kitspur. The brush, which hid opposing groups of combatants from one another in parts of the battlefield on 5 November 1854, is non-existent in the foreground and appears low on the Kitspur when this photograph was taken in 1855. The earthworks believed associated with the Sandbag Battery are visible on the crest of the Kitspur left of centre. The cliffs and headlands of the Mackenzie Heights seen on the left are on the far side of the Chernaya Valley. (Royal Collection Trust/© Her Majesty Queen Elizabeth II, 2016).

Ravine. The four Iakoutsky battalions followed, but headed for the top of the Quarry Ravine to the right of the Okhotsky. The Selenghinsky Regiment formed up to the left of Okhotsky.

Exhausted men were withdrawn from the battlefield on the British side. Pennefather now had 1,400 infantry, half of whom still held advanced positions, for the coming fight. However, reinforcements were on their way in the shape of 1,200 Guards of the 1st Division, 2,000 men of General Cathcart's 4th Division and 1,600 French soldiers. In addition, more guns were to arrive shortly.

Adams at the Sandbag Battery had been joined by Bellairs and three companies of the 49th. He now had a total of 700 men to oppose the Okhotsky. His men held their ground driving back Russian column after column. The fighting at close quarters was bloody with four young officers losing their lives. Retaining possession of the battery became tantamount even though it had little strategic value. However, the sheer weight of numbers against them caused Adams' men to fall back on Mount Head. Adams himself received a shot in the ankle with the wound eventually proving fatal.

Captain Edward Hamley had established a battery of three guns on the eastern slopes of Mount Head and initially pounded a Russian column on the far side of the Quarry Ravine. However, Russian infantry was soon advancing through the brush towards him. Firing case, Hamley stopped them in their tracks. The Duke of Cambridge then came up with 700 men of the Grenadier Guards and Scots Fusilier Guards, and moved towards the

The Kitspur today looking south from the slope further along the Inkerman Tusk. The Kitspur was the scene of fierce fighting for the control of the Sandbag Battery, which was situated on the crest at centre. The Sandbag Battery was on the far right flank of the Allied position and strategically insignificant, but it became the obsession of both sides to hold this ground and was the target of repeated Russian attacks and Allied counter-attacks. St Clement's Ravine is below and the path along its floor is visible on the right. Mount Head at the northern end of the Fore Ridge is near where the mast can be seen on the skyline. The area known as the Gap is on the far right skyline.

Sandbag Battery. The Grenadier Guards led, but their rifles were damp and failed to fire. There was no other recourse but to charge the position with bayonets, an action that swept the Okhotsky downhill. However, realising they were not being pursued, the Russians soon stopped retreating, regrouped and worked their way back up the slope. This retreat and attack cycle was continued as the Grenadier Guards held firm. The Scots Fusilier Guards were also called upon to fire on and then bayonet charge two Okhotsky columns moving up from St Clement's Ravine. The action at this location was turning into a fierce struggle for supremacy with the Sandbag Battery as the goal of both sides. About 500 men were funnelled into the fight on the Kitspur in small detachments as they arrived on the scene.

To the south-southwest of the Sandbag Battery, British troops were still at the Barrier, but there were no defenders between the two positions. This vulnerable area in British lines became known as 'the Gap'. The Gap needed to be closed to stop the Kitspur being isolated, but by whom? Help seemed to have arrived on the scene at around this time in the form of the 6th Regiment de Ligne and the 7th Léger. These French regiments had marched up to the battlefield and were behind Home Ridge. However, General Bosquet had not yet appeared and the force would not move any further forward without orders from its commanding officer. This led to some ill will between the French and British as their help was desperately needed.

The remains of the parapet of the Sandbag Battery on the Kitspur as photographed by Klembovsky in the early 1900s. The Chernaya Valley can be glimpsed on the far right indicating that the encroaching brush was not obscuring the view to the northeast at this time. (Walter Havighurst Special Collections, Miami University Libraries, Oxford, Ohio).

Pine trees have been planted nearby and dense brush has re-established itself on much of the site of the Sandbag Battery today. This platform is where the battery is most likely to have stood. The ground falls away quite steeply beyond the edge of the site as is seen in Klembovsky's image. The area has been thoroughly dug-over by souvenir hunters. A human tooth and part of a skull was found on the disturbed surface when the author visited in September 2012. The GPS reading made at the site was 44° 35.641'N; 33° 35.880'E.

Dannenberg now called on the Selenghinsky to attack the Kitspur from the east while the Okhotsky and a sapper battalion were to attack from the north. Nine battalions with 6,000 men now faced the few hundred men defending the Sandbag Battery. The slaughter continued with the Russians valiantly climbing the slopes with a firm resolve only to be met by concentrated and accurate rifle fire. Selenghinsky troops eventually rushed the parapet and some fired down at sheltering British troops from the top. The remains of the Grenadier Guards fell back to higher ground with its colours. After celebrating the capture of the battery, the Russians advanced some way before halting. Two forces stood facing each other at distances that were as short as eight yards. As ammunition dried up, rocks were hurled. At this moment, the 314 men of the Coldstream Guards arrived and the Grenadier Guards became determined to recapture the battery before their comrades. Charging with bayonets, there was hand-to-hand fighting before the Russians broke. The Coldstreams joined the line to the right of the Grenadiers and there was then a lull in fighting on this front. However, the battle for the empty battery, which had of no military significance, but had much symbolic importance to the soldiers fighting for it on both sides, was not yet over.

Cathcart had allowed 1,700 men of the 4th Division to be dispatched to various parts of the front to plug gaps in defences as was deemed necessary by Pennefather. He had none of his own troops left with him until Brigadier General Arthur Torrens arrived with 400 men from the 46th (South Devonshire) and 68th (Durham) Regiments. Although a small force, it presented an opportunity for Cathcart to engage the enemy. Pennefather and the Duke of Cambridge wanted the Gap to the left of the Kitspur to be secured, but Cathcart chose instead to strike the Selenghinsky battalions operating further down the slope to the right of the Sandbag Battery. He proceeded with this action even after Quartermaster General Airey, on behalf of Raglan, ordered him to move to the Gap. Cathcart had a 'dormant commission' from the government to take over from Raglan should he become incapacitated, but had resented not being allowed to share in Raglan's thoughts or advise on matters of strategy. This may have caused him to ignore the Commander-in-Chief's instructions and do things the way that he saw fit. This was a tragic mistake.

Cathcart ordered Torrens to proceed with his 400 men obliquely down the hillside to attack the extreme left flank of the Russian offensive. At this time another assault on the Sandbag Battery was in progress. It was being countered by the gallant actions of Captain Edwyn Burnaby and a few men on the right flank of the Grenadier Guards, who jumped from the parapet and took the fight to the assailants. A desperate close quarters struggle by men with bayonets either singly or in small groups ensued. This led to a general contagious excitement and the whole line of the Guards moved forward from the battery onto the ledge before it and into the advancing Russians. Cries from senior officers to stand fast on the high ground were lost in the mayhem. Many of the Guards plus reinforcements from the 20th, 46th, 68th and 95th regiments charged down the slope after the Russians who were retreating pell-mell. This incident was known as the 'false victory' as, although it succeeded in driving many Russians off the battlefield, it left the Kitspur perilously undermanned and vulnerable to attack. The Russians were routed, but British troops were now scattered on the slopes down towards the bottom of the Chernaya Valley where they could do nothing useful. Only ninety or 100 defenders remained on the Kitspur and two Okhotsky battalions were advancing on their positions. A few troops were able to quickly scramble back up the slope and re-join their comrades before being cut off, but for the majority it was to take some time. Nevertheless, most eventually regained the heights and threw themselves back into the conflict for the Kitspur.

Cathcart meanwhile was aware that all was not as it should be when he heard musketry from above his position aimed at his troops below engaged with the Selenghinsky Regiment. A battalion of the Iakoutsky Regiment had advanced out of the Quarry Ravine into the Gap, where Raglan wanted Cathcart's force positioned, and on past the Kitspur. The Russians now had a marvellous opportunity to turn the British right flank. Cathcart sent orders to recall his men below and moved upwards with fifty men of the 20th (East Devonshire) Regiment who had joined him from the Kitspur to confront the 700-800 men of the Iakoutsky Regiment. Many of these fifty men were killed, but not before checking the advance of the Russian column. Cathcart rode his horse up and down in front of the crest where the Iakoutsky were positioned. He knew the situation was perilous. More men arrived from below, but were without ammunition and refused to join the fight above. Cathcart, who was in a sheltered position in a rocky nook, moved out to speak with Major Charles Maitland, but was shot through the heart and fell from his horse. Colonel Charles Seymour was also killed by his side and Maitland seriously wounded. Things were going from bad to worse.

The Iakoutsky Regiment was on the northern end of Fore Ridge to the southwest of the Kitspur. It now began to fire down on the Duke of Cambridge and his men at the Sandbag Battery from the north-eastern slopes of Mount Head. The Duke's problems were compounded by two battalions of the Okhotsky Regiment, who were moving against him on his left front. A total of, by now, 150 British soldiers were being assailed by about 2,000 Russians. Almost cut off and outnumbered, the Duke decided it was time for his isolated men to get back to the main British lines. The Iakoutsky Regiment was moving to its left as it spread out on the Kitspur. As a consequence, some of those on the British left scraped past the Russian's right flank as they moved uphill while others had to fight their way through with fixed bayonets. One group with its colours was attacked in the rear by the on-coming Okhotsky, who had swept past the now undefended Sandbag Battery. Turning to face them, about eighteen soldiers led by Burnaby bravely counterattacked, but were overwhelmed. Some of those left for dead, including Burnaby, who had slipped on the wet barrel of a musket when the Russians past over him, thus avoided being 'dispatched' by following troops.

At this dark moment, the 900 men of the 6th Regiment de Ligne moved forward on orders from General Bourbaki, a senior French office who had finally arrived on the scene, and hit the Okhotsky on its right flank. Driving the Russians before them into St Clement's Ravine, the advance faltered. However, French officers were urged to continue and retake the Sandbag Battery by Captain James Armstrong, who was Brigade Major of the 1st Brigade of the 2nd Division. His entreaties did the trick and Burnaby and his colleagues were saved from capture. After the battery was secured, the French moved west to the head of St Clement's Ravine.

Of the 2,600 British soldiers that had fought on the Kitspur, almost 1,000 were now either killed or wounded. The Guards and other regiments had been depleted, but still the outcome of the battle was in the balance.

While all the above had been going on, three battalions of the Iakoutsky Regiment had descended from Shell Hill and had advanced up Quarry Ravine to the Barrier. Earlier, Mauleverer and 200 men of the 30th Regiment had defeated two battalions of the

Fenton's image entitled *The Quarries and Aqueduct in the Valley of Inkerman* looks north over the lower reaches of the Quarry Ravine and the Chernaya Valley from the Inkerman Tusk. This area of the ravine was where the stone quarries that gave it its name were located. The multi-arched aqueduct bridge that carried water into Sevastopol to operate the dry docks can be seen where the valley opens into the Chernaya Valley to the right of centre. The Post Road that ran from the Inkerman Bridge to the Barrier and across Home Ridge rounds East Jut above the quarry on the left. (Royal Collection Trust/© Her Majesty Queen Elizabeth II, 2016)

A view from the Inkerman Tusk today showing the Sevastopol-Simferopol highway, which follows the line of the old Post Road, rounding East Jut on the left. The quarries in the ravine below are obscured by dense brush that was absent when Fenton took his photograph. Caves in the ravine were used for storing munitions in the Cold War and are still military sensitive. The head of the Sevastopol Roadstead now covers land that was marsh during the Crimean War.

Fenton's image entitled *The Ruins of Inkerman* looks northeast along the Inkerman Tusk on the left and down into the Chernaya Valley on the right. The river was in flood at the time the photograph was taken in May 1855. The ruins of Kalamita Castle lie at centre on the top of the escarpment on the far side of the valley. The Russians occupied the area below and Fenton was fired upon on one of his visits. (Royal Collection Trust/© Her Majesty Queen Elizabeth II, 2016).

The view northeast along the Inkerman Tusk today with the ruins of Kalamita Castle at centre on the top of the escarpment across the Chernaya Valley. St Clement's Ravine is on the right and the Mackenzie Heights are on the skyline.

Fenton's image entitled *The Valley of the Tchernaya* which looks east over the Chernaya Valley from the Inkerman Tusk. This photograph forms a panorama with the previous image and again shows the river in flood. The ruins of Kalamita Castle are now top of the escarpment on the extreme left. (Royal Collection Trust/© Her Majesty Queen Elizabeth II, 2016).

Today's view east from the Inkerman Tusk with Kalamita Castle on the top of the escarpment on the extreme left. The river, which can be seen in the valley to the right of centre, is here confined within its banks. The embankment on the far side of the valley carries the Sevastopol to Simferopol railway. The Mackenzie Heights lie in the background.

155

Borodinsky Regiment and now he and those troops still capable of fighting faced a new challenge. The Russians made many charges, but their front ranks were driven back time and time again. However, the weight of the enemy resulted in the 30th being slowly pushed back towards Home Ridge. After contesting the ground foot-by-foot, they eventually found themselves lying exhausted behind the defence work along the crest of the ridge.

Pennefather launched 140 fresh troops belonging to the 1st Battalion of the Rifle Brigade at the Iakoutsky Regiment advancing up the slope towards Home Ridge. For a minute or so, the two sides blazed away at each other and then the Russians fell back. In hot pursuit, the Rifles pushed them back into Quarry Ravine. When the Iakoutsky battalions again emerged to resume the fight, they were met by 200 men of the 95th Regiment, who had just arrived at the Barrier. These men held their ground, but the Iakoutsky columns bypassed the obstruction and approached the crest of Home Ridge. One column was torn by canister shot from Turner's guns and sent into retreat. Another was confronted by the weary men of the 30th. These Russians also retired back down the slope.

The Iakoutsky Regiment kept up the pressure and soon more were moving on Home Ridge, but this time further to the east away from the Post Road. They were faced by 180 men of the 20th and nearly 200 men of the 57th (West Middlesex) Regiment newly arrived on the scene. The 20th moved down the slope in line and fired thus alerting Russian guns on Shell Hill to their presence. Despite this they continued, lost some coherence because of the brush, and charged. Forcing the enemy back down the hill, they inclined to the left and followed the Post Road past the Barrier and into Quarry Ravine. Going too far, they returned back up the slope. The left attack of the Iakoutsky columns were thus repulsed, but the right attack was still before Home Ridge. The 57th moved forward and heard the call '57th, die hard!' from Lieutenant Colonel Frederick Horn, a cry that was last used at the Battle of Albuera in Spain in 1811, and then the order to charge. The Russians did not immediately break this time and the fight became hand-to-hand for a while. However, the right attack of the Iakoutsky Regiment was overcome and chased into Quarry Ravine, as was its left attack moments before.

The Third Russian Offensive, 08.30 – 09.15 hours

It has been estimated that the Russians still had 17,000 infantry, which together with almost 100 guns in battery, was still a considerable force vastly outnumbering the 3,600 British and 1,600 French soldiers with thirty-six guns now on the ground. There was a lull while they organised themselves for another attack on Home Ridge. Columns were first seen pouring down the side of Shell Hill and into Quarry Ravine, which was the favoured approach bypassing the exposed Saddle-top Ridge. Four battalions of the regrouped Iakoutsky Regiment emerged from the Quarry Ravine in echelon and attacked straight up the Post Road towards the centre of Home Ridge. They were flanked by more battalions and supported by skirmishers. It was estimated that 6,000 men were now on the move. About 2,000 British and 900 French troops stood in their way. Of the 2,000 British soldiers, 600 were spread out in small groups to harass the advance and another 600 were drawn in line between Home Ridge and the Wellway. The remaining 800 were on Home Ridge or approaching its crest. The 900 men of the 7th Léger were also moving towards Home Ridge. The Russian vanguard marched either side of the Barrier, which was now held by Bellairs and 150 men of the 49th who had moved there from the Kitspur. These now isolated British troops were left unmolested.

The view west from Kalamita Castle over the Chernaya Valley towards the high ground where the Battle of Inkerman was fought. St Clement's Ravine is just left of centre with the rock-exposed slopes of the Inkerman Tusk to its right. Quarry Ravine separates East Jut from the Inkerman Tusk. East Jut is on the skyline on the far right with Shell Hill beyond to its left. Mount Head is on the far left skyline. The Kitspur, where the Sandbag Battery was located, is the high ground to the left of St Clement's Ravine.

The Russian masses first struck on the western extremity of Home Ridge and captured three of Turner's field guns. However, they did not seize the initiative to turn east along the ridge and attack more artillery, which was poorly defended. The opportunity was soon lost. Scarcely three minutes after the guns had been taken, approximately sixty Zouaves, who had absconded from other duties to take part in the battle, arrived and bayonet charged. The Russians were driven out leaving the three captured guns behind. The remainder of the enemy in this sector were attacked by the 600 men of the 21st and 63rd (West Suffolk) regiments initially positioned in the area from Home Ridge to the Wellway. This force continued to advance until fired on from Shell Hill and given the order to lie down facing northeast.

Meanwhile, Russian columns had emerged undetected from the smoke and mist to overwhelm the 100 men of the 55th defending the centre of the line on Home Ridge. Falling back from the crest-work, some were taken prisoner. Further to the east, three of Turner's guns were firing case into the enemy vanguard before being forced to limber up and retreat. The Russians were now over the crest of the eastern end of Home Ridge in many places and looking down its southern side into the 2nd Division camp. Observing the 7th Léger forming a line which had its left on the Post Road, the Russian vanguard hesitated. The 7th Léger advanced and then halted, advanced again after encouragement and then halted again before falling back. It was another moment of crisis for to lose Home Ridge was to lose the battle.

Looking southwest up Quarry Ravine from the east bank of the River Chernaya. The aqueduct carrying water to the dry docks in Sevastopol passed over the gap in the foreground on an arched bridge before entering a tunnel off to the right. The highway from Sevastopol to Simferapol, which follows the route of the old Post Road, rounds the end of East Jut above the quarry's cliff on the right. The end of the Inkerman Tusk is on the left.

The Russian artillery was still firing on Home Ridge and the camp beyond apparently unaware that their troops had reached the crest. One of their missiles mortally wounded Brigadier General Thomas Fox-Strangways, the Commander of the British artillery, while he was talking to Raglan and other shots killed horses under Headquarters staff. The situation was grave.

The 55th, not being pursued by the Russians after being pushed back from the crest-work on Home Ridge, regrouped, fired on the enemy and charged with bayonets. The Russians fell back and the 55th retook the defence works on the ridge. The Russians at the centre of the ridge had similarly not attempted a pursuit of the retiring 7th Léger. Then 200 men of the 77th under Egerton that had been withdrawn from further west to a position just to the left of the retreating French also began to move forward. While these men advanced up the slope to the left of the Post Road, the 7th Léger, after rallying, marched up the right of the Post Road in double column formation. An opportunity for the Russians had again been wasted through a lack of initiative. Those content on remaining on the ground that they had won instead of taking full advantage of a favourable situation by pursing their enemy downhill, now fell back down the northern slope of Home Ridge themselves. The crest was retaken. The 77th and the 7th Léger were halted on the reverse slope.

The site of the Barrier on the Inkerman Ridge today looking north-northwest towards the white Russian monument on the summit of Shell Hill. The highway from Sevastopol to Simferopol, which follows the route of the old Post Road, begins to descend along the north slope of Quarry Ravine at this point. The track in the right foreground leads to the head of St Clement's Ravine and then turns to the southeast to ascend Mount Head. The side road seen just beyond the track descends steeply onto the floor of the Quarry Ravine.

The foremost of the advancing enemy had been defeated, but the main body plus its flanking forces, a total of 2,000 men, were still coming forward. About 1,400 Allied soldiers now held the Home Ridge front that would bear the brunt of the main attack. Just under 1,000 were French with the rest being the remnants of the 55th, 57th and 77th Regiments. The 170 men of the 57th were actually in advance of the crest of the ridge. In addition to this force, there were two companies of Guards at Hill Bend under Colonel George Upton and 200 men of the 47th under Colonel Richard Farren on the far left.

This time the Barrier was directly in the path of the Russian advance and the men of the 49th, who had been left isolated behind the first wave, retreated. They were joined by another fifty men of the 20th and the Guards. Bellairs occasionally ordered his men to turn and fire, but few had any cartridges left. Eventually they reached the 7th Léger and retired behind its ranks to form up in support. Their retreat in front of the French had prevented the 7th Léger from firing on the Russians so that the enemy had almost reached the Allied line before a volley could be discharged. However, when it did, the effect was devastating with the Russians falling in heaps. No follow-up order was given for the French to charge and the regiment began to waver and even fall back just a few paces from the Russians. The Russians were encouraged and leapt forward, but then abruptly stopped when their right flank was attacked by Lieutenant Colonel Henry Daubeney and thirty men of the 55th.

These few men punched a way through the 600-strong column and emerged on its eastern side with far fewer numbers. The French took advantage of the Russian halt and attacked over the bodies of the Russians slain earlier. French and British mixed together as the line surged forward.

The right wing of the Russian attack ran into the 600 men of the 21st and 63rd still facing northeast. The Russians broke under fire from the extended British line and were pursued to the northeast. Changing direction to the north, the pursuers then moved forward on either side of the Post Road and ran into an obstinate mass of Russians from the centre attack. Nevertheless, they succeeded in pushing them back to the Barrier, where an unsuccessful stand was attempted. However, the Russians soon retreated down the Quarry Ravine using the Post Road and the track to its east under plunging fire from above. The left wing of the Russians was similarly pushed back with the centre force after receiving canister shot from a gun directly in its path.

The Fourth Russian Offensive, 09.15 – 10.00 hours

The Russians were not finished and regrouped once gain. Their guns on Shell Hill and East Jut continued to dominate the battlefield and there were still 9,000 fresh troops held in reserve at the rear.

A strong column forced the 6th de Ligne from its advanced position on the right bank of Quarry Ravine down to lower ground. The Russians did not pursue, but turned south on the high ground, and a French battery brought forward to Mount Head prevented them taking the Sandbag Battery. Another Russian column advanced to turn the left flank of those on the line of the Post Road. The foremost of the 21st and 63rd, who had been keeping the Russians massing below them in the Quarry Ravine at bay, now decided to fall back to the Barrier. The 7th Léger, obeying orders, moved across the front of the Barrier to join the 6th de Ligne on the right slope of the Quarry Ravine. Lieutenant Colonel Frederick Haines was now alone with his men at the Barrier. Russian columns moved up the Quarry Ravine under cover of artillery fire and attacked, but were driven back. However, the situation was becoming desperate and reinforcements were needed. A mounted officer rode to the camp and brought back 180 men. In addition, a company of the 77th and one of the 49th plus some men from the Rifle Brigade were added to the defending force. On a visit, Brigadier General Thomas Goldie had his horse shot under him and then he himself was mortally wounded.

It was about this time when two 18-pounder guns, which had been summoned by Raglan much earlier in the battle, arrived on the battlefield and were mounted at Hill Bend where they faced Shell Hill over Saddle-top Reach. These two heavy guns replaced three lighter guns and were supported by the remains of the Guards gathered in that area. The gun crews then systematically began to destroy the 100 guns of the Russian battery on the skyline. The new arrivals attracted retaliatory fire, but were protected by a parapet that absorbed round shot. Nevertheless, the 150 gunners were reduced in number by exploding shells with seventeen falling in the period of one quarter of an hour. However, the fire of the 18-pounders was relentless and the Russian guns were quite quickly rendered ineffective. The French had also brought up twelve heavy guns, which were firing from the Fore Ridge. The tide in the artillery duel had changed.

Having determined that the threat from Gorchakov's forces in the Chernaya Valley was much reduced, General Bosquet came up with almost 2,000 men followed later by General

The view north looking towards the crest of Home Ridge on the highway from Sevastopol to Simferopol. The old Post Road is also believed to have crossed the ridge at this point. A Russian column advanced up the Post Road and over the crest near here during the battle of Inkerman before being driven back. Beyond the crest, the road descends to the site of the Barrier about 440 yards further on. Hill Bend is off to the right.

The view south from near the crest of Home Ridge looking over the site of the 2nd Division's camp. The 7th Léger advanced to the left of the Post Road, and 200 men of the 77th Regiment to its right to drove back the Russians from Home Ridge during the Battle of Inkerman. The Sevastopol-Simferapol highway seen in the picture is believed to follow the line of the old Post Road at this location.

The view west over the valley known as the Wellway where the Russian column, which had advanced up the Careenage Ravine to outflank the British, was attacked from this side by the 77th Regiment and from the far side by the Grenadier Guards during the Battle of Inkerman. The column was decapitated with the Russians at its head killed or captured with those in the trunk fleeing back down the ravine.

The new memorial to the Battle of Inkerman on the site of the old British monument to the east of the road that now runs along Saddle-top Reach from the Sevastopol-Simferopol highway. This monument, which also closely resembles the original, replaced an earlier one sometime between the summers of 2011 and 2012.

d'Autemarre with another 2,000. This was a massive influx of fresh French troops to help the hard-pressed men, who had so far held the enemy off while sustaining heavy casualties.

The French Advance, Retreat and then Attack, 10.00 – 11.00 hours

The first of the French troops to enter the fray were 450 Chasseurs, who rushed to the area of the Gap where they met remnants of the 20th being pushed back by two Russian columns. They joined forces and the enemy ceased to press forward, although they had the advantage when the French moved away to the right to follow their original orders to go to the Kitspur.

Bosquet got ready a body of 3,000 infantry and twenty-four guns with cavalry support. They advanced towards the Kitspur in two columns with the Algerian Tirailleurs on the right and 3rd Zouaves on the left led by a *vivandière*. Unbelievably, many of these troops were taken straight onto the Inkerman Tusk, which had sheer sides and was in view of the Russian artillery on Shell Hill. There were no Russians to fight on the Tusk. However, the situation was soon to change when a column of the Iakoutsky Regiment suddenly climbed out of the Quarry Ravine and captured a French gun. At the same time, the Selinghinsky battalions were advancing up the Kitspur towards the Sandbag Battery when they saw the rear of the French across St Clement's Ravine to their right. Seizing the opportunity, they changed their direction of attack. Meanwhile, the Iakoutsky Regiment had gained more high ground to the west of the top end of the Quarry Ravine thus threatening to cut off and roll up the French soldiers on a precipitous spur that was the Inkerman Tusk. Galvanised into action, the Zouaves stopped the Selinghinsky in its tracks and managed to leave the Tusk without having to fight their way out. The retreat became infectious and the two battalions that had not marched on to the Tusk also fell back. Presently, most of this large French force found itself back on Home Ridge without accomplishing anything. To add to the woes, the *vivandière* who led the Zouaves had been killed.

The French artillery on the Fore Ridge fired on the Russian infantry positions to deter pursuit, but were subjected to very heavy fire from those Russian guns that could not be targeted by the two 18-pounders at Hill Bend and sustained heavy losses. The French cavalry were withdrawn after a shell burst close to a squadron of Chasseurs d'Afrique. Luckily for the Allies, the Russians did not take advantage of the situation that was now once again in their favour.

There was despondency among the French now back behind the main defensive line, but it didn't last long. As for the British, a further 350 men had joined the ranks of those still able to fight. About 200 of these were from the 50th (Queen's Own) Regiment spared from Victoria Ridge and 150 were a remnant of the 57th, who had been in the siege trenches the previous night. The two 18-pounders had also by now gained the upper hand over those Russian guns that were within their reach.

The French decided to advance their same troops that had lately retired in front of the Russians. This time the target was the Selenghinsky Regiment, which had by now taken the Sandbag Battery. Members of the Coldstream Guards that had charged now the slopes earlier that morning and who had made their way back up to the high ground lined up to their left. The Russians put up a fight with their backs to the nine to ten feet-high parapet and when at last they turned to flee, the two embrasures became choked with men. The Zouaves rushed in with bayonets and there was much slaughter. Advancing further down the hill, the Zouaves came across 100 men of the 95th who had also charged down earlier

Fenton's image entitled **French Redoubt at Inkerman** shows a strongpoint constructed at Mount Head on the northern end of the Fore Ridge to increase defensive capabilities after the Battle of Inkerman. The view is to the east over the Chernaya Valley towards the Mackenzie Heights. On one contemporary map, this fortified position is called the **'Redoubt of the 5th November'.** (Royal Collection Trust/© Her Majesty Queen Elizabeth II, 2016).

during the period known as the 'false victory' and were struggling to regain the heights. The French continued to drive the Selenghinsky Regiment down the hill and eventually off the battlefield. At the same time as the action by the Algerian Tirailleurs and Zouaves was taking place, the 6th de Ligne and the 7th Léger were directed to attack the enemy's centre, but ended up advancing on the Barrier, which had remained in British hands.

Victory, 11.00 – 13.00 hours

Three more French battalions arrived bringing the combined strength of French forces led by General Canrobert to between 7,000 and 8,000 infantry. These were posted behind Home Ridge, on the Fore Ridge and the slopes of the Kitspur. The British with a total strength of almost 3,000 were either in the centre on Home Ridge, fighting forward of this position or guarding the ravines to the west and northwest. Many of these were what Kinglake refers to as 'spent forces' and incapable of further sustained effort. Dannenberg may now have had 14,000 on the Inkerman Ridge with which to pursue the battle with 9,000 of these being the troops held in reserve. Another 20,000 men under Gorchakov were waiting for the right moment to attack the Sapoune Ridge from the Chernaya Valley. To

Today's view was taken looking east from the top of an artificial mound that can now be found on Mount Head over the area where the French redoubt would have been located. The Kitspur, which is covered in dense brush, begins to fall away towards the site of the Sandbag Battery beyond the clearing. The same hills in the Mackenzie Heights range that appeared in Fenton's picture, albeit with more vegetation than in 1855, are seen in the distance.

the amazement of the British, the French, who possessed most of the able fighting men still available to the Allies, now decided to call it a day.

Dannenberg was hoping that Gorchakov would launch his attack so that he too could return to the offensive and he bided his time. As a result, there was relatively little action for an hour. The 18-pounders at Hill Bend now controlled the field, but were running low on ammunition and were firing only intermittently. Troops at the Barrier and on the ground to its left who had been harassing the Russian artillerymen began to act more offensively. They became bold. Haines at the Barrier sent out men to edge closer to the guns on Shell Hill and Lieutenant Colonel Lord West ordered fifty-sixty men, who were the remnants of the 77th positioned near the Mikriakov Glen, to advance on a still troublesome Russian battery on the western side of Shell Hill. Lieutenant William Acton was given the job of leading the 77th and, using the brush as cover, he got within 800 yards of his objective. He organised an attack, but his men were tired and reluctant. Threatening to go alone, Acton gained some support and then the rest of the 77th came forward to help. The men were divided into three and rushed the battery from in front and on both flanks. Haines' men joined in and the position was taken, but not before the Russians had limbered the guns and made off. A company of the 49th under Captain James Armstrong then arrived at the scene. Dannenberg lost heart and ordered the remaining guns and the Iakoutsky plus Okhotsky regiments to be withdrawn covered by Vladimirsky battalions from the reserve.

Closing Stages

The four battalions of the Vladimirsky Regiment were enthusiastic and instead of holding the line moved forward quickly in a mass down Shell Hill as if to launch another attack. However, they retreated when shot from the 18-pounders repeatedly ripped through their ranks. A crushing defeat on the Russians could now be achieved if the Allies acted swiftly. Unfortunately, the French did not want to move. It was left to the batteries on Home Ridge and Fore Ridge to throw shots over Shell Hill at the departing Russians. The Lancaster gun on the Victoria Ridge also harried the retreat inflicting damage. The Allies had won the battle.

Prince Menschikov, who had remained a spectator until now, attempted to stop the retreat. However, Dannenberg was in no mood to agree to this unrealistic command. Some of the guns went back into Sevastopol on the West Sapper's Road while others went down St George's Ravine and then into the hinterland via the East Sapper's Road and Inkerman Bridge. Some Russian infantry followed the artillery while others left by way of the Post Road or the bed of Quarry Ravine. All had departed by 15.00 hours leaving behind their dead and smashed guns. Another half an hour passed before Canrobert belatedly ordered a French battery to East Jut where it harassed the Russian retreat before it was itself fired upon by Russian steamships in the roadstead. Both Raglan and Canrobert rode to East Jut where they observed the Russians making their way across the Inkerman marshes via the causeway. Lieutenant Colonel Collingwood Dickson, who had been in charge of the 18-pounders that had done so much damage to the Russian guns, also rode up. Raglan told him 'You have covered yourself with glory'.

The last action was fought by fifty-six men of the 50th under Lieutenant Colonel Richard Waddy. They had descended into the Careenage Ravine from Victoria Ridge and climbing up the other side in the direction of the West Sapper's Road had found a column of retreating Russian artillery that had been immobilised and left undefended. However, the 50th were deterred from doing anything more than fire their rifles from a distance when a superior force of Russian soldiers with guns arrived on the scene. This timely intervention enabled the Russian artillery column to escape.

Kinglake estimated that the Russians lost almost 11,000 men, killed, wounded or taken prisoner and this included six generals and 256 other officers. The British lost 2, 357 killed or wounded with 597 killed. This included thirty-nine officers killed and ninety-one wounded. The greatest losses were suffered by the Guards, who lost half their number in one hour, and the right wing of the 21st Fusiliers. Significant losses were also incurred by the 20th and 57th regiments. The French reported that they lost thirteen officers and 130 men killed and thirty-six officers and 750 men wounded.

A Visit to the Battlefield

The main highway from Simferopol, the capital of the Crimea, passes over the battlefield as it approaches Sevastopol from the northwest. This highway can be reached from Sevastopol by taking the road that now runs up the Vorontosv Ravine from near where the armoured train is on display and going straight ahead at the Dergachi Roundabout. The new British memorial to those who died in the Crimean War is off to the right about 180 yards along the highway from the roundabout. Roughly two-thirds of a mile further along, the highway dips as it traverses the head of the Careenage Ravine. The windmill that served as a landmark in the infantry camps was near the top of the north-eastern slope of this ravine close to here. The highway continues to the northeast and after a further three-quarters of a mile passes the area of the Wellway. One mile from the Careenage Ravine, it reaches Home Ridge. Parking here close to the crest, the visitor can look back down the south-southwest-facing slope where the 2nd Division were camped and forward down the north-facing slope where the Russian columns advanced in their attempts to break the defence line. The location of Hill Bend is to the east.

The highway here follows the course of the old Post Road. The location of the Barrier is 500 yards further along from the crest of Home Ridge just before where the downhill gradient suddenly increases as the highway begins to descend the Quarry Ravine. A road off to the left at this point leads past the site of the British monument to the battle and up to Shell Hill. The Russian monument on Shell Hill is off to the right near the crest of the West Jut-East Jut Ridge. The view from the monument is south-southeast over Saddle-top Reach to Home Ridge.

Returning back to the Barrier, parking is available on the left just before the surfaced side-road joins the highway. A track leads upwards on the other side of the main highway to the right of where another track falls into Quarry Ravine. This track, which was lined with fly-tipped rubbish when last visited by the author, continues straight on as a path into St Clemet's Ravine after 240 yards, The Inkerman Spur is on the left as one descends the ravine with the Kitspur on the right. Further down the slope, the site of the Sandbag Battery lies on the ridge to the right, but is extremely difficult to find amid the dense scrub.

Returning up St Clement's Ravine and re-joining the track up from the main highway, take the track upwards to the left. This leads to an open space at the location of Mount Head at the northern end of the Fore Ridge. Climb to the top of the artificial earth mound here, which others have mistaken for the site of the Sandbag Battery. From here, there are views northwest to Shell Hill and north to East Jut, which is covered with communication towers and is off-limits. The Chernaya Valley with the Mackenzie Heights are visible to the east and the view south is down the Fore Ridge.

With more time available, the visitor can explore the Inkerman Spur between the Quarry and St Clement's ravines, but this area is more sensitive, as it is closer to the communication towers and an old munitions storage facility located in caves in the Quarry Ravine. The land to the north and west of where the main highway crests Home Ridge was also the scene of much action.

8

The Cavalry Camp
and St George's Monastery

Before the Battle of Balaklava on 25 October 1854, the British cavalry camped close to a vineyard on the southern slopes of the Causeway Heights under the hillock on which No.6 Redoubt was being constructed. During the battle, the camp of the Light Brigade was trampled by some regiments of the Heavy Brigade as they charged uphill against advancing Russian cavalry. After the battle, when the Russians occupied Nos. 1-3 Redoubts on the eastern end of the Causeway Heights, the cavalry could no longer remain camped in the South Valley of Balaklava. The Light Brigade was moved close to the Windmill, a landmark on the Chersonese Plateau before Sevastopol. However, there were difficulties in this new location in providing the brigade's horses with enough forage. It was decided on 30th November 1854 to relocate the brigade closer to Balaklava. This decision came the day after Fanny Duberly, whose husband was in the 8th Hussars, wrote 'fifteen of our horses died last night' in her journal. The new location for the camp was in a comparatively sheltered valley to the west of Kadikoi.

The valley where the cavalry was camped is not named on maps dating from the Crimean War except as the location of the 'Cavalry Division' or 'Cavalry Camp'. However, the name 'Vinoy Ravine' was used in some British newspapers at the time. The area was bounded on the north by the steep rocky slopes of Frenchman's Hill, which, as mentioned previously, was also known as Vinoy's Hill. To the south, the side of the valley rose gently and then more steeply into the hills to the west of Balaklava. Guards' Hill was on the southeast corner of the valley. A broad spur from these hills also formed a barrier at its western end, gradually losing altitude towards the north to form a narrow ravine. The main route through the valley was a broad road from Kadikoi that ran along the base of Frenchman's Hill and exited through a rocky gorge at its western end. This road was built by the French and completed just before the military railway from Balaklava to the Col de Balaklava was opened, thus rendering it almost obsolete as a major transport artery from the port to the Chersonese Plateau.

William Simpson's watercolour entitled *Cavalry Camp, July 9th, 1855* shows the southern slopes of the valley looking west from high on Guards' Hill. The spur that lies at the western end of the valley is beyond the camp on the right. The track running through the camp on the right and disappearing around a headland just left of centre ran from the sutlers' bazaar at Kadikoi to the settlement of Karani. The beginning of this track obliquely crosses the hillside in the Robertson/Beato image entitled *Huts of the Royal Artillery* shown in in Chapter 6. The floor at the western end of the valley is on the extreme right.

Simpson's 'key' to the picture gives an indication as to where the various cavalry regiments where camped. The huts and tents in the foreground belong to the 6th

Simpson's watercolour entitled *Cavalry Camp, July 9th, 1855.* (Public domain work of art).

Aerial image showing the location of the Cavalry Camp on today's landscape. North is at the top. The valley where the camp was located is to the south of Frenchman's Hill and to the west of the Sutlers' Camp. (Adapted from a Google Earth™ image)

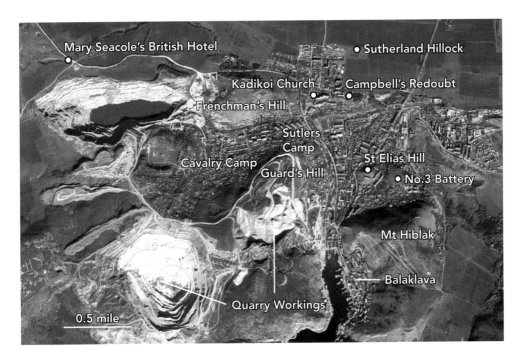

Fenton's image entitled **Cavalry Camp, Church Parade.** (Library of Congress, Washington).

The same view today looking west-northwest from the southern slopes of the valley west of Kadykovka.

Fenton's image entitled **Camp of the 5th Dragoon Guards.** (Library of Congress, Washington).

Looking northwest from the southern slopes of the valley west of Kadykovka. This image forms a panorama with the view opposite.

Fenton's image entitled *Cavalry Camp, looking towards Kadikoi*. (Library of Congress, Washington)

The view today looking over the same valley towards Frenchman's Hill and Kadykovka.

Fenton's image entitled **Military Camp.** (Library of Congress, Washington).

Today's view east from the spur at the western east of the valley where the cavalry camped.

(Inniskilling) Dragoons. The tents on the far right across the road are those of the 5th (Princess Charlotte of Wales's) Dragoon Guards. The 2nd (Scots Greys) Dragoons were above the track at centre with the 1st (Royal) Dragoons on the lower side of the road at centre. I Troop of Royal Horse Artillery had their camp on the lower slopes of the spur across the western end of the valley seen in the middle distance on the far right. The 8th Hussars camped at the bottom of the spur further to their left. The 13th Light Dragoons were left of the 8th Hussars under the same spur. Moving even further to the left, the camp below where the track to Karani bends around a headland in the middle distance was that of the 11th Hussars. Above them on the other side of the road were the 4th Light Dragoons. The 10th Hussars camped either side of the road as it disappears to the left of a plateau–like hill in the far distance.

Fenton took his photographic van into the valley in late March and early April 1855. Here he photographed many officers including Major General Sir James Scarlett, who commanded the Heavy Brigade, Brigadier General Lord George Paget, who now commanded the Light Brigade, Lieutenant Colonel George Clark of the 2nd Dragoons and Captain Henry Duberly, the paymaster of the 8th Hussars, who stands next to his wife Fanny mounted on her horse 'Bob'. Fenton also photographed the landscape.

The first of Fenton's landscapes reproduced here shows the valley from its southern slopes looking west-northwest towards the spur that descends from the left and marks its western extremity. The image, which is entitled *Cavalry Camp, Church Parade*, was taken from lower down the slope and more to the west than where Simpson was positioned. A religious service is taking place on the valley floor on the far right.

The camp seen between the tops of two bell tents in the left foreground belonged to the 5th Dragoon Guards. Above and beyond was the camp of the 13th Light Dragoons with the 8th Hussars to their right. Further to the right again, where the spur descends in the middle distance and above the tents on the valley floor at centre, was the camp of I Troop of Royal Horse Artillery. The long shed was their stables. The French-built road can be seen on the far right following the base of Frenchman's Hill. The low point on the skyline on the far right is the Col de Balaklava. Parallel tracks extend along the valley floor. The track in the foreground is the same as the one that is seen in Simpson's painting. Smoke from garbage fires show that the wind was strong and blowing from the south.

Today, apartment buildings lie on the valley floor and dachas line the slopes where the cavalry camped. Many trees grow where once only grass was found. The whole area is now an urban extension of Kadykovka to the east. The hills in the middle distance beyond the valley have been extensively quarried as has the end of the spur where I Troop of Royal Horse Artillery once camped. The steep slope of Frenchman's Hill can just be seen on the far right with the Col de Balaklava on the skyline above. Omar Pasha's Redoubt was located where a small clump of trees can be seen on the high ground on the centre skyline.

The second of Fenton's landscapes shown is entitled *Camp of the 5th Dragoon Guards*. It looks in the same direction as *Cavalry Camp, Church Parade* but was taken from a position below where the foreground track disappears on the extreme left of his first image. Beyond the dragoon's camp lie the east-facing slopes of the spur that lies at the western end of the valley with the camp of the 8th Hussars evident at its base. Trails from this camp cross the shoulder of the spur behind. The camp of I Troop of Royal Horse Artillery is on the crest of the spur at centre. The French-built road on the far right passes through a rocky gorge at the northern end of Frenchman's Hill.

The modern view looking northwest from the southern slopes of the valley where the cavalry camped forms a panorama with the image that is opposite. It shows the western end of Frenchman's Hill that lies to the north of the valley on the right. The Sapoune Ridge is on the skyline behind Frenchman's Hill with the Col de Balaklava the low point on the skyline on the left .The South Valley of Balaklava can be seen between Frenchman's Hill and the Sapoune Ridge.

The next of Fenton's images is entitled *Cavalry Camp, looking towards Kadikoi*. The view here is northeast from the slope of the spur at the western end of the valley. The tents and huts in the foreground belong to the 11th Hussars. Frenchman's Hill lies on the far side of the valley and descends on the right towards Kadikoi, which is on the far right. The tents of General Joseph Vinoy's brigade are on the summit of Frenchman's Hill on the far left. The French-built road runs along the base of the hill. This photograph was taken from near the track seen in Simpson's *Cavalry Camp, July 9th, 1855* just before it curves around a headland in the middle distance.

Today, the valley floor along the railway line that now roughly follows the course of the French-built road is industrialised. Frenchman's Hill is still recognisable on the north side of the valley. Note on the left that its lower slopes close to the valley floor have been quarried. The white apartment buildings on the far right are in Kadykovka, Beyond Kadykovka, vineyards cover the South Valley of Balaklava with the land rising to the ridge that is the Causeway Heights. The Mackenzie Heights are in the far distance.

Fenton's next photograph, entitled *Military Camp* was taken from close to the same position as the previous one only looking east along the southern slope of the valley. The southern end of the camp of the 11th Hussars is below. The track from Kadikoi seen in Simpson's *Cavalry Camp, July 9th. 1855* and in Fenton's *Cavalry Camp, Church Parade* runs along the hillside on the right. The area of tents above the road in the middle distance was where Fenton took *Cavalry Camp, Church Parade*. Guards' Hill rises up from here to the right. The white building in Kadakoi on the left is the church.

Today's view down the valley was taken from the crest of the spur at its western end, which has a higher elevation and is further north than where Fenton stood to take *Military Camp*. Dachas and low-rise apartments now occupy the grassy southern slopes of the valley. Guards' Hill rises on the right at the valley entrance. The dome-shaped Canrobert's Hill can be seen across the South Valley of Balaklava on the left. This photograph shows how the area has changed since the Crimean War.

Fenton took another image from close to the position where his previous two images were taken only looking southeast at the hills that lay to the south of the camp. This view is entitled *Camp of the 4th Light Dragoons, Soldiers' Quarters*. This camp was just above the track as it began to curve around the headland seen in the middle distance in Simpson's watercolour. The same track is in the foreground of Fenton's picture. Accommodation huts lie just beyond the road with a shed that serves as a stables further way left of centre. Tethered horses feed on the grassy slopes.

Fenton took the view looking north from the southern slopes the valley with the spur at its western end on his immediate left. He called this image *Cavalry Camp, looking towards the Plateau of Sevastopol*. Indeed, the Sapoune Ridge, which was the edge of the Chersonese Plateau and from where Lord Raglan watched the Battle of Balaklava, is on the skyline. On the high ground below the ridge, the outline of the stationary steam engine complex where wagons were hauled up the steep incline on the military railway from

Fenton's image entitled *Camp of the 4th Light Dragoons, Soldiers' Quarters.* (Library of Congress, Washington).

Kadikoi is visible to the right of the French-built road that swings past huts on its left. This road can also be seen running along the base of Frenchman's Hill, which rises on the right, before entering a rocky gorge at the centre. The camp of the 8th Hussars is in the foreground. It was in this camp that Fanny Duberly lived in a hut with her husband Henry. Fanny's drawing of her hut and its environs published in her journal suggests that it may have been the square, white-coloured cabin with the white roof seen at centre. I Troop of Royal Horse Artillery were camped beyond the 8th Hussars on the shoulder of land left of centre, which was towards the bottom of the spur seen rising on the left.

The camp of I Troop of Royal Horse Artillery was the subject of two photographs by Fenton. They were taken from the same position and differed only in the arrangement of personnel and a horse in the foreground. Only the image entitled *Major Brandling's Troop of Horse Artillery* is shown here. Fenton took this picture looking north from the shoulder of land at the western end of the valley that overlooked the troop's camp. The tents and huts in the foreground are those of I Troop, commanded by the newly-promoted Major Brandling, who had previously led C Troop as a captain. Both C and I Troops had seen action on the Bulganak, and at the Battles of the Alma and Balaklava. The troop's horses are visible tethered in lines further down the slope with the gun carriages beyond. The French-built road skirts the bottom of Frenchman's hill, which rises on the right, and then passes through a rocky gorge before emerging on the grasslands seen on the left. To the right of the road as it curves out of sight lies the stationary engine complex. Smoke can be

Fenton's image entitled *Cavalry Camp, looking towards the Plateau of Sevastopol.* (Royal Collection Trust/© Her Majesty Queen Elizabeth II, 2016).

seen omitting from a stack. This was where steam was generated to work the haulage system that dragged wagons up the incline of the military railway from near Kadikoi. This railway ran on the north side of Frenchman's Hill. Just left of the stack is a tall water derrick. The Sapoune Ridge is on the left skyline and the nearer Causeway Heights on the centre and right skyline.

Today, the same slope is heavily treed making photography difficult, but the image presented was taken close to where Fenton must have positioned himself when taking his photograph of I Troop's camp. The valley bottom now is where much of the local quarrying operations are concentrated with rock crushing plants and associated machinery. The Quarry's administration buildings now occupy the ground where the huts stood in 1855. The gorge through which the French-built road gained access to the grasslands beyond is unrecognisable and now contains stockpiles of crushed rock. However, the northern end of Frenchman's Hill is still conspicuous on the right. The location of the stationary engine was beyond and to the left of the building with the red roof in the centre middle distance. Today's main road from Balaklava to Sevastopol passes just behind this building. The Sapoune Ridge is on the left skyline with the Causeway Heights at centre to the right of the sweep of vineyards. The Mackenzie Heights are visible in the far distance on the right skyline.

The last of Fenton's pictures in the area of the cavalry camp to be shown is entitled *Road to Balaklava, Kadikoi in the Distance*. When he took this photograph, Fenton was positioned on the shoulder of the spur at the western end of the valley near where the

Fenton's image entitled **Major Brandling's Troop of Horse Artillery.** (Library of Congress, Washington).

Today's view north from the slope of the spur at the western end of the valley where the cavalry camped.

Fenton's image entitled *Road to Balaklava, Kadikoi in the Distance.* (Royal Collection Trust/© Her Majesty Queen Elizabeth II, 2016).

The view looking east down the valley where the cavalry camped from the western spur today.

The Roberston/Beato image entitled **Monastery of St George.** (Royal Collection Trust/©
Her Majesty Queen Elizabeth II, 2016).

St George's Monastery today looking east from the cliff top.

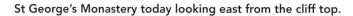

The Robertson/ Beato image entitled **Rocks near St George.** (Royal Collection Trust/© Her Majesty Queen Elizabeth II, 2016).

The view west along the coast from St George's Monastery today.

tracks can be seen crossing over the top just left of centre in *Cavalry Camp, Church Parade*. One of these tracks, which cuts into the spur, is seen in the foreground. The site was to the south of I Troop's camp. The view is east down the valley towards Kadikoi. The hillock in Kadikoi that carried Campbell's Redoubt is just beyond the entrance of the valley. Canrobert's Hill is in the distance at centre across the South Valley of Balaklava. The broad French-built road skirts the base of Frenchman's Hill on the left. Most of the tents and huts of the cavalry camp are on the slopes off the picture on the right. The parallel tracks through the camp are on the right. Figures look down onto the valley floor. Fenton's much reproduced image of Henry and Fanny Duberly was taken on this same valley floor behind where the figures are standing with Frenchman's hill as a backdrop.

The same view today looking east down the valley from lower down the slope of the western spur shows the industrial buildings that now lie on the valley floor along the quarry railway that parallels the route of the old French-built road. Frenchman's Hill is in the left with the large white apartment blocks in Kadykovka conspicuous in the middle distance to its right. To the immediate right of these tall blocks, the hillock that carried Campbell's Redoubt can be glimpsed further away. Above this hillock is Canrobert's Hill on the far end of the South Valley of Balaklava. Apartment buildings are now found on the lower southern slopes of the valley on the right.

St George's Monastery
St George's Monastery, which is situated on the coast about four and a third miles west of the head of Balaklava's harbour, was a popular place for officers to visit while off duty. It was also an Allied recuperation centre. The monastery was positioned on the top of high cliffs overlooking the Black Sea and offered spectacular views. It was a comfortable horse ride from the cavalry camp near Kadikoi and a pleasant excursion for the likes of Fanny Duberly and others.

Mrs Duberly caused a controversy by wearing a pair of trousers instead of petticoats. This did not endear her to many though it must have been practical during the cold weather of winter. Captain George Dallas of the 46th Regiment reported on a trip to the monastery in mid-February 1855:

> A day or two ago, Wombwell and I rode over to the "monastery" called St George's about 4 miles from here. I don't think I ever saw anything as lovely as the scenery, in a rocky, blustery way. It is perched on the edge of a tremendous cliff, and there are winding paths down to the sea … We walked back up the cliff behind Mrs Duberly and party, and very nice black Trousers she had.

Fanny recorded in her journal that she rode over to the monastery on 16 February 1855 with her husband and three others including Captain Stephen Lushington, who commanded the Naval Brigade. She reported that she was 'as much pleased with it the second time as seeing it the first'.

Dallas visited the monastery again a week later and wrote in a letter home on the 25 February 1855:

> Today, a party of us, Wombwell and one or two good fellows … made a pic-nic to the 'Monastery' and passed a most pleasant day. The intense enjoyment there

is getting away altogether from the horrors and noise of such a camp as ours, to a lovely spot like the one we went to, you may well conceive … We scrambled down, when full, to the beach; a most beautiful one it was to, with jolly sand like home, and I really think we would not have been much astonished if an old bathing woman or Coast-Guard, had come around the corner of a rock upon us. Scrambling up the cliff was not so amusing as sliding down we found.

He was not so impressed with the monks at the monastery and commented: 'The monks were very nasty looking beasts, with long hair like women, and faces and foreheads like apes. They seemed happy enough, laughing together, and did not seem to feel much their position, and the desecration of their beautiful home by a Company of Zouaves, who are quartered there'. He concluded by writing: 'We cannot destroy the beauty of the position, and the wonderful broken points of rock, torn to all appearances from the main cliff. I am in love with the place, and intend going often, weather and duty permitting, to hide myself from this loathsome "before Sebastopol"'.

Fenton never took any photographs of the Monastery of St George, but the Robertson/Beato team did visit and took a number of images in the area. The first of two selected shows the monastery clinging to the cliff face above the Black Sea and is entitled *Monastery of St George*. The monastery was closed and damaged during the Soviet era, but restoration work began in 1991. Today's picture reveals that some buildings have disappeared and have been replaced by other structures. The church seems to have survived intact, but its dome is now smaller than in 1855. The tower associated with buildings on the cliff top is still minus its original spire. The cliff slopes now have more trees.

Robertson/Beato's second image was taken looking west along the coast from the terrace at the monastery and is entitled *Rocks at St George's*. Its modern equivalent shows that the cliffs are essential the same as in 1855. Small boats bring holiday-makers to the secluded beach at the base of the cliff from Balaklava, but the energetic still follow paths down and up the cliffs, much as did George Dallas and Fanny Duberly. The two rocks in the sea just before the rock pillar at Cape Folient are known as Orestes and Pylades from a Greek legend.

British Army Headquarters in the Crimea
Finding Raglan's Command Centre

Soon after Balaklava was captured, Lord Raglan established his headquarters in the Tractir farmhouse at Khutor-Karagatch, which was about two-thirds of a mile to the north-northwest of the Col de Balaklava. The farmhouse had previously been in the possession of I Troop of Royal Horse Artillery, but this unit was transferred to the neighbourhood Kadikoi on 3 October 1854.

William Russell reported: 'Lord Raglan and his staff established head-quarters in a snug farmhouse, surrounded by vineyards and extensive out-offices, about four and a half miles from Balaklava on the 5 October.' The Field-Marshal died in his bedroom in the farmhouse on 28 June 1855. He was suffering from diarrhoea most likely caused by dysentery. He had also been severely depressed following the failure of the assault on the Redan on 18 June and also the death of Major General James Estcourt, whom he greatly admired, from cholera on 24 June. General Sir James Simpson, the new Commander-in-Chief, then made the farmhouse his headquarters until he resigned in November 1855. His successor General Sir William Codrington also took up residence in the building until the army returned to Britain in the summer of 1856.

The Headquarters' Complex

The watercolour by William Simpson entitled *Distant view of Lord Raglan's Head-Quarters before Sebastopol* shows the headquarters complex in the distance at the centre where the ground levels after rising from a valley. The farmhouse that served as Raglan's command centre has white walls and a red roof. The smoke beyond the building arises from batteries firing on Sevastopol. The Black Sea is on the skyline at the left with the Sevastopol roadstead and its north shore in the far distance to the right of centre. The Chersonese Plateau is on the right and is seen extending to Cathcart's Hill on the far right. When Simpson sketched this work, Captain Brandling's C Troop of Royal Horse Artillery was camped on this height and is depicted in the foreground on the left. The Heavy Brigade was also camped on the spur in the middle distance on the left. A dead horse lies in the right foreground overcome by a lack of forage and the approaching cold winter weather of 1854-55. Because the position was exposed and there was a problem transporting hay from Balaklava to the area, C Troop and the Heavy Brigade later relocated their camps to near Kadikoi.

The picture was sketched by Simpson from a vantage point on high ground to the south of Raglan's headquarters. This strategic hill was chosen as the location of a Turkish fortification known as Omar Pasha's Redoubt. The outline of this redoubt can still be seen in today's aerial

Simpson's watercolour entitled *Distant view of Lord Raglan's Head-Quarters before Sebastopol.* (Library of Congress, Washington).

Today's view looking north from near the site of Omar Pasha's Redoubt where Simpson made his preliminary sketch of *Distant view of Lord Raglan's Head-Quarters before Sebastopol.*

A magnification of today's view from near the site of Omar Pasha's Redoubt showing the treed area at the centre to the east-northeast of the retail building with the blue roof where British army headquarters was likely to have been located.

The Robertson/Beato image entitled *Lord Raglan's House.* (Royal Collection Trust/© Her Majesty Queen Elizabeth II, 2016).

photographs and is accessible by car, where there is a Second World War memorial. Walking a short distance to the northwest from the memorial, it is not difficult to see the same scene as in Simpson's picture. The location today has splendid views in all directions.

In the modern view, which was taken close to the camp site of C Troop Royal Horse Artillery, the camp of the Heavy Brigade would have been on the near spur that decreases in height from left to right across the picture. Sevastopol city can be seen in the far distance above the blue building at centre. By carefully comparing Simpson's picture and today's photograph showing the same view, the headquarters complex of the British army was determined to have been to the right and up the slope from of the large blue-coloured building at centre. Trees can be seen in this area, which is flatter ground. A magnification of the modern view shows the blue retail building on the left with a gentle slope to its right leading to the treed area on more level land. The comparison between Simpson's watercolour and a modern photograph provided some evidence for the location of British headquarters.

Some maps dating from the Crimean War show the location of both Omar Pasha's Redoubt and Raglan's farmhouse headquarters. Measurements between the two locations and their bearings from each other were noted and Google Earth™ used to determine where the headquarters site was likely to have been on today's landscape. This exercise again pointed to the headquarters complex being where the trees seen up the slope from the blue retail building were standing. Measurements made on Google Earth™ showed that the edge of this treed area to be 280 yards northeast of the nearest corner of the blue retail building.

The Robertson/Beato image entitled *Headquarters*. (Royal Collection Trust/© Her Majesty Queen Elizabeth II, 2016).

Two of Fenton's portraits taken at an entrance to the farmhouse that served as British headquarters are shown above and opposite. The steps and doorway in these images are seen on the right of the Robertson/Beato image entitled *Headquarters*.

The image above is entitled *General Estcourt and Staff* (Library of Congress, Washington). Major General James Estcourt, who is standing at centre, died of cholera on 24 June 1855, which seriously affected Raglan's morale. He was buried in a small cemetery near British headquarters.

The image above opposite is entitled *Council of War held at Lord Raglan's Head Quarters, the morning of the successful attack on the Mamelon* (Library of Congress, Washington). Raglan is on the left wearing his sun hat. Note his missing lower right arm, which was amputated forty years earlier at the Battle of Waterloo. Omar Pasha is behind the table in the centre and Marshal Pélissier is on the right. The Mamelon was captured by the French on 7 June 1855, but William Romaine, who was at British headquarters on 6 June 1855, provides strong evidence for the image being taken by Fenton that morning. An entry in his journal for 6 June reads: 'Pélissier came here at 6 AM and brought a box full of finery which he put on in order to have his portrait taken in a daguerreotype by Mr Fenton. About 10 he was still at Ld. Raglan's & he and Omar Pasha and Ld Raglan came out in front where a small table was placed with a map on it and their portraits were taken in a group.' Raglan died in his bedroom in the farmhouse on 28 June 1855, which was four days after Estcourt's death and twenty-two days after the staged council of war photograph was taken.

The Command Centre

Roger Fenton and James Robertson/Felico Beato took photographs of the farmhouse that served as the command centre in the headquarters complex. The first shown is entitled *Lord Raglan's House*. As the trees around the building are in leaf, the picture most likely taken during the pair's first visit to the Crimea in the summer of 1855. The farmhouse is seen at the top of a slope that descends into a valley. Other buildings, army sheds and tents are visible nearby on the top of the same slope. These other structures formed part of the headquarters complex. The image was taken from across the other side of the valley with another farm building in the foreground. Maps indicate that the view was to the east as the valley ran roughly from the southeast to the northwest. The road from the Col de Balaklava, past French headquarters and on to Kamiesch is shown on contemporary maps to have run behind and below the farm buildings in the foreground in 1855. Today, a multi-lane highway follows the course of this old road.

The next Robertson/Beato image is entitled *Headquarters* and shows a view of the other side of the farmhouse. The land slopes gently to the right and presumably falls more steeply into the valley behind the building. Tents and huts are visible in the background on the top of the slope on the far side of the valley from where *'Lord Raglan's House'* was taken. The view is roughly to the southwest. The photograph shows that the house was indented on its northeast side.

Of interest is a camera on a tripod seen before the end of the farmhouse on the left. It has been suggested that the man standing to the left of the camera was Roger Fenton,

Image attributed to Robertson/Beato entitled *South View of English Army Headquarters, March 1856.* (©National Army Museum, London).

Today's view of the same locality taken from behind a bus shelter at the side of the multi-lane highway that now runs along the northeast-facing slope of the valley that begins near the Col de Balaklava. The ground where the three-storey building can be seen being built at the top of the south-east facing slope of the valley falls slightly to the northwest. This fall is also noticeable at the site of the farmhouse in *South View of English Army Headquarters, March 1856.* The wooded area that was pinpointed as the location of the headquarters complex by measurements and bearings from contemporary maps can be seen behind the unfinished building.

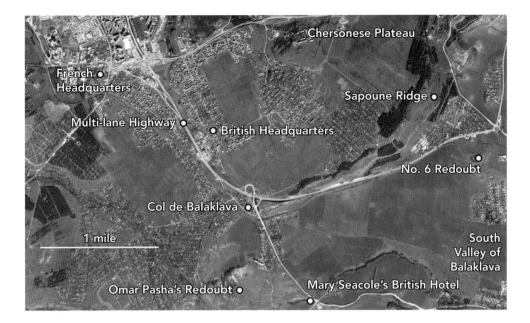

Aerial view image showing the position of the farmhouse that served as British headquarters in the Crimea from 1954 until 1856 on today's landscape. The locations of Omar Pasha's Redoubt near where Simpson sketched his distant view of headquarters and Mary Seacole's 'British Hotel' are also shown. North is at the top. (Adapted from a Google Earth™ image)

but this is difficult to substantiate. As Robertson/Beato's first visit to the Crimea is thought to have begun in June 1855, there would have been only a short period in early- to mid-June 1855 when there would have been an opportunity for them to meet. Such a meeting is not mentioned in Fenton's published communications written during his visit. Other evidence against the figure being Fenton comes from the lack of leaves on the trees in front of the farmhouse. This suggests that the picture was taken in the early spring of 1856 during Robertson/Beato's second visit to the Crimea when Fenton was in England.

Fenton took many portraits of senior officers with the headquarters as a backdrop. The door seen on the right of *Headquarters* in particular was where a number were taken. Two have been reproduced here.

The third image of the farmhouse shown is attributed to Robertson/Beato is entitled *South View of English Army Headquarters, March 1856*. The southwest face of the farmhouse also seen in *Lord Raglan's House* is viewed from across the valley. In this picture, a slight fall of the land along the top edge of the valley to the left of the farmhouse is discernible. This gentle slope was also seen in *Headquarters*. A track descends into the valley and across the floor of the valley from the house. A track cutting across the foreground from right to left is likely to be the road from the Col de Balaklava to Kamiesch. On contemporary maps, this road is shown running along the southwest slope of the valley. The ground on the valley floor and northeast slope is cultivated. The trees are bare and there appear to be patches of snow on the ground. This confirms the date of the photograph as March 1856.

Simpson's watercolour entitled *Lord Raglan's Head-Quarters at Khutor Karagatch.* (Library of Congress, Washington).

The view of what is believed to have been the site of the farmhouse from approximately the same angle today showing a three-storey building under construction.

The Location of the Command Centre Today

Knowing that the land at the top edge of the valley to the northwest of the farmhouse fell away, as shown in the images *Headquarters* and *South View of Army Headquarters, March 1856*, a location with similar topography was sought close to today's wooded area above the valley determined by map measurements to have been where the headquarters complex was situated. A site with a similar gentle slope to the northwest was found on the edge of the valley close to the blue retail building seen in the modern views taken from near Omar Pasha's Redoubt. A photograph taken from the side of today's multi-lane highway that runs along the south-western slope of the valley and which looks towards this site is presented. The ground here falls away into the valley and also to the northwest along the top edge of the valley. It seems very likely that the farmhouse was located where the unfinished three-storey apartment building seen in the photograph was situated in 2012.

The next image is of another of Simpson's watercolours entitled *Lord Raglan's Head-Quarters at Khutor Karagatch* which looks north-northwest and shows the northeast-facing side of the farmhouse. An entrance on the left leads into what could be the cellar of a separate building. A sentry paces in front of the farmhouse as messengers arrive and depart. The modern scene below looks towards the site of the farmhouse, which would have been where the three-storey building under construction is situated, from a similar angle. The track in front of this building shows that the ground falls away in a slight gradient to the northwest. Excavations close to unfinished building that were associated with its construction showed an underground cellar. This provides evidence for the existence of an older building on the site.

A Winter of Discontent:
The Initial Unsuccessful Struggle to take Sevastopol

The defences of Sevastopol were organised by Count Franz Todleben, who initially was only a captain in the military engineers. His ideas were so compelling and imaginative that Prince Menshikov gave him control over the development of fortifications. Although Vice Admiral Vladimir Kornilov wanted to sail out and take on the Allied fleet in a suicidal mission of honour, wiser heads prevailed. It was decided that five old ships of the Russian fleet, which were later joined by an additional two, should be sunk across the entrance to the Sevastopol Roadstead to block the entrance to Allied warships.

Their guns were used to reinforce batteries and their sailors formed into land battalions. Earthen redoubts were rapidly constructed on the south side of the city to augment the stone forts protecting the shoreline of the roadstead. Todleben also supervised the constant improvement of the defences during the siege so that damaged batteries were repaired virtually overnight and strong outlying positions constructed in the face of the besiegers. The rapid appearance of defence works stronger than they were before bombardments was demoralising for the Allies. Todleben's genius undoubtedly extended the siege for many months.

Another reason why the siege dragged on was because the city was never really isolated. After the Allies moved around Sevastopol to its south side, the north side of the roadstead was still in Russian hands and communications with the rest of the Crimea soon reopened. Indeed, during the early part of the siege, the Sapper's road east along the shoreline of the south side of the roadstead even allowed movement to the Inkerman Bridge and hence across the causeway to the hinterland. Supplies of food, munitions and military reinforcements were continually arriving in the city

On 27 September 1854, which was the day after the Allies captured Balaklava, there were 16,000 men on the south side with 3,500 men on the north side of Sevastopol's roadstead plus 3,500 sailors on board ships. On 30 September 1854, Menshikov's army appeared on the north shore of the roadstead 'to the inexpressible joy of the garrison' and on that day provided the city's defenders with field guns, 8,000 troops and Cossacks. Todleben reported that each day after that the garrison was augmented by column after column of soldiers until 32,000 men were ready to receive the Allied onslaught by 5 October 1854.

The decision by the Allies not to immediately attack Sevastopol in strength when its defences were at their weakest, but to wait until the city could be bombarded, was a serious mistake. While the British and French prepared their batteries, the Russians considerably strengthened their position. This led to a siege that cost many lives and lasted almost a year.

Simpson's watercolour entitled *Malakoff or Round Tower*, which shows the damaged tower on Malakhov Hill with its associated battery as it appeared from Allied lines early in the siege. Sevastopol's roadstead is visible in the background with the north shore or Severnaya beyond. (Library of Congress, Washington).

The reconstructed Round Tower today taken from an earthen bank on the site of the battery's parapet. The park that now covers Malakhov Hill lies in the background.

The Robertson/Beato image entitled **The Battery of the Ravine** shows Chapman's Battery on the 1st Parallel of the British Left Attack on the Green Hill Ridge. There is little activity indicating that the siege is over. Round shot litters the slope in the foreground. Central Hill in Sevastopol is in the distance on the far right of the photograph. The position of the city indicates that the view from the battery is to the northwest. (Royal Collection Trust/© Her Majesty Queen Elizabeth II, 2016).

Sevastopol's Defences

Sevastopol was located on the south side of a large sea inlet or roadstead that ran over four miles east from the Black Sea. The actual city with its fine buildings was a mile from the roadstead's sea entrance. To the immediate east of the city lay a one and a third mile long inlet to the south known to the Russians as the South Harbour and to the British as Man-of-War Harbour or Dockyard Creek. On the eastern side of this inlet lay the Karabelnaya district, where dry docks, storehouses, barrack buildings, an arsenal and hospital were found.

Five stone forts with batteries had originally been built along the shoreline of the roadstead to protect Sevastopol from an attack by sea. On the north shore, Fort Constantine was on a promontory that jutted out into the roadstead entrance with Fort Michael about 1,150 yards to its west. The massive Star Fort lay a little way inland to the northeast of Fort Michael. On the south shore, Fort Alexander lay opposite Fort Constantine, with Fort Nicholas to the immediate west of the entrance to South Harbour and Fort Paul to the immediate east of the same entrance. In addition, there were another three defensive works with batteries on the north shore and three others on the south side.

The Robertson/Beato image entitled **English Left Attack** overlaps with **The Battery of the Ravine** showing the view to its right. Central Hill in Sevastopol is now in the distance to the right of centre. The Vorontsov Ravine with the end of the Vorontsov Ridge beyond is on the far right of the image. The earthworks protecting the Russian's Barrack Battery can also be seen on the top of the ridge. Another British battery situated on the 2nd Parallel is visible in the middle distance to the left of centre. (©Art Institute of Chicago)

Russia's Black Sea Fleet, which before the ships were scuttled consisted of fourteen battleships, seven frigates, one corvette, two brigs and eleven steamships, lay anchored in the roadstead. All in all, the fleet had total of 1.908 guns and was crewed by 18,500 seamen.

A semi-circle of strongpoints covered the approaches to Sevastopol from the south. These began in the east with Bastion No.1 near the entrance to Careenage Bay. Then came Bastion No.2, also known as the Little Redan, followed by the Malakhov Bastion on Malakhov Hill. Next was Bastion No.3, known as the Redan to the Allies, near the end of the Voronstov Ridge. These four bastions protected the Karabelnaya district. On the high ground just to the west of the head of the South Harbour was Bastion No.4, which was called the Flagstaff Bastion or Bastion du Mât by the Allies. Turning northwest, the defensive line extended to Bastion No.5 or the Central Bastion. The last strongpoint was Bastion No.6 or the Quarantine Bastion, which lay 1,200 yards south of Fort Alexander. Initially, the bastions were lightly armed and intervening earthworks to link them together either flimsy or none existent. However, men, women, children and even convicts laboured long hours to improve the defence line.

The third in the series of Robertson/Beato images of Chapman's Battery is entitled **English Batteries**. It overlaps with **English Left Attack** to show more of the battery to the right. Russian round shot is again evident on the slope in the foreground. The view looks north and shows more of the Vorontsov Ridge beyond the Vorontsov Ravine. A line of Russian defences is visible along the crest of the ridge stretching from the Barrack Battery on the left to the Redan Bastion in the centre. The strategic location known as the Quarries is visible as a faint white scar just below the crest of the ridge on the right. (Royal Collection Trust/© Her Majesty Queen Elizabeth II, 2016).

When the Allies began constructing trenches and preparing batteries, it became clear to the Russians that the Allies had rejected plans to attack immediately. Todleben wrote that 'all in Sevastopol congratulated each other on this circumstance; all saw in it an important guarantee that the town might yet be saved'. He proceeded to strengthen the defences opposite where the Allies were working on their lines.

The First Bombardment of Sevastopol
To soften-up the Russians by reducing its defences before any assault, the Allies had been busy erecting gun platforms and digging trenches in an arc around the defences of Sevastopol. The British had taken responsibility for the siege lines east and northeast of the Great Ravine, which ran towards Sevastopol from the south, while the French controlled the area to the west and northwest, which was closest to their supply ports.

Siege train parks were established by the British on the Chersonese Plateau near a windmill to the east and the camps of the 3rd and 4th Divisions in the west. Batteries were completed

This image by Robertson/Beato is entitled **Battery before the Redan** and is a closer view of the sand-bagged battery seen on the right of **English Batteries**. Three siege guns can be seen at their embrasures pointing in the direction of the Redan. Ammunition for the guns is neatly stacked in the centre and on the far left. The view is north-northeast towards the Vorontsov Ridge which is seen in the middle distance. The scar that indicates the location of the Quarries is below the crest of the ridge on the left. Trenches of the British Right Attack are visible on the ridge at right. Malakhov Hill can be seen further away beyond the depression in the Vorontsov Ridge in the centre. (Royal Collection Trust/© Her Majesty Queen Elizabeth II, 2016).

by 12 October and armed by 16 October 1854. The British sector was divided into a Right Attack mainly concentrated on the Vorontsov Ridge and a Left Attack on the Green Hill Ridge.

On the Vorontsov Ridge, a twenty-one-gun battery, which was also known as Gordon's Battery after the captain who directed the attack, was constructed along the line of trenches of the 1st Parallel where they crossed Frenchman's Hill (not to be confused by the hill of the same name near Kadikoi). Mortars were positioned on either side and all pieces overlooked the Malakhov and Redan bastions. A single Lancaster gun, which had a revolutionary oval-shaped barrel and fired conical-headed projectiles, was placed in the Left Lancaster Battery some distance behind Frenchman's Hill. In addition, a five-gun battery, which was known as the Right Lancaster Battery after its single Lancaster gun component, was constructed on the Victoria Ridge facing Malakhov Hill. There were thirty-two pieces of artillery in total. On the Left Attack, Chapman's Battery, again named after the captain who directed the attack, was established along the trench line of the1st Parallel in this area that extended from the Vorontsov Ravine to the Great Ravine. Here, there were

Above and opposite: The topography of the foreground in Robertson/Beato images of Chapman's Battery and also the background views reveal that they were taken on the eastern side of the Green Hill Ridge. Detailed plans of the Royal Engineers showing the British Left Attack indicate that the Battery No. 1 component of Chapman's Battery was most likely to have been photographed. The modern photographs on pages 200 and 201, which overlap, show the area where Battery No. 1 was located. In the picture above, Central Hill in Sevastopol is in the distance behind and to the immediate right of the red house in the centre. The steep-sided Voronstov Ravine with the Vorontsov Ridge beyond is on the right. The site of the Redan is where the white obelisk on the crest of the ridge on the extreme right can just be seen. In the opposite picture, the undulating Vorontsov Ridge is seen across the Vorontsov Ravine. The area of the Quarries on the Vorontsov Ridge would have been just above the dark-roofed house in the left foreground. The wooded top of Malakhov Hill can be glimpsed over the Vorontsov Ridge to the right. The grassy slope in the foreground of both images is where round shot lay in the Robertson/Beato's photographs.

forty-one pieces of artillery including more Lancaster guns. All seventy-three British guns and mortars primarily opposed Russian batteries from the Flagstaff to the Little Redan Bastions, which included those at or near the Malakhov and Redan Bastions.

The French similarly positioned sixty-four guns so as to oppose Russian batteries from the Quarantine Fort (an outlying defensive position on the coast) to the Flagstaff Bastion and surrounds. However, they had not sited their weapons with as much care as the British and were open to enfilade and reverse fire. This flaw was to tell during the first great exchange of fire.

The artillery duel began at 06.30 hours on 17 October when the British embrasures were unmasked. Round shot soon began to adversely affect the hastily prepared Russian positions. Their parapets were not thick enough to resist the projectiles and the blast from their own guns caused further damage.

The French guns had initial success against bastions Nos. 5 and 6 before a Russian shell found a magazine on Mount Rodolph to the southwest of the city at 09.30 hours. The

resulting explosion killed 16 and wounded 3 men and the battery fired no more that day. After an ammunition caisson exploded elsewhere, the fire from French lines to ceased altogether at 10.30 hours. The British continued the bombardment on their own.

During the first day of the bombardment, Allied warships attacked the three forts guarding the sea approaches to Sevastopol. Fort Constantine had stone walls five-and-a-half to six feet thick with guns in two storeys of casements and others open on the top. Of its ninety-seven guns, forty-three could engage an enemy moving towards the roadstead entrance. On the opposite shore, Fort Alexander had fifty-six guns of which twenty-seven were in stone casements. Fifty-one of its guns could be brought to bear on ships approaching from the Black Sea. The third was the Quarantine Fort, which lay on the coast just outside the roadstead about a quarter of a mile to the west-southwest of Fort Alexander. This defensive position had fifty-eight guns in the open air that fired over parapets. Of these, forty-eight could fire on enemy ships.

At 13.30 hours, the French fleet opened fire on the Quarantine Fort and Fort Alexander with 600 guns. Against them, seventy-three guns in the two forts replied. Much of the French shot went east of its target and swept the empty area between it and the town. The sea-fort suffered little damage with only three guns being dismounted and thirty men killed or wounded. Three guns were also dismounted in Fort Alexander with twenty men killed or wounded. By contrast, the French ships sustained heavy damage losing 203 men killed or wounded. The British fleet, including the flag-ship HMS *Agamemnon*, took on Fort Constantine at the same time. As well as fire from the fort, guns in the Telegraph Battery on nearby cliffs could also reach the attacking ships. Despite this, twenty-two of the twenty-seven guns on the top of the Fort were silenced. However, that was the extent of the damage inflicted on the Russians. British ships were set on fire and moved out of range. It was all over at 18.30 hours. The British lost 317 men killed or wounded and much pride. Two ships were so greatly damaged that they had to be sent back to Constantinople to be refitted. A total of 1,100 British and French guns had taken on 152 Russian guns and achieved comparatively little. Sevastopol was never attacked with any great resolve from the sea again. The Allies had learnt a lesson.

While the naval bombardment had been going on, British land batteries still pounded Russian positions. Alexander Kinglake reported that 'Before half the day was spent, the

This Robertson/Beato image is entitled **21-Gun Battery.** The 21-Gun Battery, which was also known as Gordon's Battery and incorporated Nos 2-5 Batteries, was on the 1st Parallel of the British Right Attack. Sailors lounge in the left foreground indicating that the unseen guns, which would have been off the picture to the left, were manned by the Naval Brigade. The topography and abrupt end to the gabion-reinforced earthwork suggest that the position may actually have been No. 11 Battery, which lay just in advance of the 1st Parallel to the east of the 21-Gun Battery. If so, the earthworks in the immediate foreground from where the image was taken would have been those of the 1st Parallel. The two trench lines crossing the open grassland in the middle distance to the left of centre, and dropping down into the Middle Ravine, were likely to have been the 4th and 5th Parallels. The view is north over the Middle Ravine with the Malakhov Hill in the distance to the right of centre. Earthworks protecting batteries can be seen running along the crest of this hill and down to the left where the Gervais Battery was located. The Mamelon, which would have been in French hands at the time of the photograph, is on the far right. (Royal Collection Trust/© Her Majesty Queen Elizabeth II, 2016).

frail ramparts most battered by our artillery had degenerated into shapeless mounds and after the first nine hours of cannonade, there was more than one spot where they seemed to be nearly effaced'. The stone tower on Malakhov Hill was crumbling, but still stood. Its few guns in an open-air battery on top had been either dismounted or thrown over the parapet and one piece stood on end pointing to the sky. The bastion was silent.

Embrasures at the Redan were blocked by debris from accurate fire. By 15.00 hours, one third of its guns had been dismounted. Loss of life was heavy. Gunners at a number of pieces had had to be replaced twice. Fifty of seventy-five sailors sent to the Redan had been killed. Not long after 15.00 hours a shell ignited a powder-magazine located in the salient and it exploded killing 100 men. In addition, the parapet was blown into the defensive ditch and guns strewn around. At this stage, of the twenty-two guns that originally armed the work, only two manned by five gunners were left operational.

Ricocheting and overshooting round shot had also caused much damage in the rear of the bastions where the Russians kept troops on hand to counter any infantry attack on the lines. However, an assault never came. This would have been the moment to strike and it was expected by the Russians. Kinglake explains the inaction as a consequence of an agreement between the French and British that neither would attack without the other and as the French had not reduced the bastions in their sector, this was impossible.

Firing continued until dusk. The Russian guns were silent that night. Russian losses had been heavy with casualties amounting to more than 1,100. This contrasts with the reported loss of ninety-six Frenchmen and 114 Britons. The Russians suffered a further blow with their much respected defence leader Kornilov being killed by a round shot while visiting the Malakhov Bastion. Nevertheless, they were not deflated. Gangs worked hard at the Redan throughout the night to remove unserviceable guns, re-lay their platforms, make new embrasures, clear the ditch, construct a new magazine and bring forward even more powerful guns. By dawn, the Russians had replaced ten guns on the right face of the Redan with nineteen.

The next day, the bombardment was continued by the British, but the French were still silent. It wasn't until 19 October that sixty-one French guns came back into action. Every night, the Russians rebuilt their battered defences and even constructed additional batteries. On 20 October, the four 68-pounders in the Right Lancaster Battery were moved to the Right Attack on Frenchman's Hill leaving only the Lancaster gun behind. A new British work with three guns and two mortars called the Picket House Battery was also established on the French side of the Great Ravine with the aim of firing on South Harbour.

About 8,700 projectiles were estimated to have been fired by the Allies and 20,000 by the Russians on the first day. The rate of British fire diminished after the second day and was restricted after 25 October because of a shortage of ammunition. Thus the first bombardment drew to a close with the Russians in no worse a position than they were before the start. Indeed, their defences were in better shape.

The battles of Balaklava and Inkerman then diverted attention away from the siege. During this period, another trench was opened 600 yards in advance of the 1st Parallel on the British Right Attack and a position for bronze mortars prepared between the two. Embrasures in Chapman's Battery on the Left Attack were also altered so that fire could be directed at the Russians' Barrack Battery near the Redan that threatened French assaults on the Flagstaff Bastion.

The revolutionary Lancaster guns with their supposed greater accuracy and range had proved a disappointment and were reported as a failure at the end of the siege. Both Right and Left Lancaster batteries were dismantled and their guns transferred elsewhere along the siege line. One 'light' Lancaster burst on the first day of the first bombardment with other 'light' Lancasters bursting later on 23 and 27 October 1854. The 'heavy' Lancasters were less liable to burst and they continued to be used by the Naval Brigade. However,

The Robertson/Beato image entitled *Sailors' Battery* shows men of the Naval Brigade with two 68-pounder guns. One or both of these guns may be have been a Lancaster. These were positioned in No. 1 Battery on the 1st Parallel of the British Right Attack. The guns point towards the Malakhov Bastion. The high ground of the Vorontsov Ridge stretches away in the middle distance on the left. (Royal Collection Trust/© Her Majesty Queen Elizabeth II, 2016).

with the exhaustion of their special ammunition, unsuitable ordinary round shot was substituted. William Russell reported that after a Lancaster gun was struck by a Russian shot, 'several engineer officers declared their satisfaction at getting rid of the gun, in which they could place no confidence on account of its wild and uncertain firing'.

The Russians countered the Allied encroachment on Sevastopol by mounting night raids against the trenches. The French were on the receiving end of a particularly robust sortie on the night of 11-12 December 1854 when a party left the Flagstaff Bastion with two howitzers. The first the French knew about the raid was when they were suddenly bombarded with grape shot and the trenches rushed. Fierce fighting drove the Russians back. At another location, the Russians occupied and began to destroy a trench and associated earthworks before they were forced to retreat. A further four strong attacks were made against the French under cover of darkness in January 1855 that resulted in hand-to-hand combat. On all occasions the Russians were eventually defeated. The British were also attacked during this period with drowsy men being dragged from dugouts. In addition, patrols were surprised and captured. Vigilance had to be maintained at all times and the constant state of alert had the effect of wearing down the troops' mental and physical health.

After the Battle of Inkerman with its great loss of life, the British found it difficult to provide the men necessary to man the trenches and also continue the defence of the Inkerman Ridge. Sickness had also taken its toll as a result of cholera outbreaks and extremely cold weather.

Simpson's watercolour entitled **A Hot Day at the Batteries** showing part of the western section of the 21-Gun Battery in action with two 10-inch and one 13-inch mortars in the foreground. In the distance, the Redan Bastion is in the centre and the Malakhov Bastion surrounded by gun smoke on the extreme right. Sevastopol lies beyond and to the right of the Redan with the promontory that carried Fort Constantine in the far distance at the entrance to the roadstead. (Library of Congress, Washington).

It has been determined from contemporary maps that the eastern section of the 21-Gun Battery lay across this four-lane highway at this location. The highway, which carries today's traffic from Yalta and Simferopol along the Vorontsov Ridge into Sevastopol, begins to descend more steeply at this point.

In December 1854, only 350 men could be spared to defend almost a mile of front on the Right Attack and on one occasion on 29 January 1855 it was down to just 290. The situation was becoming critical and threatened the continuation of the siege. On 2 February 1855, an agreement was reached by which the French took over responsibilities for manning the fronts on Victoria Ridge facing the Malakhov Bastion and also the Inkerman Ridge. This was in addition to their continuing operations to the northwest and west of the Great Ravine. This left the British to pursue the siege against the Redan from the Right Attack on the Vorontsov Ridge and the Left Attack on the Green Hill Ridge. British guns also supported the French flanks across the Middle and Great Ravines by maintaining fire on the Malakhov Bastion and covering French attacks against the Flagstaff Bastion. The British were now very much the junior partner. The decimated brigade of Guards, who had been camped east of the windmill on the Chersonese Plateau, were sent to Balaklava for recuperation and the 2nd Division moved from behind Home Ridge on the Inkerman Ridge to west of the Vorontsov Road between the Light and 4th Divisions.

Winter Deprivations – Chaos at Balaklava

The British army was 'in deep gloom' following the Battle of Inkerman. Men endured long hours in the trenches and were often soaked to the skin. Wood for cooking and warmth was also in short supply as the Chersonese Plateau was virtually devoid of trees. The most memorable event that occurred between the Battle of Inkerman and the onset of the exceptionally harsh winter of 1854-55 was the Great Storm which began in the early morning of 14 November 1854.

The wind began to increase during the night. Russell reported that while sleeping listlessly in his tent, he 'became aware that the sound of the rain and the noise of its heavy beating on the earth had been swallowed up by the roar of the wind, and by the flapping of tents outside'. He then found that 'the sides of the canvas, tucked in under big stones, began to rise, permitting the wind to enter and drive sheets of rain right into one's face'. He recalled that later, 'the pole of the tent bent like a salmon–rod; the canvas tugged at the ropes, the pegs yielded. A starling crack! A roar of wind again, the pole bent till the 'crack' was heard again. Finally, Russell next recollected that 'a harsh screaming sound, increasing in vehemence as it approached, struck us all with terror'. He continued 'As it neared us we heard the snapping of tent poles and the sharp crack of timber'. Russell's tent collapsed and he struggled for the exit creeping out into the mud. He found the whole headquarters'

Opposite top: Simpson's watercolour entitled *The Gale off the Port of Balaklava, 14th November 1854* shows the ships *Prince* and *Rip van Winkle* in the foreground in their last moments before being dashed on the rocks. Other vessels are seen in trouble in the left middle distance. The entrance to the harbour is the break in the line of cliffs in the centre. The ruins of the Genoese fortress on Castle Hill are on the right. (Library of Congress, Washington).

Opposite bottom: The photograph of the cliffs at Balaklava as they look today was taken from close to where Simpson must have sketched the outline for his watercolour. Pleasure boats that ferry swimmers and sunbathers to narrow beaches under the cliffs are emerging from the harbour entrance.

Simpson's watercolour entitled ***Sebastopol from the 26-Gun Battery, on the Extreme Right of French Attack*** shows an advanced parallel in the harsh winter of 1854-55. The view is north along the Great Ravine, also known as the Picket House Ravine, which divided the French Left or Town Attack from the British Left Attack. The Flagstaff Bastion is on the distant high ground on the extreme left. The South Harbour crossed by a pontoon bridge is in the centre distance with Fort Paul visible at the entrance to the roadstead. The Barrack Battery and then the Redan are on the high ground to the right. The tower of the Malakhov is depicted on the extreme right. (Library of Congress, Washington).

The Great Ravine today taken from lower down its slope. The South Harbour is in the centre distance with the section of the Vorontsov Ridge that carried the Barrack Battery on the skyline in the centre right.

camp beaten flat to the earth with people 'running in all directions in chase of their effects or holding on by the walls as they strove to make their way to the roofless barns and stables'.

This scene was being repeated all over the Chersonese Plateau as the ferocious storm battered the camps. Most tents ended up flying through the air. In addition, wagons were overturned and 'barrels could be seen bounding along like cricket balls'. Marquees sheltering the sick collapsed tossing their occupants onto the muddy ground. Shingle roofs were torn away and even part of the roof of the farmhouse that served as Lord Raglan's home was carried off. Wagons were overturned. The situation was even worse in the marine camps on the heights above Balaklava where the winds blew belongings across the bay and 'men had to cling to the earth to avoid the same fate'. Those in the siege trenches passed a particularly miserable night. The light of morning revealed a scene of utter devastation. At noon, the wind changed direction and became colder. Sleet fell and then snow. Some men were found dead. The storm raged until late in the day.

Fanny Duberly was on board the *Star of the South* within Balaklava harbour. She reported the water 'seething and covered with foam' with the ships 'swinging terribly'. She also described how 'the spray was dashing over cliffs many hundred feet high and falling like rain' and how ships in the crowded harbour were 'all adrift, all breaking and grinding each other to pieces.' She confided to her journal that she half expected the figurehead of the *Medway,* the next ship to the *Star of the South*, to be in her cabin that night.

The greatest tragedy occurred at sea where a large number of ships lay off the coast, many of which had been unable to enter Balaklava harbour to unload because of congestion. Twenty-one were lost with a great number of sailors. Some ships were dashed on the rocks as they made a run for the narrow harbour entrance. The most serious loss was the *Prince*, a screw steam-ship that was driven into the cliffs at the end of its maiden voyage. Her masts were cut away to lighten her and the steam turned on to get her out to sea. Unfortunately, the rigging of her mizzenmast got entangled in the screw and, without power, she drifted towards the cliffs. The *Prince* was carrying winter clothing, blankets, shoes, boots, shirts and medical supplies. Ten million rounds of bullets for Minié rifles went down with the *Resolute* and enough hay to feed all the horses and mules for twenty days with the *Progress*. The loss of supplies were sorely missed during the winter.

The weather did not improve. On 23 November, 'the rains swelled into torrents'. Men arriving wet through in camp from the trenches in the morning wondered if they were going to survive when they set off again on duty that evening. The tracks from Balaklava to the Chersonese Plateau were becoming impassable with mud and supplies of ammunition for the guns were slow in getting to their destination. Oxen and horses used to pull wagons were either too weak to work, dying or dead. Carcasses lay on the ground and marked the route. Forage was running short for cavalry horses. They were reported as eating their own tails with three dying of cold and hunger in each regiment every night. In addition, the army was put on half rations and men died from exhaustion at their posts overnight. It got so cold that torn, dirty and deteriorating uniforms were patched, augmented by blankets tied with string and sheep skin leggings, Coats were described as rags tacked together, Some unfortunates had neither socks nor shoes and others bound their legs with bands of straw and hay. The lack of suitable clothing was becoming critical. Sickness peaked in January and February with hospitals being overcrowded. On 1 February, 19,219 British soldiers were under arms with 18,028 sick – almost half the army. However, as the weather improved later on, so did the health of the men.

Opposite top: Fenton's image entitled **Mortar batteries in front of the Picquet House, Light Division** shows a position with three 13-inch sea-service mortars – two in the immediate foreground and another on the other side of a shelter or powder magazine. This battery was established with two mortars in March 1855 and another was added in early April 1855. It was located over 1,000 yards to the southeast in the rear of the 21-Gun Battery on the 1st Parallel of the British Right Attack. These particular mortars were regarded as unwieldy and labour-intensive. This battery was eventually dismantled with the weapons being positioned elsewhere. The photograph was believed to have been taken on 23 April 1855 immediately after Fenton had visited the 'Valley of the Shadow of Death'. (Library of Congress, Washington).

Opposite bottom: The same mortar battery as in the previous image also featured in Fenton's photograph entitled **Quiet Day in the Mortar Battery**, which was taken at the same time as the one above. Here gunners pose as if relaxing or bored. An observatory or look-out was located about sixty yards in front of the battery. This could be the feature on the skyline just right of centre. (Royal Collection Trust/© Her Majesty Queen Elizabeth II, 2016).

There appeared to be little organisation at Balaklava during the winter months with ships lying in wait to enter the harbour and unload. The harbour was becoming a cesspool as every piece of waste was thrown into its increasingly murky waters where it sloshed backwards and forwards. Dead horses, mules, camels, dogs, cats and even men floated with the debris and detritus. The quayside was also in chaos with goods piled high or scattered in the filth. Ill and starving Turks fell down and died in the streets. Rats and dogs scavenged for food.

Fanny Duberly summed it all up when she wrote in her journal on 3 December 1854:

> If anybody should ever wish to erect a 'Model Balaklava' in England I will tell him the ingredients necessary. Take a village of ruined houses and hovels in the extremist state of imaginable dirt; allow the rain to pour into and outside them, until the whole place is a swamp of filth ankle-deep; catch about, on an average, 1,000 Turks with the plague, and cram them into the houses indiscriminately; kill about 100 a day, and bury them so as to be scarcely covered with earth, leaving them to rot at leisure-taking care to keep up the supply.
>
> Onto one part of the beach drive all the exhausted bât ponies, dying bullocks, and worn-out camels, and leave them to die of starvation. They will generally do so in about three days, when they will begin to rot, and smell accordingly. Collect together from the water of the harbour all the offal of the animals slaughtered for the use of the occupants of above 100 ships, to say nothing of the inhabitants of the town – which, together with an occasional floating human body, whole or in parts, and the driftwood of the wrecks, pretty well covers the water – and stew them all up together in a narrow harbour, and you will have a tolerable imitation of the real essence of Balaklava. If this is not piquante enough, let some men be instructed to sit and smoke on the powder-barrels landing on the quay; which I myself saw two men doing today, on the Ordnance Wharf.

Fenton took other images showing the view from in front of the mortar battery. The two overlapping and cropped photographs shown here make up a panorama entitled *Distant View of Sebastopol, with the Mamelon and the Malakoff tower, the lines of Gordon's Battery in the Middle Distance.*

The first picture was taken looking northwest with the dark line on the skyline at the left being Gordon's or the 21-Gun Battery on the crest of the Vorontsov Ridge. The trench line seen running from left to right and then disappearing behind a fold in the land was the 1st Parallel. The high ground shown in part in the distance on the extreme right was the Malakhov Hill. Sevastopol is largely unseen in the haze to its left with the north side of the roadstead just visible. (Royal Collection Trust/© Her Majesty Queen Elizabeth II, 2016).

The second image looks north with the Malakhov Hill on the left and the Mamelon to its right in the distance. The ground falls away into the Middle Ravine, which separated the British Right Attack from the French Right Attack, in the middle distance. These views show the bare and stony landscape outside Sevastopol. Because the bedrock was close to the surface, it was difficult terrain to dig the trenches and build the earthworks that were needed for protection from enemy fire. (Library of Congress, Washington).

Because of the view to the Malakhov and Mamelon, the mortar battery was a favourite location to watch actions in the French sector of attack. On 22 March 1855, William Romaine, who was the Deputy Judge-Advocate for the Army of the East, went there when he heard that there was to be an attack on the rifle pits in front of the French advanced works. He reported seeing Generals Brown, Jones, Airey and Estcourt. On 10 April 1855, Fanny Duberly visited the location 'to watch the practice of the Sea-service mortars'. She was also there on 8th June 1855 with General Bosquet to watch the attack on the Mamelon when a navvy was decapitated by round-shot forcing a move to a safer position. Fenton also witnessed and wrote about this macabre event. (Library of Congress, Washington).

Eupatoria under Threat

On 17 February 1855, the port of Eupatoria, which was close to where the Allies disembarked on 14 September 1854 and had been left garrisoned by Turks and some French in the middle of Russian-occupied territory, was attacked. The plan had been hatched by Russia to again distract the Allies from the siege. Lieutenant General Khrulev was in charge of the operation and under him was a force of about 20,000 infantry and cavalry with 108 guns. This force faced an equally strong garrison with the advantage of being behind a ditch and earthworks. Khrulev planned an attack from three sides. A diversionary column coming from the northwest would initiate the assault and draw fire while columns moving later from the north-northwest and northeast would press home the attack.

Seventy-six Russian guns opened fire at daybreak from a line of earthworks that they had constructed overnight. This seemed to be having some effect as defensive fire slackened because of one Turkish battery being disabled. However, when his first column that was meant as a feint advanced, it was soon stopped by fire from British ships and the port's defences. Omar Pasha, who was in charge of Eupatoria's defences, was aware of Russians assembling near a cemetery on the northeast side of the town. British and French gunboats were directed to an area offshore where they could fire into their ranks. When the guns became silent, the Russians surged forward to within twenty-five yards of the ditch, but were repulsed. After two rallies, they gave up and tried to retreat back to the cemetery, but they were intercepted by a battalion of Turks emerging from a town gate and were driven northwards. Two hundred Turkish cavalry joined in the pursuit, which only stopped when the Russians formed a hollow square. At 10.30 hours, Khrulev called off the attack believing that to continue would be costly. He had lost 769 men killed or wounded to 387 Turk and French soldiers.

In April, Omar Pasha felt the situation was secure enough for him to bring 15-18,000 of his men from Eupatoria to the Chersonese Plateau in further support of his British and French allies.

The White Works and the Mamelon

Large-scale bombardments had been mostly put on hold during the winter, but old batteries were being improved and new ones prepared as the trench lines moved closer to the Russian works. Russian sharpshooters in lodgements in advance of their lines made life difficult, but two gun batteries were constructed on the 3rd Parallel of the British Left Attack and also a mortar battery to the right of Chapman's Battery on the 1st Parallel. In support of the French, the British began construction of a new battery on their 2nd Parallel of the Right Attack on the Vorontsov Ridge. In addition, two batteries were established on either side of the Inkerman Ridge to the north and west of Shell Hill. The former, known as St Laurent's Battery, was to throw shot and shell at Russian ships in the roadstead, while the latter, known as Artilleur Battery, was to fire on the Malakhov Bastion. A large redoubt on Thistle Hill on the Victoria Ridge, which had been started by the British, was also finished by the French. However, this was 1,200 yards behind their 1st Parallel and too far for any guns placed here to do any damage.

The Allies had by now realised that the Malakhov Hill was the key to the defence of Sevastopol and that once taken the city would be untenable. Priority was given to its capture. The Russians also were aware of its importance and began to improve defences in this area by establishing new redoubts in advance of their present lines.

On the night of 21 February 1855, eight battalions of Russians emerged from Sevastopol and began building a strongpoint on the brow of the Inkerman Ridge to counter any moves against the Karabelnaya district that the Allies might be considering in the area. Work continued the next few nights with the French unsuccessfully attacking the position in the early hours of 24 February. Soon, what was known as the Selenghinsky Redoubt was armed and work had begun on the Volynsky Redoubt to its left front. Twenty-two 24-pounder guns were in place in the two redoubts by 3 March. These new Russian strongpoints became known as the *Ouvrages Blancs* or White Works because of the colour of the soil that was disturbed during their construction.

The White Works were not the only new defensive positions to be developed in advance of the main defensive line around the city. A hillock called the Mamelon lay forward of the Malakhov Hill with its summit about 730 yards to the southeast of the Malakhov Tower. The French on Victoria Ridge saw the importance of this geographical feature in their operations against the Malakhov Bastion, but before they could make a move to establish a presence, the Russians beat them to it on the night of 11 March. The construction of the Kamchatsky Lunette over subsequent nights was another blow to the Allies. It was armed with ten 24-pounders and covered in the rear with ten others by 21 March. As the French trench lines were getting closer, the Russians used their new strongpoint as a springboard for a sortie in strength against the French and British lines.

At 22.00 hours on 22 March, 5,500 Russians left the flank of the lunette on the Mamelon and began an advance en masse up the Victoria Ridge. After meeting determined resistance, they eventually drove back a French working party and some Zouaves from an advanced parallel. Meanwhile, three French battalions had gathered to oppose the Russians, who could not take any more ground. The Russians were spent and fell back to the lunette before the stubborn French, who lost 184 killed and 371 wounded.

While this night-time battle was in progress, the Russians also sent out sorties against the British Right Attack, which was defended by 1,200 men of the Light Division under the command of Lieutenant Colonel Richard Kelly of the 34th (Cumberland) Regiment. Half of

Simpson's watercolour entitled ***Quarantine Cemetery and Church, with French Battery No. 50*** was sketched in the grounds of Sevastopol's main cemetery to the west of the city and outside the Russian main defensive line. The view over the valley known as the Cemetery Ravine is to the northeast. The cemetery was the scene of fierce fighting on 22 and 23 May 1955 when the French successfully fought and dislodged Russians from counter approaches. Many tombs were damaged in bombardments at this time. (Library of Congress, Washington).

Today, the cemetery has many more trees and shrubs than in 1855 and these mask the view of the two churches seen in Simpson's watercolour. The ridge in the background with apartments served as the final forward French position before Sevastopol on their Left or Town Attack. To the east, the French trenches looked over the Zagorodnoy Ravine towards the curtain wall between the Quarantine and Central Bastions.

these guarded the 3rd Parallel, which was the most advanced trench at the time. There was also another body of 300 men digging trenches in the rear. Kelly had time to send some of his men to where he saw the line was in greatest danger.

The Russians came forward in four separate bodies. One emerged from the Middle Ravine and attacked the extreme right wing where it met seventy to eighty men of the 97th (Earl of Ulster's) Regiment. Despite being outnumbered by ten to one, the 97th moved forward to face the column of Russians, who fired a volley and then quickly retreated. The men of the 77th (East Middlesex) and 88th (Connaught Rangers) regiments faced another nearby Russian column and also sent it packing. An hour passed without much happening and then another body of Russians attacked the left flank of the Vorontsov Ridge, surprised the trench guards and then worked their way along to the 2nd Parallel. Kelly rushed forward ahead of the men of the 7th (Royal Fusiliers) Regiment and mistook some Albanians in the service of the Czar for his own men. He tried to fire his gun with the safety catch on and was instantly felled and taken prisoner. The Russian force moving east ran into men of the 34th Regiment, the 7th Fusiliers and members of working parties of Royal Engineers, who were now armed, moving west. A struggle then ensured around a mortar battery, with the Russians giving way and retreating towards the Redan.

The fourth body of 500 Russians advanced on the 4th Parallel of the British Left Attack on the Green Hill Ridge and drove out a detachment of the 20th (East Devonshire) Regiment. Soon they had reached the 3rd Parallel where 250 men in working parties were strengthening parapets of the as yet unarmed batteries Nos. 7 and 8. Here they stayed for half an hour before being driven out by some men in the working parties who had rallied and were now armed. The Russians withdrew, carrying abandoned British pick-axes and shovels. Little damage had been done to the batteries. The British reported sixteen killed and sixty-four wounded that night. The Russian lost 1,200 men in all.

A burial truce was arranged for the 24 March and both sides 'fraternised in a friendly fashion' while removing their dead under the white flag. During this period, a Russian artillery officer is said to have arranged a dual between a British 68-pounder gun called 'Jenny' manned by the Naval Brigade and a Russian gun on the Mamelon. At noon the next day, other guns stopped firing and 'Jenny' and the Russian gun took it in turns to fire at each other. The third shot from 'Jenny' went through the Russian gun's embrasure and victory was anticipated. Yet the Russian gun wasn't silenced and gave 'Jenny' 'a nasty thump' with the next shot. However, the Russian gun was 'knocked clean over' by about the seventh shot from 'Jenny' and the sailor gunners loudly cheered. In return, the Russian gunners climbed the parapet and removed their hats in an acknowledgement of defeat.

The Second Bombardment of Sevastopol

Reinforcements had arrived in the Crimea and the French army stood at 70,000 men at the beginning of April 1855. The British army still had only 20,500 able-bodied men, although more and more were returning to duty from sick leave. More work had been undertaken establishing batteries in preparation for another bombardment with more mortar batteries ready for action on the British Right and Left Attacks. In addition, Nos. 7 and 8 batteries on the Left Attack that had been occupied by the Russians while unarmed now had guns. The French also continued to build new positions with thirty-nine batteries west of the Great Ravine and eight on their front against the Malakhov. A military railway constructed between Balaklava and the camps on the Chersonese Plateau was now complete and was

Simpson's watercolour entitled *Fortress at Yenikale, looking towards the Sea of Azoff*, shows the old Turkish-built strongpoint that commanded the narrow straits between the Black Sea and the Sea of Azov. It contained twenty-five guns when captured by the Allies of which fourteen were mounted on a swivelling base. One gun is shown being confiscated. The hospital, which contained Russian wounded when captured, was the building with the red roof seen over the walls to the right of the tree. (DeGolyer Library, Southern Methodist University).

bringing ammunition up to the front. Although horse–drawn, except for a section beyond Kadikoi where a steam engine pulled the wagons up a steep incline, it was an improvement on the old road.

The garrison in Sevastopol consisted at this time of 34,000 infantry plus 9,000 artillery and sailor gunners. There were eighty-six new batteries and 996 guns, or which 466 could reach the Allied siege batteries. However, the Russians had fewer mortars and guns capable of firing shells, which meant that the Allies had a greater number of weapons that could drop exploding missiles from above. In addition, the Allies had the height advantage. Gun powder was also in short supply in Sevastopol, which meant the Russians had to limit their firing.

The second bombardment commenced shortly after 05.30 hours on 9 April 1855 with eventually over 400 guns in action. The weather was not good with heavy rain and poor visibility, but towards evening the view became clearer and the Allies saw that considerable damage had been inflicted on the Russian defences. The lunette on the Mamelon and the White Works were in a state of ruin. However, the Russians replaced dismounted guns and

Simpson's watercolour entitled **Straits of Yenikale, with the bay and town of Kertch, from the old fortress at Yenikale** looks southwest from the walls of the strongpoint. The parapet is being repaired on the left with the far Asiatic shore of the straits on the horizon on the far left. The Allies landed on the Crimean side of the straits seen in the far distance left of centre and marched around through Kertch, seen on the far side of the bay on the extreme right, to get to Yenikale. A new earthwork is nearing completion to the right of the fortress beyond which is a military camp. Another defensive earthwork is visible half a mile away beyond the tents. (DeGolyer Library, Southern Methodist University).

repaired most of the damage during the night so that an infantry attack the next morning was not regarded as feasible. The bombardment continued on the 10 April and the White Works were again so badly affected that they would not have withstood an assault. In addition, all but two guns had been silenced at the Flagstaff Bastion.

Nevertheless, infantry attacks were not sanctioned because of a reluctance by the French, and a golden opportunity to take both the Flagstaff Bastion and the White Works was lost. Instead, the bombardment continued. A magazine at Battery No.9 on the British Right Attack was hit by a shell and exploded on 16 April. A crater was formed, the parapet was partially destroyed and all but one gun buried in debris. However, the one remaining gun kept firing with the senior officer receiving the Victoria Cross. On 17 April, the bombardment stopped. The British had lost 205 men killed or wounded, the French 1,585 and the Russians 6,130.

The British took action against the more advanced of the Russian rifle-pits that opposed new sap trenches on the Right Attack at 21.00 hours on 19 April, when Colonel Thomas

Egerton with a detachment of the 77th Regiment assaulted and captured these 'lodgements'. Within four to five hours, Royal Engineers had connected one of the lodgements to the head of the sap trench. A battalion of the Vladimirsky Regiment and others tried to take back the lodgements at 01.00 hours and succeeded in driving in British troops, who were occupying outlying captured positions. However, they could not take the main position and were eventually driven back. Sixty-eight British soldiers were killed or wounded in the fierce fighting including Egerton. The newly-taken lodgement was afterwards known as 'Egerton's Pit' in his memory.

Napoleon III back in Paris then thought that he should personally take command of French operations in the Crimea and intended to arrive from Constantinople with the French Army of Reserve. This idea fell through, but any assault was delayed until 28 April when extra men were expected to arrive and become available for action. Unfortunately, since 23 April, the Russians had greatly increased their presence on the ground between the Redan and Egerton's rifle-pit. This ground, which previously had been unoccupied, now had more rifle pits connected by trenches. In addition, a location known as the Quarries had been fortified. An assault to take the Redan was going to be more difficult than before. On the plus side, the Sardinians had entered the war on the side of the Allies and troops for the Crimea were soon on their way.

On 10 May 1855, an Allied expedition to capture the strategic port of Kertch on the shore of the straits leading from the Black Sea to the Sea of Azov set sail, but the French portion was almost immediately recalled because Canrobert had received an instruction from Paris that an operation in the hinterland was to begin as soon as the Army of the Reserves reached the Crimea. The British could not go ahead on their own so Raglan had no alternative but to postpone the mission. In the middle of May, the plans of the proposed field operation arrived from Paris, but they assumed participation of the British and that a Franco-Turkish force would man Britain's portion of the trenches. However, neither Canrobert nor Omar Pasha could see a way to accomplish this so Canrobert resigned and went back to his old role as General of Division. He was replaced by General Aimable Pélissier, who assumed overall command of the French forces on 17 May 1855.

Pelissier was stronger and more determined than Canrobert. He brushed aside the misgivings of General Niel, who, as the new French Chief Engineer, had sought to delay assaults and also choose not to kowtow to the wishes of Napoleon III. Pélissier wanted to continue the siege now that an end was in sight and forget about diversionary land attacks elsewhere in the Crimea. He knew that the Allies, with 100,000 French, 28,000 British, 45,000 Turks and 15,000 Sardinians, now greatly outnumbered the defenders.

On the night of 21May1855, the Russians had begun preparing two new counter approaches, a name coined for advanced defensive positions, against the French at the head of Quarantine Bay and parallel to the boundary of the Quarantine Cemetery. When complete, these new works would threaten the French Left Attack in this area. Pélissier acted immediately and sent 6,000 French troops into the attack on the night of 22 May. The Quarantine Bay position was soon captured, but fighting raged at the cemetery position, which was taken and retaken five times. However, it was finally won and held by the French the next night. They lost 1,724 killed and wounded to the Russians 2, 569. Pélissier's no-nonsense approach and dynamism was reinvigorating the French campaign.

The Expedition to Kertch

The expedition to Kertch and the Sea of Azov that had been recalled by Canrobert went ahead under Pélissier. The region to be attacked was considered important because it was on supply routes to Sevastopol from the Russian hinterland. The British ships were commanded by Rear Admiral Lyons and the French ships by Vice Admiral Armand Bruat. According to Russell, the British contingent amounted to 3,000 or more infantry from the 42nd (Royal Highland), 71st (Highland Light Infantry), 79th (Cameron Highlanders) and 93rd (Sutherland Highlanders) regiments plus fifty Royal Engineers and fifty from the 8th Hussars. The French sent 7,000 troops under General d'Autemarre and the Turks 5,000 under Rashid Pasha. All were under the overall leadership of Lieutenant General Sir George Brown.

The expedition embarked on the evening of 22 and the morning of 23 May. Moving east, the ships met off Cape Takili, which is at the southern entrance to the straits that separate the Black Sea from the Sea of Azov and twenty miles from Kertch, on 24 May. The expeditionary force landed unopposed at Ambalaki, which was about twelve miles from Cape Tikali and six from Kertch. The Allies then began marching the short distance to the coastal batteries at Cape Paul. Fearing they would be cut off, the Russians spiked their guns and blew-up the magazines before escaping.

The Russians had 6,000 infantry and 3,000 cavalry in the Kertch area under the command of Lieutenant General Baron Wrangel. When he heard of the arrival of the Allied ships, he decided not to directly oppose the Allies, but to move his forces west down the main road that served the Kertch Peninsula. Before he left, he destroyed supplies of wheat and flour.

Wrangel did leave orders that government vessels should take on board government property before leaving. The Russian steam-schooner *Argonaut*, having secured her cargo, left Kertch only to be chased and fired upon by the British gunboat HMS *Snake*. Two other Russian steamers, the *Goets,* which was sent to aid the *Argonaut,* and the *Berdiansk*, also became involved. However, the *Snake* barred the passage of the *Berdiansk* and her master ran her aground where she was burnt. The other two vessels seem to have escaped. Most other boats that had not left Kertch were destroyed by the Russians except for four war-steamers that managed to escape into the Sea of Azov at 19.00 hours that evening. That night, the Allies landed more men, horses, guns and stores.

Early on the morning of 25 May, HMS *Miranda*, notwithstanding fire from Russian battery on the Cheska Spit, began marking a channel through the straits to the Sea of Azov that had a depth of sixteen feet. By 06.00 hours, Allied troops were marching on Kertch and, on entering, destroyed the iron foundry where guns were cast. At 13.00 hours, they were in possession of Yenikale, about six miles to the east and opposite the narrows through to the Sea of Azov. The guns in the coastal battery here had also been spiked and the magazine exploded. Discipline appears to have broken down on the march with many Turkish soldiers now running amok in Yenikale in an orgy of looting and vandalism. Houses were broken into and a few fires started.

The next day, Brown appointed a French officer as commandant, who showed zeal in suppressing the Turks, but could not restrain his own men. A civilian deputation came from Kertch to report that law and order had broken down with the Turks and French plundering and destroying property. Brown, who had been asked the previous day by Kertch's remaining citizens to provide a garrison, again refused. Later, Brown learnt that even French and British sailors were contributing to the mayhem with the captain of HMS *Furious* reporting that order in the town was worse than ever. Again Brown did very little other than to organise a hussar patrol twice a day from the captured Quarantine Station near Kertch. The state of anarchy continued. Priceless artefacts in the Kertch museum were plundered and hospitals ransacked.

The lawlessness prevailed for quite some time and became a stain on the reputation of the Allies. Roger Fenton, who travelled with the fleet to Kertch without his camera, was particularly disgusted. In a letter home concerning his arrival on the outskirts of Kertch on 25 May he wrote:

> On each side and in front as far as we could see, the country was covered with stragglers, Turkish and French, but principally the latter, intent on plunder. We could see the French rushing through the plantations into the houses and coming out again laden with fowls, geese, looking-glasses, chairs, ladies' dresses and everything useful they could lay their hands on. As they got into the contents of wine casks they got more outrageous, discharging their muskets right and left at fowls, pigs and birds.

At Yenikale, he reported:

> Going out of the fort I came to the town itself, which lies under the cliff and up its sides. There was a terrible scene: French, Turks, and I am sorry to say a few Highlanders, were breaking into the houses, smashing the windows, dragging out everything portable and breaking what they could not carry away. The inhabitants had all fled with the exception of the Tartars and a few Russians, amongst whom was a priest; from the treatment of those that were left, it was lucky that they had.

During their occupation, the invading force either appropriated or destroyed grain supplies and coal stockpiles. About 100 spiked artillery guns left in coastal batteries and elsewhere were also captured. Much had been achieved without the loss of a single man in combat.

For three weeks after the capture of Kertch and Yenikale, Allied ships under Captain Lyons, the son of the admiral, raided and burnt coastal towns around the Sea of Azov and sank many Russian vessels including those that had escaped from Kertch. Supplies destined for the garrison and citizens of Sevastopol were destroyed as far as Taganrog on the estuary of the Don River. After decimating the region, the Allies returned to the Chersonese Peninsula leaving 7,000 men behind to maintain control. The expedition was judged to have been a great success and, as a consequence, a morale raiser for the Allies.

Sevastopol Falls!
Victory Finally Achieved

Marshal Pélissier and Lord Raglan decided that the next move against the Russians in Sevastopol would be to capture the White Works, the Mamelon and the Quarries as a necessary prelude to taking the city itself. This endeavour was to go ahead after a fresh bombardment in early June.

The Third Bombardment of Sevastopol

The Russians had 36,000 troops with 1,174 pieces of artillery defending Sevastopol on the southern shore of the roadstead on 5 June 1855. Of the guns, 571 were aimed at the Allied batteries while the others provided flanking fire or interior defence. They had also constructed a new battery in the rear of the White Works. Facing the Russian guns were 544 Allied guns of which 385 were in the French sectors and 159 in the British sector.

The bombardment began at 14.30 hours on the next day. Again the redoubts comprising the White Works and the Mamelon were severely punished with the Kamchatsky Lunette on the latter's summit having its embrasures destroyed, its ditches filled, its guns covered with debris and its personnel slaughtered. It was reduced to silence that evening. The left faces of the Flagstaff and the Redan Bastions also suffered with the right half of the Malakhov Bastion almost silenced. That night, the Russians repaired the damage, but the lunette was so badly affected that it could only be partially restored. The bombardment resumed early on 7 June and by 08.00 hours mastery of all Russian guns east of the Middle Ravine appeared to have been achieved. However, the Redan kept up its fire and at 10.00 hours hit the magazine of Battery No. 9 on the British Right Attack.

It was decided at midday that the Russians were sufficiently weakened for an assault to go ahead later that day. Orders were given for the fire from mortars of the British Right Attack was to be concentrated on the Mamelon until the French attack went ahead and then the Malakhov beyond. Most of the guns were ordered to fire on both targets until the lunette fell and then they were to concentrate on the Malakhov. The targets of fourteen of the guns were to be the Redan Bastion and Barrack Battery. Most of the guns on the British Left Attack were also to be aimed at these strongpoints.

At 18.30 hours, after a barrage of bursting mortar shells had given the Mamelon the appearance of a volcano, Pélissier signalled the French troops to attack the White Works and Mamelon. The White Works were defended by about 450 Russians divided between the Volhynsky and Selenghinsky Redoubts. These men were considerably outnumbered by the attacking French. The positions were taken relatively easily by two columns of the 3rd Corps with little loss of French lives, and the Zabalkansky Battery on the northern end of the Inkerman Ridge was also seized. The five guns in this battery were spiked and the embrasures destroyed. However, unlike the two other positions, it was too far advanced to be held. After thirty minutes, two battalions of Russian troops attempted a counter-attack by marching out of the Karabelnaya district and crossing over the Careenage Ravine on the viaduct. Bosquet had anticipated this move and two French battalions lay in ambush on the slopes of the Inkerman Ridge. Attacked from the rear as they climbed the path up to the redoubts, the Russians tried to get back from where they had come. However, four-fifths of the force, which was about 400 men, surrendered and were taken prisoner.

Three French columns attacked the lunette on the Mamelon – the Algerian Tirailleurs on the right, the 50th de Ligne at centre and the 3rd Zouaves on the left. These troops were soon in the lunette and the three 8-inch guns in Battery No. 9 on the British Right Attack opened fire with shrapnel on the Russians retreating back to the Malakhov. Unable to restrain themselves, the French troops chased after the Russians until fire halted them close to the bastion and they sought shelter. At about this time, Russian reserve troops had come forward and the French were driven back to the Mamelon. The Russians then retook the hill. Allied artillery fire was once more concentrated on the lunette and, when it stopped, two fresh French brigades left the protection of the trenches to recapture the position. The Russians were driven out for a second time and the French consolidated their gains.

When the French first took the Kamchatsky Lunette, a British column consisting of 200 men from the 49th (Hertfordshire) Regiment attacked the right flank of the Quarries from advanced sap trenches while another column of 200 men from the 7th (Royal Fusiliers) and 88th (Connaught Rangers) regiments moved against the left flank from the 3rd Parallel. At the same time, 300 men of the 34th (Cumberland) and 88th regiments left the 3rd Parallel to advance on the collateral trenches that extended across the Vorontsov Ridge to the east. A further 300 men of the 47th (Lancashire) Regiment acted in support. The ground between Egerton's Pit and the Quarries was afterwards found to be strewn with explosive devices that detonated when trodden upon. Luckily, few seemed to have been injured by these devices because the troops did not assault the Quarries head on.

The 300 Russians manning the Quarries were quickly driven out by the bayonet and survivors retreated back to the Redan. A number of the victorious assault troops pursued them some distance and then sheltered to fire at the embrasures. With their troops no longer in the way, the Russians fired at the Quarries. These batteries stopped firing from time to time when the Russians counter-attacked. The first counter-attack at dusk by components of the Kamtchatsky, Volhynsky and Minsky regiments drove the British out of the Quarries, but they immediately rallied and returned to expel the enemy.

Earthworks protecting the captured Russian trenches and defences had now to be established on the reverse side that faced the Redan. About 800 men that followed the attacking troops were to form working parties to fortify the newly won positions. However, most had to join the fight to retain the won ground rather than attempt to construct new defence works. Only 250 could be spared to begin work on reconstructing the captured lines and positions.

Another counter-attack by the Volhynsky Regiment when it was dark was also driven off, but not before Russians had entered the captured works. After falling back and regrouping the Russians tried again only to fail as before. Just before daybreak, there was a third attempt. The defenders were by this time exhausted and could hardly stand. However, a few rose to pour fire into the advancing column and, by making much noise, convinced

Above: The Robertson/Beato image entitled *Valley of the Shadow of Death* looks northwest from behind the 2nd Parallel on the British Right Attack close to the crest of the Vorontsov Ridge The picture takes its title from the Vorontsov Ravine seen on the left. Neat stacks of round shot mark what is likely to have been the site of No. 14 Battery on the 2nd Parallel. The 3rd Parallel runs across the ridge further away and is connected to the 2nd Parallel by a communications trench seen between the two on the left. The Egerton's pit area lies on the right beyond the 3rd Parallel with the Quarries visible further away as a light-coloured bank. Beyond the Quarries in the far right distance lies the Redan Bastion. The head of the South Harbour can be glimpsed beyond the entrance to the Vorontsov Ravine with the city of Sevastopol in the centre and right distance. The Green Hill Ridge, which was the area of the British Left Attack, is beyond the Vorontsov Ravine on the far left. Above this ridge in the distance lie the heights where the Russian Garden Batteries were located. The Flagstaff Bastion would have been just off the picture here on the left. (Royal Collection Trust/© Her Majesty Queen Elizabeth II, 2016).

Opposite: The view today, which looks west-northwest, was taken from the top floor of an apartment building that was under construction on the site of the 2nd Parallel of the British Right Attack near the crest of the Voronstov Ridge. The northern end of the Green Hill Ridge on the other side of the Vorontsov Ravine is in the middle distance on the far left. The domed white building in the wooded area further away is the museum housing the siege panorama. The Russians had their Garden Batteries in this area. The city of Sevastopol is in the distance on the right. The Redan Bastion was situated in the middle distance in the trees seen above the larger of the two pointed turrets on the house with the red roof on the far right.

the Russians that they were many more than they actually were. The Russians stopped and resisted the strenuous efforts of officers to get them to advance. Retreat was then inevitable. When dawn broke, the British still held the ground that had now been connected to and incorporated into the Right Attack's front line.

The construction of new batteries began at the Quarries under the cover of the bombardment, which continued until 11 June. The prevailing view at this time was that an assault on the main bastions after another bombardment would be successful and result in the city being taken.

During the assaults to take the White Works, Mamelon and the Quarries, the Russians reported 5,000 men killed wounded or missing. The French toll was a substantial 5,443, while the British lost 671, which included forty-seven officers.

The Fourth Bombardment of Sevastopol

On the day before the fourth bombardment, the Russians had 1,129 pieces of ordnance south of the roadstead with 549 opposing the siege batteries, 319 for flanking fire and 261 for interior defence. The infantry garrison had 43,000 men. In addition, there were 10,997 men and sailors servicing the artillery. The French had 422 guns and had extended their trenches to include the redoubts at the White Works and the lunette on the Mamelon, all of which now had batteries. The British Left and Right Attacks had 166 pieces of ordnance with four 8-in mortars and three 32-pounder guns now at the Quarries. While the Russians had 140 rounds for each gun and sixty rounds for each mortar, the Allies had 400-500 rounds for each piece.

At daylight on 17 June, the Allied batteries opened fire. The British concentrated on the Redan, but also directed shells onto the Malakhov. The heavy guns at the former soon

Above: The Robertson/Beato image entitled **8-Gun Battery** overlaps the **Valley of the Shadow of Death** on the left to form a panorama. The 8-Gun Battery, which was official designated Battery No. 9, is shown in the foreground. It was located on the 2nd Parallel of the British Right Attack on the crest of the Voronstov Ridge. The 3rd Parallel is visible further away running from left to right across the ridge. The disturbed area seen above the line of the 3rd Parallel on the left was known as the Quarries. This feature is cleaved by a large trench that probably served as the main entrance after its capture from the Russians. The Redan can be seen on the left beyond the Quarries with its curtain wall extending to the right and down the slope into the Middle Ravine. The Great Barracks that formed part of the White Buildings in the Karabelnaya district are in the distance just to the right of centre. Ships are visible on the roadstead in the far distance to the right of the barracks. (Royal Collection Trust/© Her Majesty Queen Elizabeth II, 2016).

Opposite: Today's image looks northwest from the apartment building on the site of the 2nd Parallel with the city of Sevastopol in the centre distance. The elongated white building on a promontory on the far side of the roadstead visible above Sevastopol is Fort Constantine. The dockyard cranes on the right are near where the dry docks were situated in the Karabelnaya district. The 3rd Parallel, which was within about 150 yards of the 2nd Parallel at this location, probably ran between the two houses with red roofs in the left foreground. The Redan Bastion was situated in the middle distance in the trees seen above the larger of the two pointed turrets on the house with the red roof on the far left.

ceased to fire with vigour, although showers of hand grenades and small mortar shells caused casualties at the Quarries. The Malakhov was virtually reduced to silence by 09.00 hours. About 4,000 Russians were lost that day.

After two hours of bombardment the next day, the plan was for the French to assault the Malakhov first and when it was taken, the British were to attack the Redan. However, Pélissier changed his mind and decided it would be best to launch the assault at dawn on 18 June. This was inexplicable given that it was well known by now that the Russians were experts at repairing damage and repositioning guns overnight. However, the significant plan modification was believed to have been because of the difficulties Pélissier had hiding his attack troops from Russian view in daylight. Pélissier had also dismissed General Bosquet from his command of the French 2nd Corps on the eve of battle because of the latter's objection to a decision not to include an attack on the Flagstaff Bastion. The omens were not good. Lord Raglan, with Britain now the junior partner in the alliance, agreed to the modified attack plan.

At 02.00 hours on 18 June, which was the anniversary of the Battle of Waterloo at which he had been present, Raglan and his staff set out for Mortar Battery No. 7 on the 3rd Parallel of the British Right Attack from where they intended to watch the coming assaults. Bugles were blowing in Sevastopol as the Russians had observed the Allied troop movements in preparation for the attack despite the precautions taken to assemble them under cover of darkness. Russian infantry manned the parapets and heavy guns were loaded with grape.

The Roberston/Beato image entitled **Sebastopol before the last Bombardment** looks northwest towards the Great Barracks or White Buildings seen in the distance with the north side of the roadstead beyond. The view is from the 2nd Parallel on the British Right Attack on the Vorontsov Ridge with the 3rd Parallel, which was about fifty yards away from the camera at this point, in the foreground. The 4th and 5th parallels cut across the landscape beyond the 3rd Parallel with the Russian curtain wall leading down towards the Middle Ravine the furthest away. The Redan Bastion is out of the picture on the left and the Malakhov Hill out of the picture on the right. However, the Gervais Battery, which is at the foot of the western slope down from the Malakhov, is visible on the far right on the eastern side of the Middle Ravine. (Royal Collection Trust/© Her Majesty Queen Elizabeth II, 2016).

Three French columns were earmarked to move on the Malakhov area and rockets from the site of the Right Lancaster Battery were to signal the attack to begin. However, General Mayran, who was in command of the right column waiting in the Careenage Ravine, mistook a trail of light from a shell's fuse as the signal and attacked prematurely. The French advanced 800 yards to the curtain wall between the Point and Little Redan bastions, but were driven back by guns and muskets plus fire from six Russian steamers anchored at the mouth of Careenage Bay. Mayran was killed.

By the time Pélissier reached his station, the attack on the right was underway and he could do little else but order the signal rockets to be fired twenty minutes before time. Unfortunately, General Brunet's brigade in the centre hadn't properly got into position and left the trenches in some confusion. The French were almost immediately subjected to crossfire from guns in the Little Redan and along the east face of the Malakhov and the ground became covered with their dead. Nevertheless, they managed to advance to the ditch in front of the curtain wall that ran between the two fortifications before being forced to retreat because of a lack of numbers. Brunet was one of the many killed during the unsuccessful attack. Four battalions of the French Imperial Guard in reserve behind the Victoria Redoubt joined the fight on the right, but were driven into the Careenage Ravine.

The left column under General d'Autemarre had moved forward at the same time as Brunet's men, but was better protected from fire as it advanced along the Middle Ravine. Its task was to breach the curtain wall near the Gervais Battery on the right flank of the Malakhov and then swing around to capture the bastion. The wall below the Gervais Battery was breached by one contingent that continued on into the Karabelnaya district and the

The third of today's views taken from the apartment building on the site of the 2nd Parallel of the British Right Attack shows a comparable view to *Sebastopol before the last Bombardment* only from more to the west. The slope down to the Middle Ravine is on the left with the university buildings in the distance occupying the area where the barracks stood in 1855. The ground where the Gervais Battery was situated is on the shoulder of land on the far right. The north side of the roadstead is in the far distance with white Fort Constantine on the left at the end of its promontory.

The Robertson/Beato image entitled *Trenches before the Malakoff* shows a similar view as seen in their image *21-Gun Battery* only from much closer. The view is to the north over the Middle Ravine from the 3rd Parallel of the British Right Attack. The fortified position in the centre foreground was associated with Battery No. 19, which held two 10-inch mortars during the final bombardment. The end of Battery No. 18, which contained seven 13-inch mortars, is to its right. Battery No. 21, which had two 8-inch guns, is on the far left. The 4th and 5th parallels can be seen on the left. Malakhov Hill is at centre in the middle distance. Parapets run along the summit with the flag on its far right indicating the location of the Malakhov Tower. The Mamelon is the lower hillock it its right. The Gervais Battery is to the left of Malakhov Hill. (Royal Collection Trust/© Her Majesty Queen Elizabeth II, 2016).

Opposite: Today's equivalent image of *Trenches before the Malakoff* was again taken from the top floor of an apartment building built on the site of the 2nd Parallel of the British Right Attack. The view is north with the Malakhov Hill in the centre and the Mamelon closer and to its right. The north side of the roadstead can be seen in the distance either side of a wooded Malakhov Hill.

Gervais Battery itself taken by another. Hopeful officers sent back for reinforcements to exploit the situation, but a murderous fire now opened up on them from the Redan and the Malakhov. The advance slowed and finally stopped. An hour passed before Zouaves in support began to march towards the Middle Ravine, but by this time d'Autemarre had been forced to vacate the Gervais Battery in the face of strong Russian counter-attacks. The Zouaves were halted. It had all ended badly for the French.

When the Gervais Battery had been taken by the French, the order was given for the British attack on the Redan to commence. The plan was for two columns to simultaneously attack each of the bastion's two faces and for another to attack the salient a little later. Lieutenant General Sir George Brown was to be nominally in charge with the body assaulting the right flank led by Lieutenant General Sir John Campbell and the body assaulting the left flank led by Colonel Lacy Yea. The guns of the Redan were silent that morning and it was hoped that the pounding of the day before had caused serious damage. This was to prove a false hope as the Russians had made good their repairs.

Campbell's storming party consisted of 400 men of the 57th (West Middlesex) Regiment, who were to follow 100 men of the 1st Battalion of the Rifle Brigade deployed in open line.

The Robertson/Beato image entitled **Interior of the Mamelon Fort** looks north towards the Little Redan Bastion and the far side of the roadstead from the northern slope of the Mamelon. French soldiers stand in the foreground next to a half-buried Russian gun and wicker gabions used to strengthen earthworks. A four-gun battery with parapets made of gabions and sandbags lies beyond. (Royal Collection Trust/© Her Majesty Queen Elizabeth II, 2016).

The north-facing slope of the Mamelon today looking towards the site of the Little Redan Bastion. The foreground is disturbed, but it is not known if the earthworks and trench-like depression date from the Crimean War.

Simpson's watercolour entitled *Interior of the Mamelon Vert, Looking South*, shows the scene inside the Kamchatsky Lunette on the Mamelon after its capture by the French. A Russian gun lies dismantled in the left foreground and a gun carriage behind has lost a wheel. After capture, the strongpoint was reconfigured so that guns pointed in the opposite direction at the Malakhov Bastion. (Public domain work of art).

The summit of the Mamelon today where a ridge of earth can be found around a slightly depressed inner basin. It is not known if these earthworks date from the Crimean War or were part of more modern defence position. The view is north towards the Malakhov Hill, which is visible in the background.

Klembovsky's image taken from the Mamelon in the early 1900s showing a raised Victoria Redoubt on the skyline. The view is southeast along the Victoria Ridge with the Careenage Ravine on the far left and the Inkerman Ridge beyond. Before the successful attack on the Kamchatsky Lunette on 7 June 1855, the advanced trenches of the French were on the opposite slope seen crossed by paths. An earth bank that looks like it may have been a parapet is visible beyond the disturbed ground nearer the camera. (Walter Havighurst Special Collections, Miami University Libraries, Oxford, Ohio).

The view to the southeast from the site of the Kamchatsky Lunette on the Mamelon today shows how the suburbs of Sevastopol have spread up the Victoria Ridge obstructing the line of sight to the site of the Victoria Redoubt. The Careenage Ravine is on the far left. A ridge of earth is again visible in the foreground, but whether it is the same as that seen in the previous image is not known.

There were also twelve engineers, fifty soldiers carrying wool bags for filling the ditch, and sixty soldiers and sixty sailors with twenty scaling ladders. The 800 men in support were from the 21st (Royal North British Fusiliers) and 17th (Leicestershire) regiments and commanded by Colonel Lord West.

As soon as the leading wave of riflemen had cleared the parapet, they were subjected to grape shot and musket fire from the western face of the Redan. There were 470 yards of open ground to cover before the target area was to be reached. The attacking force hung back seeking what little shelter they could find and this halted those with the wool bags and ladders coming up behind. They were all encouraged to move forward by Lieutenant Colonel Richard Tylden, who, before he was seriously wounded, implied that because of the extremely fraught situation, the salient was as good a target as the more remote west face. As the few remaining men carrying wool bags and ladders advanced again, the riflemen supposedly ahead had disappeared. In addition, the assault troops could not be seen coming up at the rear. There seemed no point in continuing. The carrying party had no option other than to retreat back behind the parapet.

The storming party had been delayed by soldiers of numerous regiments, who had wanted to take part in the assault unofficially, crowding the trench line that was to launch the main attack. As a result, the men of the 57th had to move further west where they emerged from behind the end of the parapet to face heavy fire from the western face of the Redan and the Artakov Battery, which was situated between the Redan and the edge of the Voronstov Ravine. They were not now behind the party carrying the wool bags and ladders needed to cross the ditch and scale the earth banks and were being subjected to an intense barrage of grapeshot. Campbell was soon killed and Lieutenant Colonel Thomas Shadworth, his back-up senior officer with the assault group, quickly met the same fate. Lieutenant Colonel Henry Warre was now in charge and encouraged his men to make for the Artakov Battery. Now joined by the survivors of the 100 men of the 1st Battalion Rifle Brigade and others from various regiments who wanted to participate, they skirted the abattis to the left and got within thirty yards of the ditch from where they fired on the embrasures. Additional troops would be needed to seize the battery. Reinforcements were called for from the support troops.

West, who was now in command of the right flank operation and back with the support column, was not aware of the situation in front of the Artakov Battery and he assumed all the assault troops had been killed or dispersed. He only knew of those that had returned to the attack trench with their ladders. He attempted to once again get these men into action and follow them with his support troops. However, as only the sailors seemed undaunted, the soldiers with the ladders having disappeared, he had to organise more men to help. Even so, there were only four men to carry each ladder and not six as previously. The ladders were brought out over the parapet and the men lay down with them to await the covering troops. However, men climbed over the parapet only to advance in a few places. No concerted effort to attack was made. West became cautious and sent back for advice from Brown as well as calling for fresh troops. Brown told him to reform the attacking column, but not to advance without orders. West replied that reforming the column was hopeless and again requested more men. There was no answer from Brown. The attack did not eventuate. Warre and the 57th in front of the Artakov Battery had to withdraw.

Meanwhile, Yea's attack on the left or eastern face of the Redan had also gone ahead with its covering party of 100 riflemen, 12 engineers, 180 soldiers and sailors carrying wool-

Above: Simpson's watercolour entitled *The Town Batteries, or Interior fortifications, of Sebastopol. From the Advanced Parallel of Chapman's Attack, 23rd June 1855.* The view is northwest towards the head of the South Harbour from the end of the Green Hill Ridge on the British Left Attack. The Vorontsov Road emerges from the Vorontsov Ravine on the right and passes in front of the Russians' Creek Battery at the end of the harbour before climbing up the slope into Sevastopol, whose Central Hill is on the right skyline. The Crow's Nest Battery is on the hill seen on the far left. The ruined cottages on the flats to the left are as far as Major General Eyre's brigade penetrated on 18 June 1855. The end of the Barrack Battery is on the high ground on the extreme right. (Public domain work of art).

Opposite: The same view as it looks today. The South Harbour can be glimpsed in the middle distance to the right of centre with Sevastopol's Central Hill behind on the right skyline. The wooded high ground on the left where the Garden Batteries were located is now a park. Railway yards and Sevastopol's railway station now occupy much of the flat land in front of the South Harbour. The end of the Vorontsov Ravine is below on the right with the end of the Vorontsov Ridge that carried the Barrack Battery above. A residential suburb stretches back along the Green Hill Ridge behind the camera, but ends before reaching the 1st Parallel of the British Left Attack where the location of Chapman's Battery can still be visited.

sacks and ladders and 400 men of the 34th Regiment as the storming column. Once more, grape-shot filled the air as these men scrambled over their parapets. Those riflemen that survived made it to the abattis, a barricade of sharpened branches that lay eighty yards in advance of the Redan's earthworks that did not seem damaged by the previous day's bombardment. They lay down finding cover in irregularities of the ground, but Russians recklessly standing on the parapet of the Redan were able to look and fire down on them.

Ladders lay on the ground next to the few men left to carry them The commanding engineer, Lieutenant A'Court Fisher, sought advice from Yea who had come charging up with sword in hand ahead of the remains of the storming party, but Yea was shot dead at that moment. Fisher turned to Captain William Jesse who was also killed before answering. Others were similarly hit as he tried to get direction. As on the left flank attack, none of the 800 support troops, this time comprised of men from the 7th and 34th Regiments, could be seen coming up to help. However, they had been slowly advancing under Colonel Daniel Lysons against heavy grape-shot and musket fire which was cutting down their numbers. Indeed, they only stopped and retired when they saw the men at the abattis withdrawing. This happened when Fisher, judging himself to be the most senior officer left in the field and unsupported, ordered a retreat.

Provision had been made for a third body of men led by Major General Henry Barnard to attack the salient of the Redan from the right of the Vorontsov Ravine, but this was compliant on the success of the two flank attacks. Barnard's men were held in their advanced position awaiting orders. Raglan and Major General Sir Harry Jones, who had succeeded Sir John Burgoyne as Chief Engineer, had been observing the action from behind the parapet of Mortar Battery No. 7 on the Right Attack. Here, they were in danger and Jones was wounded on the forehead by a grape-shot. Raglan then changed his position to the right of the 1st Parallel.

Simpson's watercolour entitled *Valley of the Tchernaya, looking North* shows the view from a Sardinian position on the north-eastern slopes of Mt Hasfort. The settlement of Karlovka is on the right with its octagonal tower. The River Chernaya flows west from here past the conical-shaped and rock-ridged Telegraph Hill on the left. This hill was a Sardinian outpost on 16 August 1855 when the Russians attacked from the hills in the centre middle distance. An aqueduct bridge has been depicted at the bottom of the hill on the left. The river then turns north and meanders into the far distance past the site of the Tractir Bridge and then through the narrow valley between the Inkerman Ridge on the left and the Mackenzie Heights on the right. At the Battle of the Chernaya, the main Russian force moved across the valley seen above and to the right of the summit of Telegraph Hill from right to left to attack the French on the Fedioukine Hills on the far left. (Public domain work of art).

The bridge carrying the aqueduct over the Chernaya River as it looks today.

The modern view shows the Chernaya Valley from a location on the northwest slope of Mt Hasfort. The settlement of Karlovka, which still boasts its octagonal tower, is off the picture on the right. However, the settlement of Chorgun is visible in the cleft between the hills just right of centre. Telegraph Hill with its rocky spine is on the far left. The Mackenzie Heights are on the skyline.

When the last retreating British troops had reached the safety of the trenches, the bombardment of the Redan and Malakhov was resumed. Within forty-five minutes, the two bastions were so badly damaged that fire from them all but ceased. Raglan went to see Pélissier with the intention of unleashing Barnard's troops on the salient of the Redan. However, the French had not had time to reinforce d'Autemarre's force at the Gervais Battery and the opportunity for further gains was deemed to have passed. Pélissier recalled his men from all fronts and Barnard's troops were also withdrawn. The attempt to capture the Malakhov and Redan that day was over.

The only military success for the Allies that morning had been achieved by Major General Sir William Eyre and 2,000 men of various regiments who advanced along the Great Ravine to the west of the British Left Attack to take a line of rifle pits manned by troops of the Okhotsky and Tomsky Regiments. The Russian positions were in full view of the right face of the Flagstaff Bastion and protected by a stone wall that ran from a small cemetery to the crest of a knoll at the northwest corner of the Green Hill Ridge. Despite heavy fire, the troops rushed the wall and held the captured pits all day. Some houses further on were also taken. Later, these houses were abandoned on advice of the engineers, but other positions were retained and fortified. Eyre's force suffered serious losses with more than a quarter of the attackers being killed or wounded.

The casualties on 18 June amounted to about 1,500 Russians, 3,500 French and 1,500 British. Todleben, the brains behind the stubborn Russian defence, received a debilitating wound and had to retire from duty, but the greatest losses had been amongst the Allied assault commanders with four out of six being killed leading their men. The whole episode had been judged to have been poorly planned and mismanaged with too few troops being allocated to the British attacks.

The Allies were despondent while many Russians now believed that their city would never fall.

Above: Klembovsky's image taken in the early 1900s looks northwest down the Chernaya Valley from the summit of Telegraph Hill, which was a Sardinian strongpoint when the Battle of the Chernaya began. The course of the River Chernaya is marked by a line of trees in the valley below. The Sardinians were driven from the hill and back over the River Chernaya by the Russians during the early stages of the fighting. The main Russian force then attacked from right to left in the middle distance and unsuccessfully tried to dislodge the French from their positions on the low Fedioukine Hills seen on the left. The higher Sapoune Ridge on the edge of the Chersonese Plateau covers most of the skyline before it drops down into the Chernaya Valley on the far right. The high ground to the immediate left of the valley at this point is the Inkerman battlefield. The high ground in the distance on the other side of the valley on the extreme right is part of the Mackenzie Heights. (Walter Havighurst Special Collections, Miami University Libraries, Oxford, Ohio).

Opposite: Today's view from the summit of Telegraph Hill shows a similar scene. The River Chernaya, which is hidden by trees, still follows roughly the same course down the valley. A track runs along a disused railway embankment to the left of the river. The settlement of Khmelnitsky, the edge of which is seen on the far left, now lies where the North Valley of Balaklava enters the Chernaya Valley. The Fedioukine Hills are in the middle distance on the left. The Tractir Bridge was located in the trees that obscure the river at the far end of the wooded slope of the Fedioukine Hills. The Sapoune Ridge on the edge of the Chersonese Plateau is visible on the skyline. In the distance on the far right, the River Chernaya passes through a gap between the uplands where the Battle of Inkerman took place and the Mackenzie Heights.

Raglan was deeply affected by the failure and his outward appearance changed. This was noticed by an officer of the Coldstream Guards, who said to some of the headquarters' staff 'Do you not see the change in Lord Raglan? Good God! He is a dying man!' Raglan became grief stricken soon afterwards on the death of his friend General Estcourt, whom he greatly admired, from cholera on 24 June. On 26 June, Raglan became unwell and died on the evening of 28 June in his bedroom in the farmhouse that served as headquarters.

He was suffering from diarrhoea that may have been caused by cholera. The much admired Field Marshall was mourned the next day by the senior Allied command. Pélissier was said to have 'stood by the bedside for upwards of an hour crying like a child'. On 3 July, Raglan's coffin was carried on a gun carriage from headquarters to the port of Kamiesch under full military honours. Double ranks of infantry lined the seven-mile route and cavalry accompanied the cortege. At Kamiesch, his body was placed in the launch from the British flagship and taken to HMS *Caradoc* for the journey home to England. Lieutenant General Sir James Simpson, who was serving as Raglan's Chief of Staff, reluctantly took over as Commander-in–Chief of the British army.

The defeat of 18 June called for a rethink of strategy. Pélisier was almost sacked by Napoleon III, who wanted some field operation against the Russian army of the interior from Aloushta, a coastal town northeast of Yalta. However, he survived by giving lip service to Napoleon's ideas. On the Town Front, also known as the French Left Attack, the Russians had taken advantage of a lack of active operations to strengthen the defences in the area of the Flagstaff and Central Bastions. However, an attack on these two bastions was not high on the allied agenda.

The British and French Chief Engineers met to discuss the technical aspects of the future of the siege and they decided that, before any more advances could be made against the Redan and the Malakhov, marked superiority over the guns in these bastions and also those in the Little Redan had to be achieved. Sir Harry Jones and General Adolphe Niel also believed that the Russian army in the field had to be beaten or driven off so the at the garrison could no longer be continually renewed and that, if Sevastopol had not fallen before the next winter, the siege should be lifted. The Commanders-in-Chief did not altogether agree with this rather pessimistic view of the situation.

The Battle of the Chernaya – Russia's Last Attempt at Breaking the Siege

Before the next planned bombardment of Sevastopol, another event of importance took place along the Chernaya River where it flowed past the Fedioukine Hills on its way to Sevastopol's roadstead. This area had been won by the Russians at the Battle of Balaklava, but, although occasionally sending out Cossack observers as far as the Causeway Heights, they had essentially relinquished their absolute authority over most of their gains to the southwest of the river at the end of 1854. On 19 April 1855, twelve battalions of Turks under Omar Pasha supported by British and French cavalry plus field artillery had advanced on the Chernaya to determine if its surrounds had been abandoned by the Russians. The enemy were not seen. General Alfonso La Marmora arrived in the Crimea on the 8 May with the first of 15,000 Sardinian troops, who established themselves at Karani, which lay two and a quarter-miles to the west-southwest of Kadikoi. On 25 May 1855, the Sardinian army occupied nearby Mt Hasfort and pushed across the river to establish outposts near the village of Chorgun. The French under Canrobert also moved forward that day to take control of the Fedioukine Hills and construct a defensive fortification on the far side of the Tractir Bridge while two Turkish divisions camped in the North Valley of Balaklava. The ground west of the Chernaya was now firmly in the hands of the Allies. In early June, the French reconnoitred the Baidar Valley further along the Vornotsov Road from Kamara and then established a cavalry camp with some British squadrons and Turkish infantry.

Prince Menshikov was dismissed as Commander-in-Chief of the Russian forces on 15 February 1855 and replaced by Prince Mikhail Gorchakov. He was the brother of Prince Pyotr Gorchakov, who had participated in the battles of the Alma and Inkerman. On 2 March 1855, Czar Nicholas I had died of pneumonia and was succeeded by his son Czar Alexander II. Under a new Czar, the Russian High Command began thinking about how to utilise its 70,000-man army in the Crimean hinterland. Pressure mounted for action to alleviate the siege of Sevastopol. Although Count Todleben advised against it from his sick bed, General Vrevsky, who had only recently arrived in the Crimea and whose views carried much weight, ardently promoted the attack option. The Russian army had been ensconced on the Mackenzie Heights for some time. Gorchakov finally agreed to assault the Allied lines along the Chernaya River.

The attack took place on 16 August 1855. The French with 18,000 men and forty-eight guns were at this time guarding the line of the Chernaya River along the northeast facing escarpment of the Fedioukine Hills. In addition, they had established a position on the far side of the river at the Tractir Bridge. The Sardinians, with 10,000 men and thirty-six guns were on Mt Hasfort and at a few outposts across the river. Two divisions of Turks were to the rear of the Sardinians with French and British cavalry and field artillery nearby in reserve. The Russians plan was to attack the French positions in force centring on the Tractir Bridge with another force attacking Sardinian positions and take Mt Hasfort. The ultimate aim was

Opposite top: Robertson/Beato's image entitled *The Tractir Bridge* shows where the road from the Mackenzie Heights to Balaklava crosses the Chernaya. The British army camped here on 25 September 1854 before occupying Balaklava the next day. This location was also the scene of fierce fighting during the Battle of the Chernaya on 18 August 1855. The view is to the north-northeast from the slopes of the Fedioukine Hills and shows the edge of the aqueduct that fed water to the dry docks in Sevastopol in the foreground. (Royal Collection Trust/© Her Majesty Queen Elizabeth II, 2016).

Opposite bottom: Today's photograph shows the location of the Tractir Bridge from the same position as it was taken by Robertson/Beato. The grassy area is an island in the River Chernaya with the site of the old bridge, which no longer exists, in the trees where the eastern channel flows. A monument to the Battle of the Chernaya is just out of view on the right. The Mackenzie Heights are on the skyline.

Klembovsky's image taken in the early 1900s showing the open ground to the immediate west of the Tractir Bridge. The track from the bridge cuts across the picture from left to right and enters a valley that takes it though the Fedioukine Hills. The channel of the no longer functioning aqueduct can be seen rounding the escarpment of the Fedioukine Hills on an embankment in the centre middle distance and then following the contours into the valley entrance. It was on the slope above the aqueduct that Robertson/Beato's image of the bridge was taken. The Russians penetrated the valley on the right after crossing the river and aqueduct, but were driven back by the French. (Walter Havighurst Special Collections, Miami University Libraries, Oxford, Ohio).

The view today shows that the same ground as in Klembovsky's picture with the entrance to the valley that took the track through the Fedioukine Hills on the right. The embankment on the left was constructed for a now abandoned railway, which cut through the end of the escarpment in the centre. Nothing now remains of the aqueduct.

Simpson's watercolour entitled *Battle of the Tchernaya, 16th August 1855*, shows French Zouaves repelling a Russian attack at the aqueduct bridge while a fresh column of Russian troops march over the Tractir Bridge in the background. The little octagonal house depicted in the middle distance on the far right is also seen on the lower right of Robertson/Beato's image entitled *The Tractr Bridge*. This building is where Raglan spent the night of 25 September 1854 when the Allied army was on its flank march around Sevastopol. It was one of many to be found along the course of the aqueduct. (Public domain work of art).

The view is east towards the Chernaya from the entrance to the valley through the Fedioukine Hills. The approximate position of the aqueduct bridge would have been in the foreground. The over-bridge in the picture carried the now abandoned railway over the entrance to the valley. The narrow paved road up the valley today follows the route of the track to Balaklava taken by the British army on 26 September 1854 for some distance.

A modern aerial image of the area of the British Right Attack superimposed with the parallels and other trench lines at the time of the final bombardment of Sevastopol to show approximately where they can be found today. Key: 1, 2, 3 etc. refer to designated battery numbers and 1st, 2nd, 3rd, etc., to the parallels mentioned in the text. The road running from lower right to upper centre is the main highway that today carries traffic from Yalta and Simferopol into Sevastopol. [Adapted from a Google Earth™ image]

to advance towards Balaklava and the Sapoune Ridge. Gorchakov wanted arrangements to be flexible enough for a large reserve to take advantage of whichever thrust proved the most successful. To this end, two divisions with the cavalry and most of the guns were to be held in reserve to exploit any breakthrough. He ordered General Read to attack the Fedioukine Hills with the 7th and 12th Divisions while General Liprandi was to attack Mt Hasfort with the 5th and 17th Divisions.

The Russians on the left began at dawn by driving in the Sardinian outposts from the far side of the Chernaya River, which included an elevated position known as Telegraph Hill. Batteries then opened on the Sardinians on Mt Hasfort. Read on the right fired on French positions as soon as light permitted from across the Chernaya River, but the shot fell short. Then, misinterpreting ambiguous orders from Gorchakov, he began a premature assault on French positions aided by mist. The river in August was fordable in most places so it was no obstacle for attacking troops. It was easily crossed after French earthworks protecting the Tractir Bridge were enveloped. Further advances on the left bank of the river were rendered difficult because an aqueduct, which was about eight feet wide and four feet deep and supported by a steep embankment, ran along the base of the slopes of the Fedioukine escarpment and hindered movement. This aqueduct had supplied the dry docks at Sevastopol with water before the supply was cut off by the Allies. Despite this obstacle, progress was made along the track from the Tractir Bridge that crossed over the aqueduct and entered a valley between the Fedioukine Hills. The French hurried reinforcements to the scene and soon their rifle fire from the surrounding hills began to tell. The Russians were driven back to the aqueduct and then across the river. The Russians attacking further downstream were subjected to grape and round shot from French artillery on the escarpment and finally broke when bayonet-charged by descending French troops. The first assault had failed. It was now 07.30 hours.

Hearing of Read's problems, Gorchakov stopped Liprandi's advance and ordered the 5th Division down the right bank of the Chernaya in support of Read. When the regiments of this division began to arrive on his left flank, Read inexplicably decided to send in the first of the new arrivals piecemeal. First to go forward was just one battalion of the Galitsky Regiment, which was unsupported and suffered considerably as a consequence. It retreated soon after reaching the left bank. Read's next move was to order an attack by four battalions of the Kostromosky Regiment, which were forced to retire after having half their numbers killed or wounded. Unbelievably, the survivors of the Galitsky battalion were then ordered forward again with disastrous results. The Arckhangelogorodsky, Volgogodsky and Kostromosky Regiments plus the remaining three battalions of the Galitsky Regiment were then sent in together against the Tractir Bridge. Initial progress was good as morning fog obscured the scene from the French gunners and those defending the bridge were again driven back. However, the mist lifted as the Russians were clearing the river and they became an easy target for the French batteries and the tide of battle turned once again. The French artillery fire was devastating. The divisional commander was killed, as were the two brigade commanders and the four regimental commanders. Read was also killed by a shell and Gorchakov took charge of operations in this sector himself.

At 08.00 hours, Liprandi's 17th Division was turned against the French defending the south-eastern end of the Fedioukine escarpment. This force made some headway crossing the river and aqueduct, but Sardinian troops bolstered the defence. Other Sardinians intervened on the Russians' left flank, which was caught in an enfilade. The 17th was bloodily repulsed after the arrival of French support.

By 10.00 hours, the Russian infantry was in retreat back across the Chernaya Valley to the Mackenzie Heights covered by their artillery and cavalry. During the battle an artillery round decapitated General Vrevsky, the man who had urged Gortchakov to go on the offensive. Gorchakov blamed Read, who was also conveniently dead, for the failure of the attack by crossing the river early without orders.

The Russians lost 2,273 men killed and 4,000 wounded with 1,742 were reported as missing. The French had 1,800 killed or wounded with the Sardinians having 250 casualties including fourteen killed. The Russian dead and wounded with their muskets and swords lay in heaps on the battlefield. The Tractir Bridge was blocked by a pile of corpses with other bodies strewn along the banks of the river. The water in the river ran red in places. The Russians had failed miserably to divert attention from the siege. In addition, Pélissier could claim to have engaged in a field battle with the Russian army of the hinterland that Napoleon III craved.

Mary Seacole, whose store and restaurant at Spring Hill were on the road to the Col de Balaklava from Kadikoi, took her wagon on to the battlefield after the Russians had departed to see what she could do to help the wounded. She reported:

> The ground was thickly encumbered with the wounded, some of them calm and resigned, others impatient and restless, a few filling the air with their cries of pain – all wanting water, and grateful to those who administered it, and more substantial comforts. You might see officers and strangers, visitors to the camp, riding about the field on this errand or another. And this, although – surely it could not have been intentional – Russian guns still played upon the scene of action. There were many others there bent on a more selfish task. The plunderers were busy everywhere. It was marvellous to see how eagerly the French stripped the dead of what was valuable.

Mary attended the wounds of many and helped lift them into the ambulances. One Russian, who was shot in the lower jaw, bit so hard on her finger as she sought to locate the ball that it left a scar. She took a French officer wounded in the hip back to Spring Hill for 'out-patient' treatment and also helped save a Cossack colt who was in danger of being shot to put it out of its misery. The latter recovered under her care and returned with her to England.

A Visit to the Chernaya Battlefield Today

Those wishing to visit the battlefield should leave Sevastopol on the Yalta Highway and take a turning to the left almost three miles further on from the roundabout at the bottom of the Sapoune Ridge. This intersection is just 340 yards before the turnoff to Kamara on the left. The side-road follows the base of the west-facing slope of Mt Hasfort and offers views to the left over the eastern end of the North Valley of Balaklava. After just over one-and-a-quarter miles, this road intersects with another on the outskirts of a village that lies in the gap at the entrance to the North Valley of Balaklava from the Chernaya Valley. Turning right at this intersection, the road crosses a bridge over the Chernaya River after a quarter of a mile. A track along the river bank to the right before the road bridge leads to the old stone bridge that took the aqueduct over the Chernaya. A parking area on the left just over the road bridge is where walks up to the top of Telegraph Hill begin. This is a steep climb with no obvious path, but the view north-northwest down the Chernaya Valley and over the battlefield is spectacular. On the summit, there was a Sardinian outpost abandoned soon after the battle began.

Returning to the car park, take the road back over the river bridge and through the village. Go straight on where the road from the Yalta Highway enters from the left. The road runs along the bottom of the east-northeast face of the Fedioukine Hills defended by the French during the battle. Continue on this road, which has the Chernaya River on its right, for just under three-quarters of a mile to where there is a gap in the Fedioukine Hills to the left. A narrow, surfaced road off to the left here goes someway along a valley, where the British army marched on its way to Balaklava on 26 September 1854, after passing under a disused railway bridge. A walk up the slopes of the Fedioukine Hills to the northwest of the valley entrance affords views over this area to the southeast of the Tractir Bridge that was the scene of fierce fighting. The bridge no longer stands. Returning to the Chernaya Valley road under the railway bridge, find the path on the other side that leads to a weir and then onto a large open space. A Russian monument to the battle is found here on what is today an island in the river. The probable site of the bridge is further on in the trees lining the other channel of the river. In 2012, there was a covered picnic table and a miniature concrete replica of the old, two-arched bridge across the stream at this location.

The Fifth Bombardment of Sevastopol

After the fourth bombardment, the siege guns continued to fire intermittently until the end of June 1855. In July 1855, an average of 800 rounds were fired a day with an occasional increase, such as on 19 July when trenches on the Right Attack were advanced. During the next month, the rate of fire varied from ninety rounds on the 10 August to 800 on the 16 August.

More batteries were constructed. On the British Left Attack, Battery No. 15 was added to the 3rd Parallel, Battery No. 16 to the 2nd Parallel and Battery No. 17 established in front of the 2nd Parallel on the edge of the Vornotsov Ravine. A 5th Parallel was being prepared which was completed on 21 August. On the Right Attack, Batteries Nos. 18 and 19 were completed in front of the 3rd Parallel and Battery No. 20 added to the two others in the Quarries. In addition, the Russian trenches captured on 6 June were being converted to 4th and 5th Parallels. Again, this work was not finished until 21 August. A signal station was also established behind the Right Attack at a viewpoint known as the Picket House so that observers here could communicate troop movements seen in Sevastopol to HMS *Hannibal* anchored off the mouth of the roadstead and to the artillery in the trenches.

The fifth bombardment began at 05.00 hours on 17 August when a salvo of three shells were fired into the Redan from Battery No. 13 on the British Right Attack. Through misunderstandings, Batteries Nos. 7, 8 and 14 on the 3rd Parallel of the British Left Attack were unsupported by French batteries on their left until 07.00.h and the batteries manned by the Naval Brigade remained silent This enabled thirty to forty Russian guns to concentrate on the 3rd Parallel and overwhelm the three batteries by superior firepower. By 9.30 hours, four out of six 32-pounder guns in Battery No. 7 were out of action and then a fifth was struck and broken. When the final gun was silenced, the commanding officer marched his men back to camp. All three batteries were so badly damaged that they were not manned again until 8 September.

Despite this setback, the heavy allied firing on the 17 and 18 August subdued the guns in the Redan and Malakhov enough for trenches to be extended closer to these bastions. However, work in front of the Redan had been slow. Although the 5th Parallel was completed, a sap in the direction of the bastion could not be taken any closer because of fire from the Russians and the fact that the ground was solid rock. The Brançion Redoubt on the Mamelon, which had been constructed on the site of the Kamchatsky Lunette, exploded on 28 August and almost destroyed the work. This delayed progress and postponed the inevitable assault for a few days.

Above: Robertson/Beato's image entitled ***Malakoff from the Mamelon.*** **The view is to the northwest with the earthworks of the Malakhov Bastion on the hill on the skyline. A hut and semaphore erected by the French on the remains of the Tower after its capture are visible on the summit. The Gervais Battery was located on the slope on the left. French sap trenches on the slopes of Malakhov Hill encroach upon the bastion. It was from these advanced trenches that French troops in the first wave of the attack rushed forward to the ditch and then up the earthworks. A French gun battery in the foreground is protected by gabions and sandbags.** (Royal Collection Trust/© Her Majesty Queen Elizabeth II, 2016).

Opposite: The view of a wooded Malakhov Hill from the largely undeveloped Mamelon today. The buildings in the distance to the left of the hill are on the north side of the roadstead. The Black Sea is beyond.

Russian losses on 17 August amounted to 1,500 men with the average on the following days of bombardment being 1,000. Even when the fire was less intense after 22 August, about 500-600 were killed or wounded daily. A floating bridge was constructed from Fort Nicholas in Sevastopol to the north side of the roadstead by the Russians during August in readiness for a retreat. With their army in the field defeated on the Chernaya, the Russians in Sevastopol now had no hope of relief.

The Final Bombardment of Sevastopol

The British army had reorganised following Raglan's death. By the end of August, Lieutenant General Sir James Scarlett commanded the Cavalry Division and the 1st Division was led by Lieutenant General Lord Rokeby with its old Highland Brigade becoming the basis for a new Highland Division under Lieutenant General Sir Colin Campbell. The 2nd Division was commanded by Lieutenant General Frederick Markham, the 3rd Division by Lieutenant General Sir William Eyre, the 4th Division by Lieutenant General Henry Barnard and the Light Division by Lieutenant General Sir William Codrington.

On 1 September 1855, the garrison of Sevastopol was down to 50,000 men of whom 4,000 were sailor-gunners. Despite reduced numbers, ever effort was put into strengthening damaged positions and replacing inoperable guns. There were still 982 guns in the city, and even though some of these had been dismounted during the fifth bombardment and not available, there were 600 guns facing the siege batteries.

The Chief Engineers of the Allies had a final conference and agreed that another assault should take place in the very near future. However, it was acknowledged that, while the guns protecting the Malakhov had been mastered, this was not the case for those covering the Redan and Flagstaff bastions. Pélissier was hesitant and seemed inclined to wait for the arrival of more mortars, but to delay had its own dangers. A three-day bombardment prior to an assault was fixed to begin on 5 September.

By that date, three new batteries, Nos. 18, 19 and 20, had been completed on the British Left Attack, and Battery No. 21 for two 18-inch mortars on the British Right Attack.

A magnification of part of Robertson/Beato's image entitled *8-Gun Battery* showing the Quarries after its capture by the British. The area of disturbed earth that constituted the Quarries was on the upper northern slope of a bank on the far side of a depression that ran cross the Vorontsov Ridge at this point. The deep trench seen at centre ran up to Mortar Battery No. 16. Battery No. 17 ran across the top of the Quarries from the centre to the right corner where Battery No. 20 was situated. A trench can be seen as an arc beyond the Quarries. This was the 5th Parallel from where the main force for the unsuccessful attack on the Redan Bastion gathered on 8 September 1855. Beyond this is the line of the abattis and then the formidable earthworks of the Redan. The buildings beyond are on the Central Hill in Sevastopol. (Royal Collection Trust/© Her Majesty Queen Elizabeth II, 2016).

The bank where the western section of the Quarries was found in 1855 as it looks today. The view is northwest from the depression that crosses the Vorontsov Ridge below the site of the Quarries. The track at centre is Dashi Sevastopol's'koi Street.

Unfortunately, there was not enough time before the bombardment commenced to mount three guns in Battery No. 22 constructed in the vicinity of Egerton's Pit and an extra two guns in new emplacements prepared in Battery No. 18. These had been intended to direct fire into the flanks of the Redan. The French had also prepared new trenches and batteries on the Inkerman Ridge though they had lost a significant number of men achieving this goal. These positions were designed to prevent Russian ships supporting Sevastopol's defenders as had been the case in the past. The British had 183 pieces of artillery and the French 620.

The barrage opened at 05.00 hours and the guns on the Malakhov were soon silenced. However, the guns of the Redan and its surrounds including the Barrack Battery, were still active. In addition, the guns in the Crow's Nest and Garden Batteries that provided flanking fire for the protection of the Redan were unsubdued. Although artillery in Battery No. 14 on the British Right Attack played on the east face of the Redan, the west face was not seriously challenged. This was to have consequences when the British assault was made.

The bombardment slackened at nightfall with only the mortars continuing. A Russian ship caught fire and lit up the sky so that the mortar shells could be seen to be falling with accuracy into the enemy's works. All that night, as during the day, ammunition was brought up to the Chersonese Plateau in trucks on the military railway and then transferred to carts for transportation to the trenches and batteries. The bombardment continued for another two days and nights. The intensity increased at dawn on 8 September with the advanced batteries on the British Left Attack, which had been abandoned during the fifth bombardment, again opening fire. The French guns battering the Malakhov suddenly became silent at noon, which was the hour scheduled for the attack in this sector.

The plan was for the main attack to be delivered without signal by the French on the Malakhov Front and, should the assault be successful, for subsidiary attacks to be made in the area of the Central Bastion on the Town Front and against the Redan Bastion to divert attention and prevent recapture of the ground won. For the attack on the Malakhov, the French were to utilise sixty-one battalions comprised of 25,300 men under the overall command of General Bosquet. The Malakhov on the left was to be attacked by General MacMahon's division with its two brigades led by Decaen and Vinoy. General de Wimpffen's brigade from General Camou's division and two battalions of the Zouaves of the Guard were in reserve. The Little Redan on the right was to be attacked by General Dulac's division with its two brigades led by Saint-Pol and Bisson with Marolle's brigade of Camou's division and a battalion of the Chasseurs of the Guard in reserve. In addition, the curtain wall between the two bastions was to be assailed by General La Motte-Rouge's division comprising the brigades of Bourbaki and Picard with two regiments each of Grenadiers and Voltigeurs of the Guard in reserve. When and if the Malakhov was occupied, the French and British flags were to be hoisted at Brançion Redoubt on the Mamelon as signals for attacks by the French in the area of the Central Bastion and by the British on the Redan Bastion to commence.

The 1st Zouave Regiment led the charge against the Malakhov Bastion leaping from trenches close to the defensive ditch. The ditch was crossed and the steep hill slope climbed; the colonial troops then stormed through the embrasures in the parapet. There were only the gunners and a few Russian soldiers eating their mid-day meal present beyond the parapet and these were rapidly overwhelmed. The tricolour was soon seen on the ramparts. The second wave arrived and Decaen's brigade secured the salient.

The Gervais Battery to the west was similarly secured by Vinoy's brigade. The Russian reserves, which had been forced to retreat some distance away when the French guns began to fire on the rear of the Malakhov at 11.15 hours, rushed forward and a fierce hand-to-hand fight ensued. Combat was so close that rifles and muskets could not be reloaded. As well as the bayonet, soldiers attacked each other with whatever was at hand. The Russians fought desperately under General Khrulev and launched counter-attack after bloody counter-attack, but could not dislodge the French from their footholds on Malakhov Hill.

Further to the northeast, the Russians were again taken by surprise at lunch. However, the French had further to run to reach the curtain wall from their forward trenches and the opening of the attack on the Malakhov had alerted the Russian gunners, who had enough time to fire canister and disable many troops rushing towards them. Despite this, the French were soon over the wall and pushing forward. The Russians rallied to force the French back from a second line of defence, only to be cut down by French rifle fire from the wall and to their right on Malakhov Hill. The French pushed forward again and retook a twelve-gun battery, which exploded when its powder magazine was hit, most likely by a Russian shell. This caused confusion and the French again pulled back to the wall but, regaining their composure, they drove back the Russians a second time.

At the Little Redan, even further to the northeast, the mid-day meal was again interrupted by the French attack on a garrison that was below full strength. The French had fifty yards to run from their trenches to the bastion and quickly scrambled into the work. On this occasion, the Russian counter-attack aided by artillery fire from a flanking battery drove the French back over the parapet to their trenches. Regrouping, a second assault was launched which retook the ramparts, but failed to secure the bastion. A third assault by the Chasseurs of the Guard also failed. Finally, the Grenadiers of the Guard attacked and managed to drive the Russians back to their second defence line where they turned and let loose with rifle and musket fire plus grape and canister. Counter-attacking, the Russians pushed the French out of the bastion. They then turned in an attempt to clear the French from the curtain wall, but by now they were too well established and retook only a small section.

Gorchakov on the north side of the roadstead sent reinforcements into the city over the new pontoon bridge and on to the Karabelnaya district to join the fight. As the Malakhov was the key to the defence of Sevastopol, it had to be retaken at all costs. Moving forward from behind the second line of defence, they strove to find a way into the now well-defended French positions, but to no avail. By 17.00 hours, the fate of the city was virtually decided.

Over on the Town Front, the French 1st Corp consisting of fifty-seven battalions with 20,580 men under General de Salles had attacked at 14.00 hours with the main thrust directed against the Central Bastion and its associated redoubts. Two mines were exploded under the strongpoint, but when the French troops rushed forward to take advantage of the situation they were met by intense musket, grape and canister fire which decimated their ranks. De Salles himself was shot in the head. At 15.00 hours, the attackers returned to their trenches and French batteries resumed firing on strongpoints. Another attack was being prepared against the Flagstaff Bastion by d'Autemarre's Division and a Sardinian brigade when Pélissier, who knew by then that the Malakhov was safe in French hands, called it off. The French had triumphed, but at a great cost in human life.

Klembovsky's image taken in the early 1900s of the view towards the Redan, which can be seen on the horizon at left, from the approximate location of the 5th Parallel of the British Right Attack. The white monument in the centre background was erected by the British in memory of those who died trying to capture the strongpoint. This memorial was destroyed in the Second World War. A fragment of the monument with the inscription was recovered from a garden of a dacha in Dashi Sevastopol's'koi Street and can now be found near the location of the Redan's salient. (Walter Havighurst Special Collections, Miami University Libraries, Oxford, Ohio).

Today's view looks northwest along Dasha Sevastopol's'koi Street from above the location of the Quarries towards a low wall in the distance that indicates the line of the right salient of the Redan Bastion.

When British and French flags were seen flying from the Mamelon shortly after noon, General Simpson gave the order for a cluster of rockets to be fired as the signal for the British to attack the Redan. The plan was for a covering party of 200 men of the 2nd Battalion of the Rifle Brigade to lead the assault. Their job was to protect a party of 320 men bringing up forty ladders from an advanced sap by firing on the Redan's parapets. Next would come the main storming force of 1,000 men starting from the 5th Parallel with 1,500 support troops waiting in the 4th Parallel. An armed working party of 200 men was also assembled plus an additional 3,000 support troops in the 3rd Parallel.

The Rifles advanced in extended order towards the salient, but before the ladder party got clear of the sap trench, raw recruits in the storming party rushed forward prematurely in a disorderly manner brushing aside the ladder bearers. This was not a good beginning, but the leading soldiers passed through the abattis, which had been damaged by artillery fire, and soon got to the ditch.

Men from the 19th (1st Yorkshire North Riding), 88th (Connaught Rangers), 90th (Perthshire Volunteers) and 97th (Earl of Ulster's) regiments in the Light Division, under Colonel Charles Windham, had moved forward on the left while men in the 3rd (East Kent), 30th (Cambridgeshire), 41st (Welch), 55th (Westmoreland) and 62nd (Wiltshire) regiments of the 2nd Division, under Colonel Horatio Shirley, advanced on the right. The Russians had had advanced warning because they had seen unusual movements in the British trenches and were on full alert since the attack on the Malakhov had commenced. There was about 250 yards of open ground from the sap trench to the salient of the Redan and about 400 yards from the 5th Parallel. Although the actual salient was wrecked, other guns were still operable and the approaching soldiers were raked with grape and canister fire.

The ditch before the Redan was fifteen feet deep, but not difficult to descend. Ladders were thrown down from above and then placed against the slightly higher far side. Some men used these ladders to climb over the parapet while others scrambled up the rubble to the embrasures despite heavy musket fire. Work began to tear down the ramparts to form a ramp so that ladders wouldn't be needed for those that followed – some used their bare hands.

The Russians retreated to a second defence line at the rear of the bastion. This was a formidable barrier lined with soldiers and guns. Many British troops reaching the Redan lay down behind the ramparts and exchanged fire with the Russians at the far end of the bastion. Few had the courage to move into the bastion even when encouraged to do so by their officers. Those that did set about spiking the guns and setting fire to the gabions and fascines in the embrasures. Support troops arriving at the Redan could not get through the obstruction caused by those who did not want to advance further. Some officers organised the more determined attackers to scale other sections of the ramparts, but the assault was failing through a lack of determination. Many were leaderless, their officers exposing themselves to fire in a bid to exalt their men to greater efforts having been shot down. Although reluctant to go forward, there was also a reluctance to retreat. Men looked around for the reserves. This led to a stalemate for a while until the Russian counter-attacked in force with a bayonet charge that drove the British out of the Redan. Moving into the salient, the Russians were counter-attacked in turn and driven back by British fire from behind parapet. There was even an attempt at a bayonet charge by the British, but it was driven back. Russian reinforcements hit the flank of their attackers and drove them out of the battery where the retreat took them back to the trenches.

The British officers that still remained alive or uninjured at the salient of the Redan repeatedly tried to rally troops for an attack on the rear barrier in the bastion that was held by the Russians, but the rank and file, who were generally untried in battle, wavered and wouldn't go. There may have been a belief that the bastion's interior was mined, but the lack of spirit was probably more to do with inexperience. Whatever the reason, the reserves were now urgently needed at the Redan to continue the push if there was to be any hope of a victory. However, despite many requests carried by officers back across the open ground strewn with bodies, no one came.

Codrington, in overall command of the attack, has been accused of dithering and even in denial about what was happening. Windham, who led the 2nd Division's storming party and had been trying unsuccessfully to stimulate an advance across the interior of the Redan, eventually decided to seek help himself. Although he persuaded Lieutenant General Markham to release the 1st (Royal) Regiment he needed General Codrington's final permission. He sought Codrington's approval as he was preparing to lead this body of fresh troops to the Redan, but was pulled down from the lip of the parallel and advised not be in such a hurry. Although there as an urgency, Codrington for some reason wanted to find out what the French were doing. Asked by Codrington the chances of success, Windham argued his case as best he could and admitted the difficulties and uncertainties. He informed Codrington that the fresh troops should attack to the left of the salient. However, time was running out.

The inevitable soon happened. The Russians fired a volley of muskets and guns loaded with grape-shot across the interior of the bastion and then charged the salient with bayonets. The remaining British troops refused to challenge the onslaught despite pleas from the few officers left and turned to flee. There was a crush to get through the embrasures and over the parapet by those who had found shelter inside the bastion. These men collided with those outside and many fell into the ditch. Others were carried down into the ditch by the earthworks giving way under the weight of the retreating mass of soldiers. The upturned bayonets of those in the ditch when the ramparts collapsed impaled their comrades tumbling down the slope. Many others were crushed by the fall and knocked unconscious. Men were still struggling to get to their feet and clambering over the dead and dying when the Russians reached the parapet and saw the mayhem below. A deadly fire was unleashed and hand grenades thrown, which served to further increase the chaos and panic of those in the ditch. Those that survived managed to scramble out and either run or limp back to the trenches. It was impossible to renew the attack with the demoralised and shamed men who had returned uninjured. No more attempts were made to capture the Redan that day. It was all over two hours after it began.

The failure was another case of gross mismanagement by those in command, who sent in untried and ill-disciplined troops in far too few numbers without adequate back-up. The day had ended in total defeat for the British. What compounded the humiliation was that the French had succeeded in taking the Malakhov, which resulted in the Russians leaving the now untenable Sevastopol overnight across the pontoon bridge. The only consolation was that the siege was over at last.

In the actions on that day, the Russians lost 2,684 killed, 7,193 wounded and 1,763 missing, the French lost 1,584 killed, 4,513 wounded and 1,410 missing, and the British lost 390 killed, 2,043 wounded and 177 missing. Many of the British dead were soon to be buried where they had fallen in the ditch before the Redan.

Cathcart's Hill

Infantry Camps and Views of Sevastopol

When Sevastopol was first invested, the British had responsibility for manning the siege line to the west of the Great Ravine, which ran south from South Harbour. This was a huge area. The 2nd Division camped behind Home Ridge on the Inkerman Ridge to the northeast and had responsibilities in this area. They were supported by the 1st Division (except the 93rd Regiment defending Balaklava at Kadikoi), who were camped northeast of the Middle Ravine not too far from the landmark known as the Windmill. The Light Division camped on the Chersonese Plateau on the southeast side of the Vorontsov Height and to the northeast of the Vorontsov Road. The 4th Division camp was near the summit and on the southeast-facing slope of Cathcart's Hill to the southwest of the Vorontsov Ravine and southeast of the Green Hill Ridge. The 3rd Division camped on a ridge further to the west and slightly forward of the north-facing slope of Cathcart's Hill.

Because of heavy casualties at the Battle of Inkerman, the British effectively became the junior partner to the French and relinquished responsibility for the manning of the siege lines northeast of the Middle Ravine. As a consequence, the regiments of the 2nd Division moved camp to the Chersonese Plateau just east of the 4th Division camp and to the southwest of the Vorontsov Road. The 1st Division was sent down to Kadikoi to join the 93rd Regiment in the defence of Balaklava. The Guards Brigade of the 1st Division camped on the slopes of Guards' Hill where they stayed until June 1855 and then relocated back to the plateau between the Vorontsov Road and the Col de Balaklava to re-join those besieging Sevastopol.

Roger Fenton began photographing the infantry camp on the Chersonese Plateau in April 1855. At this time, the regiments of 3rd and 4th Divisions manned the trenches of the British Left Attack while the regiments of the 2nd and Light Divisions manned the trenches of the British Right Attack. The first of his images to be presented is entitled *Cathcart's Hill, looking towards the Light Division and Inkerman*. The view is northeast looking over the Chersonese Plateau from the eastern slopes of Cathcart's Hill. Above the hut in the left foreground is a depression, which is the head of the Vorontsov Ravine. The Vorontsov Road, which connected Sevastopol with Yalta and beyond, lies beyond the ravine and can be seen running across the flat landscape in the middle distance on the left. Given these landmarks and a plan of the camps, the tents and huts of various regiments can be identified. Fenton's picture was taken from where the 4th Division was camped looking over the area where the regiments of the 2nd Division were located. The cluster of tents and huts in the left foreground were those of the 57th (West Middlesex) Regiment. The three rows of tents in the middle distance just right of centre belong to the 62nd (Wiltshire) Regiment with the huts of the 41st (Welch) Regiment to their right across the track. On the far right are the huts of the 49th (Hertfordshire) Regiment. Above and beyond the tents of the 62nd is an enclosure containing huts. This was the headquarters of the Light Division. The Vorontsov Road passed just behind this headquarters complex. On the far side of the Vorontsov Road were the camps of the regiments of the Light Division. The huts beyond and to the left of headquarters were the accommodation for the 77th (East Middlesex) Regiment. To their left were the huts of the 88th (Connaught Rangers) Regiment and the 19th (1st Yorkshire North Riding) Regiment. The tents beyond the Vorontsov Road on the far left belonged to the 90th (Perthshire Volunteers) Regiment. More Light Division regiments were camped further away on the left. Beyond them on the far left skyline is the slightly elevated Inkerman battlefield

The next image is a merger of two of Fenton's photographs entitled *View from Cathcart's Hill, looking towards Simferopol* (on the left) and *Kamara Heights in the distance, Artillery Waggons in the foreground* (on the right). These two images show the view to the right of *Cathcart's Hill, looking towards the Light Division and Inkerman*. The centre of the merged

Aerial image of the Chersonese Plateau with the approximate locations of the British divisional and Naval Brigade camps identified. The straight road that runs from upper centre to lower right is the Sevastopol-Yalta highway, which roughly follows the course of the old Vorontsov Road in this area. This road twists as it descends the Sapoune Ridge in the lower right corner. The summit of Cathcart's Hill is identified, as is the French camp where Fenton took several photographs. North is at the top. The site of Fort Nicholas in Sevastopol City lies almost four miles to the north-northwest of Cathcart's Hill. (Adapted from a Google Earth™ image).

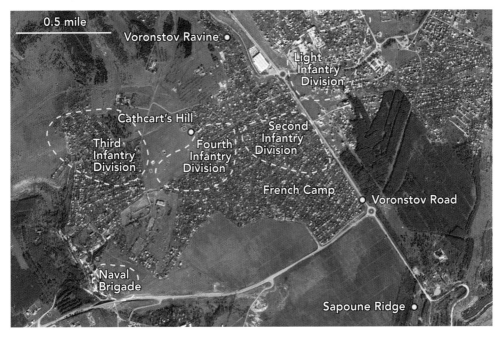

Fenton's image entitled **Cathcart's Hill, looking towards the Light Division and Inkerman.** (Library of Congress, Washington).

A merger of two of Fenton's images entitled, from left to right, **View from Cathcart's Hill, looking towards Simferopol** and **Kamara Heights in the distance, Artillery Waggons in the foreground.** The tent next to where washing lies on the ground on the extreme right of the image above is the same tent that can be seen at the far end of the first row of tents on the left of this image. (Library of Congress, Washington).

image looks roughly southeast across the Chersonese Plateau towards the Sapoune Ridge. The artillery park in the right foreground is marked on a contemporary map of the camps in 1855 and indicates that the rows of tents on the lower slope of Cathcart's Hill on the left are those of the 20th (East Devonshire) Regiment in the 4th Division. The tents in the distance at centre are believed to be French. It was from the French camp that Fenton took a view looking back in the direction of Cathcart's Hill entitled *Picquet House, Cathcart's Hill, from General Bosquet's Quarters*, which is shown later.

James Robertson and Felice Beato took photographs in the same area later in 1855. All their pictures were entitled *Camp at Sebastopol*. They reveal that not much had changed during the months that had elapsed since Fenton took his images earlier in the year. Their first image shows the head of the Vorontsov Ravine, which was also seen in Fenton's *Cathcart's Hill, looking towards the Light Division and Inkerman*. Contemporary maps of the time indicate that there were springs and three reservoirs at this location. Reservoirs can clearly be seen in the foreground with the rows of tents belonging to the 62nd Regiment on the right. The ravine exits to the left where it becomes more pronounced and deeper. The walled enclosure at centre contained the headquarters of the Light Division with the huts of the 77th Regiment in a row on the left with tents behind. The Vorontsov Road ran between the huts of the 77th Regiment and divisional headquarters. The view is looking east from the eastern slopes of Cathcart's Hill.

The same view over the head of the Vorontsov Ravine today shows the area is covered by a dacha suburb. The slope down into the basin that is the head of the ravine seen on the far left of the Robertson/Beato image is also seen on the left of today's view. A water storage tank now stands on the edge of the far side of the head of the ravine. The reservoirs of 1855 would have been on the floor of the basin in the centre. The Sevastopol-Yalta Highway, which is believed to closely follow the route of the old Vorontsov Road in this locality, runs unseen across the background 140 yards behind the water tank.

The second of Robertson/Beato's photographs with the title *Camp at Sebastopol* shows the view to the right of their first image. It looks southeast with the head of the Vorontsov Ravine, which is now on the left, merging into a fold of the Chersonese Plateau grasslands. The rows of tents of the 62nd Regiment are now on the left. Behind the tents of the 62nd are the huts of the 41st and 49th regiments. The French camp is in the distance on the far right. The Vorontsov Road runs unseen from left to right across the middle distance.

In today's picture, the fold in the Chersonese Plateau to the south of the head of the Vorontsov ravine visible in the Robertson/Beato image is just discernible despite the landscape now being dominated by dachas and their treed gardens. This depression in the landscape is noticeable when driving on the dirt road from the Sevastopol-Yalta Highway to the old British War Memorial on Cathcart's Hill. The turnoff for this dirt road is on the right just past the Dergachi roundabout when coming out of Sevastopol. The area as it looks now is in complete contrast to 1855. Photographing any vista within the dacha suburb is difficult because houses, fences and trees obstruct the view.

The third Robertson/Beato photograph entitled *Camp at Sebastopol* was taken very close to where Fenton took *View from Cathcart's Hill, looking towards Simferopol*. It shows the tents of the 20th Regiment partly obscured by a cabin in the foreground. This wooden-walled hut does not appear on Fenton's picture of the same camp taken a few months earlier. Rifles are stacked in groups to the left of the tents. The end of the artillery park seen

Robertson/Beato's first image entitled **Camp at Sebastopol** looking east from the eastern slopes of Cathcart's Hill. (Royal Collection Trust/© Her Majesty Queen Elizabeth II, 2016).

The head of the Vorontsov Ravine today from the eastern slopes of Cathcart's Hill.

The second of Robertson/Beato images entitled **Camp at Sebastopol.** (Royal Collection Trust/© Her Majesty Queen Elizabeth II, 2016).

The view to the southeast from the eastern slopes of Cathcart's Hill today.

in Fenton's *Kamara Heights in the distance, Artillery Waggons in the foreground* is on the right. The cluster of tents and huts below and to the right of the 20th camp is identified from contemporary maps as the headquarters of the 2nd Division, which was under the command of Lieutenant General John Pennefather at the time. As in Fenton's picture, the three rows of the tents of the 62nd Regiment are in the middle distance on the left with the huts of the 41st and 49th Regiments to their right. The camp of the 47th (Lancashire) Regiment would have been the tents in the middle distance on the far right. The camp of the 77th Regiment with the camp of the 88th Regiment on the extreme left are again seen beyond the camp of the 62nd. The depression that leads into the head of the Vorontsov Ravine is visible immediately above the open-sided tent on the left. The Mackenzie Heights are on the skyline.

The modern view was taken looking east from the southern slopes of Cathcart's Hill just south of the dacha suburb that now covers the mid-level slopes. Here the view is not obstructed by buildings, trees or fences. The rising land in the middle distance is where the 2nd Division camped. The Sevastopol-Yalta Highway, which follows the line of the Vorontsov Road across the Chersonese Plateau, runs from left to right in this area. Further away on the left, another dacha suburb stands where the Light Division camped. The camp of the 31st (Huntingdonshire) Regiment, part of the 1st Division, would have been on the slope to the right. The limestone cliffs of the Mackenzie Heights are visible on the centre skyline.

William Simpson's watercolour entitled *Camp of the Light Division* looks southeast from the Vorontsov Road where it begins to climb up the slope of the Vorontsov Height. The road itself is seen on the extreme right. The 88th Regiment is shown on the parade ground with the camps of the 90th and 77th beyond and to the right. The camp of the 19th is depicted on the left of the parading 88th. The 97th Regiment, the 23rd (Royal Welch Fusiliers) Regiment, the 7th (Royal Fusiliers) Regiment and the 2nd Battalion of the Rifle Brigade are camped further to the left with the Siege Train-Right Attack on the shoulder of land behind. This vista takes in a ninety degree view.

The modern photograph was taken just where the Vorontsov Road would have started to rise up the Vorontsov Height, which is behind the camera. The Sevastopol-Yalta Highway, which is its modern equivalent of the Vorontsov Road, is just off the picture to the right. Yet another dacha suburb now extends along and up the slope of the Vorontsov Height on the left. The parade ground in Simpson's picture was most likely beyond the long wall at centre right. This would place it where today's road from Inkerman approaches the Dergachi roundabout near the present British War Memorial.

Fenton spent some time with Bosquet at his headquarters in the French camp on the Chersonese Plateau. Here he photographed the general, his staff and a *cantinière* - a woman attached to a French regiment who managed a canteen and sold brandy to the troops. While at the camp, Fenton also took a landscape photograph looking towards the high ground that separated the Chersonese Plateau from the slopes before Sevastopol. This image, which is reproduced, was entitled *Picquet House, Cathcart's Hill, from General Bosquet's Quarters*. The hill seen in the left background is Cathcart's Hill. It was from these slopes that Fenton and Robertson/Beato took their views shown earlier in this chapter. The high ground on the right is the Vorontsov Height, which was also known as Picket House Hill. The Vorontsov Road can be seen ascending the hill with the ruins of the Picket House on its immediate right as it disappears over the skyline. Beyond the Vorontsov Height, the

Robertson/Beato's third image entitled **Camp at Sebastopol**. The view is east from the southern slopes of Cathcart's Hill. Today, this area is covered with dachas and trees. (Royal Collection Trust/© Her Majesty Queen Elizabeth II, 2016).

The view today looking east from the southern slopes of Cathcart's Hill. The image above would have been taken from a location within a dacha suburb that lies further to the northeast, which is off this picture to the left. Note that the profile of the Mackenzie Heights in the far distance is almost identical to the skyline in the contemporary image.

Simpson's watercolour entitled *Camp of the Light Division.*

The view southeast from the same location on the line of the Vorontsov Road today.

Vorontsov Ridge descended towards Sevastopol and the Redan Bastion. This was the area of the British Right Attack. The depression between the Vorontsov Height and Cathcart's Hill is the head of the Vorontsov Ravine. This ravine separated the British Right Attack from the British Left Attack closer to Sevastopol.

The tents visible on the slopes of the Vorontsov Height to the immediate right of the Vorontsov Road belonged to the 90th Regiment with the camp of the 97th Regiment further to the right. The rows of tents on the slopes of Cathcart's Hill on the far left were most likely those of the 20th and 57th Regiments in the 4th Division. The camp of the 2nd Division, which would have been below and to the right of these tents, is hidden.

The location of the French camp today is where yet another dacha suburb, seen on the right of the modern photograph, is now found. Today's image was taken from a road that runs west-southwest from a roundabout on the Sevastopol-Yalta Highway half a mile before it reaches the edge of the Sapoune Ridge. The neglected vineyard in the foreground is waiting for still further suburban development. The military railway would have run across this ground in the middle distance on its way to a terminus on the Vorontsov Road. Cathcart's Hill is on the left with the Vorontsov Height mostly obscured by trees on the right. The high point on the height is where the tall communications mast is seen. This mast is not far from the location of the Picket House ruins.

Simpson's watercolour entitled *Camp of the Fourth Division, July 15th, 1855* is yet another sweeping panorama that covers almost 180 degrees of view over the southern slopes of Cathcart's Hill. On the far left are the camps of those regiments, such as the 20th, featured in Fenton's images taken from the southeast slopes of Cathcart's Hill. In the foreground on the extreme left behind the barrel is the small stone building that served as accommodation for Lieutenant Colonel Thomas Shadforth of the 57th. He was photographed by Fenton with fellow officers outside this hut before his death at the Redan on 18 June 1855. In the middle distance on the extreme right is the camp of the 1st Battalion of the Rifle Brigade with the 48th (Northamptonshire) Regiment to the right of centre and the 39th Regiment of the 3rd Division beyond in the far distance.

Again, it is impossible to cover all the ground shown in Simpson's picture in one photographic image. According to a contemporary map identifying the positions of the regimental camps in 1855, the 1st Battalion of the Rifle Brigade would have been camped in the foreground of today's photograph showing the upper southern slope of Cathcart's Hill with the 21st (Royal North British Fusiliers) Regiment in the dacha suburb beyond.

Fenton took three photographs, which form a panorama, on Cathcart's Hill featuring the western end of the camp of the 4th Division. The first, which shows the view to the south-southwest, is called *Looking towards St George's Monastery, tents of the 4th Division in the Foreground.* The monastery is almost five miles distant on the coast and is not visible. Two tents in the foreground on the right are protected from ground water running down the slope by sizable earth banks. The tents are likely to have been those of the 46th (South Devonshire) Regiment. The modern image is of roughly the same area, which is southwest of the summit of Cathcart's Hill and still open country.

The second image, which overlaps with the previous one on the left, is entitled *General Garrett's quarters and tents of the 4th Division*. Major General Robert Garrett commanded the 2nd Brigade of the 4th Division when this image was taken. He seemed to be a favourite of Fenton's as several portraits of him exist including one with officers of the 46th Regiment next to a hut with a subterranean interior. It is likely that the tents and huts on the right

Fenton's image entitled *Picquet House, Cathcart's Hill, from General Bosquet's Quarters.* (Royal Collection Trust/© Her Majesty Queen Elizabeth II, 2016).

Today's view looking towards Cathcart's Hill and the Vorontsov Height from the Chersonese Plateau.

Simpson's watercolour entitled **Camp of the Fourth Division, July 15th, 1855.** (© National Army Museum, London).

Fenton's image entitled **Lieutenant Colonel Shadforth and officers of the 57th Regiment.** (Library of Congress, Washington).

Today's view over part of the camp of the 4th Division with the Chersonese Plateau below.

belonged to the 63rd (West Suffolk) Regiment camped to the north of the 46th. The view is to the southwest, as is today's view, which overlaps on the left with the modern equivalent of *Looking towards St George's Monastery, tents of the 4th Division in the Foreground.*

The third Fenton image in the panorama is entitled *Camp of the Third Division, French tents in the distance.* It shows the view even further to the right and features the end few tents and huts of the camp of the 63rd Regiment. The tents and huts of the 3rd Division can be seen in the middle distance on the ridge of high ground that lay to the west and southwest of the summit of Cathcart's Hill. The French tents in the distance are hardly discernible, but can be seen beyond the camp of the 3rd Division in a high definition image. These tents were beyond the Great Ravine, which divided the British and French zones of attack. The view overlaps with the previous image.

The modern equivalent of Fenton's image looks west from the flat summit of Cathcart's Hill with the ridge where the 3rd Division camped in the middle distance. The large apartment buildings on the skyline on the left are in a south-western suburb of Sevastopol. The Black Sea is in the far distance on the right.

Simpson's watercolour entitled *Camp of the Third Division, July 9th, 1855* is a closer view of the camp of the 3rd Division than in Fenton's image. His initial position when he sketched the scene must have been near to the tents of the 4th Division seen in the centre of Fenton's picture *Camp of the Third Division, French tents in the distance.* Simpson reports that, because of rain, he finished his preliminary sketch in a tent of the 63rd Regiment. Tents of the 63rd are seen in the foreground on the far left of his watercolour. The ridge in the middle distance is where most of the regiments of the 3rd Division and

Fenton's image entitled **Looking towards St George's Monastery, tents of the 4th Division in the Foreground.** (Library of Congress, Washington).

Today's view looking in the direction of St George's Monastery from the plateau of Cathcart's Hill.

Fenton's image entitled *General Garrett's quarters and tents of the 4th Division.* (Library of Congress, Washington).

The view today showing approximately the same area on the flat-topped Cathcart's Hill.

Fenton's image entitled **Camp of the Third Division, French tents in the distance.** (Library of Congress, Washington).

Today's comparable view looking west from the flat summit area of Cathcart's Hill.

Simpson's watercolour entitled **Camp of the Third Division, 9th July, 1855.** (Public domain work of art).

The same view today looking west from Cathcart's Hill.

Simpson's watercolour entitled **Camp of the Naval Brigade before Sebastopol.** (Library of Congress, Washington).

Today's view to the west-northwest from the site of the camp of the Naval Brigade.

A merger of two of Fenton's images entitled, from left to right, *The Cemetery, Cathcart's Hill; the Picquet House, Victoria Redoubt and the Redoubt des Anglais in the distance* and *The Cemetery; Redoubt des Anglais and Inkerman in the distance*, to form a panorama showing the summit of Cathcart's Hill in 1855. (Library of Congress, Washington).

two regiments from other infantry divisions were located. As in many of his pictures, the view encompasses a ninety degree or more of panorama. The regiments depicted as camping here from left to right were the 17th (Leicestershire), the unnamed 89th, the 38th (1st Staffordshire), the 28th (North Gloucestershire), the 44th (East Essex), the 50th (Queen's Own), the 1st Battalion of the 1st (Royal) Regiment and the 4th (King's Own), as well as the Royal Engineers. Kamiesch Bay is in far distance in the centre and the smoke on the right emanates from a Russian battery at the Flagstaff Bastion in Sevastopol. In the valley on the right a relief force is going down to the trenches of the Left Attack. Fenton photographed his iconic image entitled *The Valley of the Shadow of Death*, which is shown in Chapter 13, further down this valley.

Today's photographic equivalent cannot hope to capture all the terrain shown in Simpson's panorama, but it does feature the ridge where the 3rd Infantry Division camped, which is now a wooded dacha suburb. This picture was taken from the western slope of Cathcart's Hill from a location where it was believed the 63rd Regiment camped.

Simpson also painted a picture entitled *Camp of the Naval Brigade before Sevastopol*. The site of this camp was above a steep-sided valley that was a fork of the Great Ravine. This valley, which was crossed at the camp by a rope suspension bridge, ran north from the camp towards Sevastopol west of the ridge that was occupied by the 3rd Division. A burial ground was located on the valley's western slope to the northwest of the camp.

The Naval Brigade was a large detachment of marines and seamen from ships of the Royal Navy which supported the army on shore by manning gun batteries and also taking part in assaults on Russian lines. The brigade was led by Captain Lushington, who was promoted to rear admiral on 4 July 1855. He is one of the group of figures in the right foreground. Captain Lushington's marquee is within an enclosure on the left next to a 'Union Jack'. Captain William Peel, who is another officer depicted in the group, won the Victoria Cross for gallantry during the Crimean War. On 18 October 1854, the second day of the first bombardment of Sevastopol, he picked up a live shell with the fuse still burning and threw it over the parapet of his gun battery. He also helped defend the colours of the Grenadier Guards at the Battle of Inkerman and led a scaling party on the first attack against the Redan Bastion.

Today's photograph looks roughly west-northwest from the centre of the camp area over the steep-sided valley that lay just beyond. The ridge behind the white building seen over the edge of the valley is the same ridge depicted beyond the camp in Simpson's watercolour. The hillock on the right of Simpson's picture is now wooded and is on the extreme right of the photograph. A new road that connects the Sevastopol-Yalta Highway to the Sevastopol-Balaklava road now runs through the southern section of the camp site

The View from Cathcart's Hill

Cathcart's Hill dominated the higher ground at the north-facing edge of the Chersonese Plateau to the southwest of the Vorontsov Road. The 4th Division camped close to the summit and from its eastern and southern slopes there were views over other infantry camps on the Chersonese Plateau to the Inkerman Ridge, Mackenzie Heights, and the mountainous region to the southwest of Balaklava. Contemporary images showing these views were reproduced in the previous section headed 'Infantry Camps on and around Cathcart's Hill'. To the north of Cathcart's Hill, the land fell away towards Sevastopol and the British Left Attack on the Green Hill Ridge providing a magnificent viewpoint for those who wished to observe bombardments or assaults on Russian positions.

A stone-walled cemetery for officers who fell in the Battle of Inkerman was established on the flat summit area of Cathcart's Hill at a site of an old ruined fort, which may have been built by the Tartars. Lieutenant General Sir George Cathcart, who gave his name to the hill, was its most illustrious occupant. The cemetery was expanded in 1882 when more land was granted by the Russian government for the centralisation of British memorials and head stones from other burial places. However, no bodies from these other sites were re-interred on Cathcart's Hill. The cemetery was planted with shrubs and trees and old photographs show it had neat gravel paths with borders. Although neglected at the time of the First World War, it was well looked after in the 1920s, but was fought over during the Second World War and headstones levelled. In the early 1960s, the cemetery was destroyed on the orders of Soviet Premier Nikita Krushchev and dachas later built on the site.

Fenton and Roberston/Beato took photographs of the cemetery and Simpson painted a watercolour. A panorama formed by the merger of two of Fenton's images entitled *The Cemetery, Cathcart's Hill; the Picquet House, Victoria Redoubt and the Redoubt des Anglais in the distance* and *The Cemetery: Redoubt des Anglais and Inkerman in the distance* shows how it appeared in the spring of 1855. The direction of the view at the centre of the panorama is to the northeast. In the cemetery, the cross in the group of headstones on the left marks Cathcart's grave. The grave of Brigadier General Thomas Goldie is to its left with the grave of Brigadier General Fox Strangways to its right. The headstone with a cross just right of centre belonged to Captain Edward Stanley of the 57th Regiment. All were killed at the Battle of Inkerman.

Fenton's image entitled **French Left Attack, Kamiesch in the distance, tents of Sir John Campbell in the foreground.** (Library of Congress, Washington).

View to the west-northwest from Cathcart's Hill.

Fenton's image entitled **Distant view of Sebastopol from the front of Cathcart's Hill.**
(Library of Congress, Washington).

The view north-northwest from Cathcart's Hill today.

The camp of the Light Division on the Chersonese Plateau is below on the far right. When the area in the middle distance above the solitary man in the centre of the cemetery is magnified, the Vorontsov Road can be seen running along the Vorontsov Height and past the ruins of the local landmark known as the Picket House. The Picket House was so named because a picket of the Light Division was established here when the siege began. The building, which may have been a Post House or farm, was soon demolished for its timbers, which were used to construct siege gun platforms. Like Cathcart's Hill, the Picket House was a favourite location for those wishing to view attacks on Russian lines. The Victoria Redoubt on the Victoria Ridge is also visible in the far centre distance.

Mary Seacole visited Cathcart's Hill during the siege of Sevastopol and on 18 June 1855 she recalled:

> So I reached Cathcart's Hill, crowded with non-combatants, and, leaving there the mules, loaded myself with what provisions I could carry, and – it was a work of little difficulty, and danger – succeeded in reaching the reserves of Sir Henry Barnard's division, which was to have stormed something. I forget what; but when they found the attack on the Redan had been a failure, very wisely abstained.

In mid-August 1855, Mary reported:

> I spent much of my time on Cathcart's Hill, watching, with a curiosity and excitement which became intense, the progress of the terrible bombardment. Now and then, a shell would fall among the crowd of on-lookers which covered the hill; but it never disturbed us, so keen and feverish and so deadened to danger had the excitement and expectation made us.

Fanny Duberly was on Cathcart's Hill on 5 September 1855, to witness the opening of the final bombardment and wrote:

> We reached Cathcart's Hill this afternoon in time to see a perfect explosion of guns from the French line of attack. Every gun and mortar appeared to fire at once; those that did not go off at the precise moment following with the rapidity of file firing. It was indeed 'a noble salvo shot', and was loudly cheered by the English soldiers who were looking on. Presently, we met the brigade of Guards marching down to the trenches.

Mary Seacole visited the hill again on the morning of 8 September 1855, which 'broke cold and wintery', to witness what was to be the final assault on the Malakoff. She recalled:

> Very early in the morning I was on horseback, with my bandages and refreshments, ready to repeat the work of 18th June last. A line of sentries forbade all strangers passing through without orders, even to Cathcart's Hill; but once more I found that my reputation served as a permit, and the officers relaxed the rule in my favour everywhere. So, early in the day, I was in my old spot, with my old appliances for the wounded and fatigued; little expecting, however, that this day would so closely resemble the day of the last attack in its disastrous results.

Fenton's image entitled **Sebastopol with the Redan, Malakoff and Mamelon; Colonel Shadworth seated in the foreground.** (Library of Congress, Washington).

The same view today has far fewer surface rocks in the foreground. Buildings and trees on the right now obscure the view of the Mamelon and Malakhov Hill.

Fenton's image entitled *Colonel Shadforth and men of the 57th Regiment, Inkerman in the distance.* (Royal Collection Trust/© Her Majesty Queen Elizabeth II, 2016).

The eastern slope of Cathcart's Hill today is covered with dachas and their gardens.

It was noon before the cannonading suddenly ceased; and we saw with a strange feeling of excitement, the French tumble out of their advanced trenches, and roll into the Malakoff like a human flood. Onward they seemed to go into the dust and smoke, swallowed up by hundreds; but they never returned, and before long we saw workmen levelling parapets and filling up ditches, over which they drove, with headlong speed and impetuosity, artillery and ammunition-waggons, until there could be no doubt that the Malokoff was taken, although the tide of battle still surged around it with violence, and wounded men were borne from it in large numbers.

Fenton, having moved his camp to near headquarters from Balaklava, was invited to visit Sir John Campbell of the 4th Division on Cathcart's Hill. He wrote home on the 19 April 1855:

At Cathcart's Hill Major General Sir John Campbell commands the Division, and having received a message from him offering assistance if I would come there, I presented myself to him and at once told him my difficulties about a servant and was immediately invited to take up my quarters with him. 'Meanwhile', said Sir John 'come down and take a glass of sherry', and he led the way into a hole in the ground, a natural cavern which he had found and took possession of just before the storm of 14th of November. I tried to take pictures of the town but the day, though fine, was hazy, and I could not succeed.

On 24 April 1855, Fenton mentioned a gathering on Cathcart's Hill:

In the middle of last week everyone was at Cathcart's Hill looking out for the explosion of a great mine which the French had driven under the Garden fort; the time was announced for 4 p.m. As I had private information of the fact I was ready with my camera at the precise time, but no event coming off I shut up, and it was soon announced that it was postponed till half past six. Long after that time the hill was crowded with officers and soldiers.

Fenton took photographs from the summit of Cathcart's Hill that allow an appreciation of the view towards Sevastopol. He does not report the dates on which he took his photographs, but it seems likely that it was during the middle and latter half of April.

Fenton's image *French Left Attack, Kamiesch in the distance, tents of Sir John Campbell in the foreground* shows the view to the west-northwest from the summit of Cathcart's Hill. The area of the French Left Attack before Sevastopol is in the distance on the right with the French supply port of Kamiesch six miles away on the far left. Under magnification, warships can be seen off shore in the centre. The northern part of the ridge, where the 3rd Division was camped, runs across the picture from left to right in the middle distance as it lowers. The tents on the far left would most likely have belonged to the 4th Regiment, which was in the Light Division, but camped in the same area as the 3rd Division. Sir John Campbell's tents are on the right and this location was presumably where his cave was also found. He was killed on the assault on the Redan on 18 June 1855 and buried in Cathcart's Hill Cemetery

Today's view also looks west-northwest from Cathcart's Hill, but may have been taken further to the west than from where Fenton took his image. The northern end of the ridge, now wooded, where the 3rd Division camped lies in the middle distance. A track in the valley before the ridge was the route taken by the men of the 3rd Division when they marched to and returned from the trenches on the British Left Attack. Closer to Sevastopol, the same valley was photographed by Fenton as the 'Valley of the Shadow of Death'. This iconic image of war is shown in the next chapter. The suburbs to the west of Sevastopol stretch away to the left.

Fenton's photograph entitled *Distant view of Sebastopol from the front of Cathcart's Hill* overlaps on the left with *French Left Attack, Kamiesch in the distance, tents of Sir John Campbell in the foreground.* They were most likely taken from the same spot. The tents of Sir John Campbell are now in the foreground on the far left with Sevastopol at the centre in the far distance. Beyond the city, the north side of the roadstead is visible. The view is to the north-northwest and looks down the length of the ridge that leads to Green Hill on the British Left Attack. The disturbed ground on this ridge in the middle distance would have been an area known as the 'Lime Kilns' which became an artillery park on 1 August 1855. It was from an observation point just to the north of the Lime Kilns that Raglan watched the attack on the Quarries on 8 June 1855. According to William Romaine:

> They had chosen a place for Lord Raglan in front of the Lime Kilns of 4th Division but on going there I found you could only see the crest of the Mamelon and therefore not the French advance so I went to a spot in front and right of Cathcart's Hill, where both attacks could be seen.

Frenchman's Hill on the Vorontsov Ridge that carried the 21-Gun Battery lies to the right of the three figures.

The modern image also looks north-northwest from Cathcart's Hill from very close to where Fenton must have positioned his camera. The slight wooded rise in the middle distance is where the Lime Kilns were situated. Sevastopol city can be glimpsed over the trees at centre. The wooded area in the distance on the left is the park that now stretches from the site of the Flagstaff Bastion, through the area where the Garden Batteries was situated and on to the city. The domed museum that holds the siege panorama painting can be seen rising above the trees in this park on the extreme left. The north side of the roadstead is visible in the far distance to the right of centre.

Sebastopol with the Redan, Malakoff and Mamelon; Colonel Shadworth seated in the foreground is another of Fenton's images taken close to where *Distant view of Sebastopol from the front of Cathcart's Hill* was taken and looks roughly north with the Lime Kilns now being in the middle distance on the left. The Vorontsov Ridge is seen on the far side of the Vorontsov Ravine in the distance to the right of centre. The Vorontsov Road is unseen on this picture, as it would have been running along the floor of the Vorontsov Ravine. However, a road or track is visible on the side of the ridge and this swings across towards the location of the 21-Gun Battery on the 1st Parallel of the British Right Attack. The Mamelon is in the far distance on the extreme right with Malakhov Hill protruding slightly above the Vorontsov Ridge to its left. The Redan is just right of centre.

The view of many of the main Russian defensive positions is today obstructed by trees and buildings as can be seen from the modern image taken near to where Fenton took his

The flat summit of Cathcart's Hill today from the Flagstaff Bastion in Sevastopol - a distance of over two and a half miles.

photograph. Rows of white apartment buildings can be seen on the Vorontsov Ridge. Malakhov Hill is masked by the leaves of the tree in the foreground on the right and the trees on the far right mask the Mamelon. The wood on the site of the Lime Kilns denies a view of the area where the Redan was situated. The buildings on the far distance are on the north side of the roadstead. The Black Sea is in the background.

The last image by Fenton entitled *Colonel Shadforth and men of the 57th Regiment, Inkerman in the distance* looks to the east from Cathcart's Hill and brings the reader full circle back to just north of where his first image in this chapter was taken. The 57th (West Middlesex) Regiment is assembled in companies with two furled colours in the centre and two drummers on the left. The regiment formed the storming party on the assault on the Redan on 18 June 1855 and sustained heavy losses.

It is believed that the tents to the left of the 57th may have belonged to the 17th Regiment. The camps of the 57th and the 17th, which were both in the 4th Division, were adjacent to each other on the eastern slope of Cathcart's Hill.

The slope in the middle distance seen just above the tents in the far left foreground falls into the head of the Vorontsov Ravine. The lone tent seen in grasslands beyond is approximately where the Vorontsov Road ran across the background from left to right. Above the parading men of the 57th, the neat rows of tents in the middle distance belong to the 62nd Regiment with the huts of the 41st Regiment behind. Both of these regiments were in the 2nd Division camped on the Chersonese Plateau on the west side of the Vorontsov Road. The widely spread camp of the Light Division, which lay on the east side of the Vorontsov Road, is visible in the distance on the left.

Today's image, which was taken a little to the north of the same area, looks to the east-southeast rather than east. It shows the difficulties in photographing the view from within the dacha suburb that stretches from the line of the old Vornotsov Road, now the Sevastopol-Yalta Highway, up the eastern and south-eastern slopes of Cathcart's Hill and over the site of Cathcart's Hill Cemetery. The slope where the 57th paraded is now covered with dachas and gardens planted with trees and shrubs. However, the area where the 2nd Division camped is visible beyond on the plateau. The line of the Sevastopol-Yalta Highway can vaguely be seen as it crosses in front of the red-roofed house on the right.

The last modern photograph, to put the views towards Sevastopol reproduced here into perspective, shows Cathcart's Hill as it looks today from the site of the southwest-facing battery at the Flagstaff Bastion in the city. The dacha suburb that has crept up to the summit is amongst the trees on the left skyline. The site of the cemetery is in this area. The site of the camp of the 4th Division was mainly on the unseen reverse slope over the skyline. The white walled structure seen on the skyline in the centre is the 1993 British Memorial to the Crimean War, now quite dilapidated because of the poor quality of its construction. It has been superseded by a new memorial at the site of the camp of the Light Division near to the Dergachi roundabout on the Sevastopol-Yalta Highway.

13

The Valley of the Shadow of Death
Images of Round Shot on Roads

The 'Valley of the Shadow of Death' should not be confused with the more famous 'Valley of Death', which was the North Valley of Balaklava where the British Light Cavalry Brigade charged a Russian field battery with great loss of life during the Battle of Balaklava. Roger Fenton and the James Robertson/Felice Beato team used the term 'Valley of the Shadow of Death' in the titles of photographs taken of two different valleys within range of the Russian batteries in Sevastopol. The one thing that both valleys had in common was that they were dangerous places to loiter as evidenced by the expended round shot and unexploded shells that were found in them. Because of the risk of being hit by missiles by those who may have ventured to walk down these valleys, the name chosen for them, which comes from the 23rd Psalm, would seem apt.

Fenton's Image Entitled 'The Valley of the Shadow of Death'
On 23 April 1855, Fenton and his assistant Marcus Sparling borrowed a couple of mules from Major General Sir John Campbell, who was in command of the 4th Division, and took their photographic wagon down a shallow ravine to the northwest of Cathcart's Hill. They arrived at their destination, where the ravine had accumulated Russian round shot that had overshot the batteries on the British Left Attack, just after 15.00 hours. Because a couple of Russian missiles landed near Fenton as he reconnoitred on foot, he retreated back up the valley to a position he described as '100 yards short of the best point'. It was here where the wagon was parked and he set up his camera. While he was doing this, another Russian missile bounced on the hill fifty yards to his left and rolled down to his feet. His second position was clearly not that much safer than the first. However, this is where he stayed to capture the scene.

Fenton reports that he was in the valley for one-and-a-half hours and in his own words 'got two good pictures'. One picture was of the track along the bottom of the valley with cannonballs packed in the gutters on either side while the other image showed cannonballs both on the track and in the gutters. Both images were taken from exactly the same spot. Evidence suggests that the image of the track devoid of round shot was taken first with cannonballs arranged on the track for dramatic affect in the second picture. Fenton obviously used his artistic licence to produce a more powerful image, but he did not mention what he had done in his letters sent to England.

The location where the two photographs were taken was discovered by Errol Morris, the writer and filmmaker, after he walked backwards and forwards along the upper reaches of a ravine marked on an old map as the *Valley of the Shadow of Death*. He discovered that the two images were taken looking between north and north-northwest

Fenton's contrived masterpiece in war photography entitled *The Valley of the Shadow of Death*. The round shot on a dirt track running through a desolate landscape combine to deliver a powerful message. (Library of Congress, Washington).

The same scene today taken from very close to where Fenton positioned his camera looks north-northwest towards the centre of Sevastopol. Chapman's Battery on the 1st Parallel of the British Left Attack was about 1,100 yards away over the low hill on the right. The distance to the Redan was 2,550 yards in the same direction.

Robertson/Beato's image of the Vorontsov Ravine entitled *The Valley of the Shadow of Death, Woronzoff Road*. One soldier in the centre has hoisted a round shot to his shoulder for the camera. Gordon's Battery on the 1st Parallel of the British Right Attack was a few hundred yards away on top of the ridge behind. (Royal Collection Trust/© Her Majesty Queen Elizabeth II, 2016).

Today's view is easily recognisable. New dachas are under construction on the ridge above.

down the ravine towards Sevastopol and not away from Sevastopol as had been previously believed.

Robertson/Beato's Image Entitled 'The Valley of the Shadow of Death, Woronzoff Road'

Fenton wrote letters home so we know of many of his activities and the dates, even times, when certain photographs were taken. No similar resources are available for James Robertson or his brother-in-law and assistant Felice Beato and so it is often unclear when many of their photographs were taken. However, it is believed that their image of the deep-sided ravine referred to by them as the 'Valley of the Shadow of Death' was taken soon after the fall of Sevastopol in 1855.

The gorge that was the subject of the photograph by the Robertson and Beato team was the Vorontsov Ravine through which ran the Vorontsov Road on its way into Sevastopol after descending from the high ground to its east known as the Vorontsov Ridge. The location where round shot had accumulated on the road was the subject of their famous image. In the photograph, soldiers can be seen seemingly idling on the Vorontsov Road, which has a scattering of round shot. One holds a cannonball on his right shoulder in a pose reminiscent of a shot putter before a throw. The road, which descends away from the camera, turns abruptly to the left as it follows a sharp bend in the Vorontsov Ravine. The steep slope of the side of the ravine with its line of caves dominates the background. Soldiers are visible at the entrance to the caves, which were used to store powder and for shelter. A contemporary map also indicates that a station of the electric telegraph was located in one of the caves. The lack of heed of the soldiers on the road, which would normally have been in range of stray Russian missiles overshooting Gordon's or the 21-Gun Battery on the 1st Parallel of the British Right Attack, indicates that the need for caution in this dangerous place has ended. Well-worn paths climb the ravine side from the road to the caves and beyond.

The same photograph held by the Royal Collection Trust has the title *The Victoria Ravine*, which was another lesser used name for the same ravine. The French called the same ravine the 'Ravin du Laboratoire.

Opposite top: Simpson's watercolour entitled *Valley of the Shadow of Death–Caves in the Woronzoff Road, behind the 21-Gun Battery*. The title indicates that the name 'Valley of the Shadow of Death' for the Vorontsov Ravine was known by many. In a description of the painting, attention is given to the 'shot and shell' from Russian guns overshooting the 21-Gun Battery on the Vorontsov Ridge above accumulating on the Vorontsov Road. The sketch that formed the basis of the watercolour was drawn before the second bombardment of Sevastopol and the comment is made that afterwards the road was virtually paved with round shot of all calibres so that horses had difficulty in picking a way through them. The caves were occupied at this stage by the reserve guard of the trenches who were protected from missiles coming over the ridge behind. (Library of Congress, Washington).

Opposite bottom: Today's view below looks south from the Vorontsov Ridge down into the Vorontsov Ravine The caves seen in Robertson/Beato's image and Simpson's watercolour are around the near rock overhang on the far left.

An aerial image showing the positions of Fenton and Robertson/Beato when they took their photographs of the two different ravines both named the *Valley of the Shadow of Death* to the south-southeast of the city of Sevastopol. Both sites can be visited today. North is to the top of the image, Key: BC = Bicentennial Arch on the Sevastopol-Yalta Highway; V = Vorontsov Ravine with road. [Adapted from Google Earth™ image]

Another Robertson/Beato photograph showing the Vorontsov Ravine, this time taken from the Vorontsov Ridge, is entitled *Valley of the Shadow of Death*. This image is the first shown in Chapter 11.

Simpson painted the same scene photographed by Roberston/Beato and his watercolour was also called the *Valley of the Shadow of Death* with the subtitle *Caves in the Woronzoff Road, behind the Twenty-One Gun Battery.*

The Locations of the Two Valleys of the Shadow of Death
The position selected by Fenton for his photograph involves a long walk from the line of the 1st Parallel of the British Left Attack. Cars can be left along the straight road seen cutting across the Green Hill Ridge at the top left corner of the aerial image. Those with a hire car they don't mind mistreating could try driving nearer to the spot in low gear over the rough, stony track. However, this is not advised and certainly not during wet weather. An alternative would be to walk over the grasslands from the Robertson/Beato site.

Access to Robertson/Beato's position, which is also the same location where Simpson sketched the basis for his watercolour, is easier. The straight road that cuts obliquely across the above image from the lower right to the upper centre is a busy four-lane highway that carries traffic from Yalta and Simferopol northwest into Sevastopol along the Vorontsov Ridge. A large arch across this highway commemorates the bicentennial anniversary of the founding of Sevastopol and is major landmark useful for orientation. One can park off the highway on the dirt side streets seen at upper centre and then walk down the steep slope of the ravine to where the photograph was taken.

However, this approach is only recommended for those who are fit and have a good sense of balance. The alternative and best route for those with a hire car would be to drive along the road that today runs up the Vorontsov Ravine. This starts at a right turn just past the armoured train display on the road running east at the head of the South Harbour. There is a small pull-off at the bend to the immediate southeast of where the Robertson-Beato photograph was taken (see aerial image). The road at this point is one-way out of Sevastopol. Caution needs to be taken as traffic usually moves quickly along this twisting thoroughfare.

The Fall of Sevastopol Until the End of Occupation

14

At 18.00 hours on 8 September 1855, Prince Gorchakov realised that the French, who now possessed the Malakhov Bastion, were there to stay and reluctantly ordered the evacuation of the Sevastopol. He knew that Allied guns on Malakhov Hill would soon be able to fire on the defences on the southern and eastern sides of the city and make it impossible to maintain a perimeter. The retreat from the south side to the north side of Sevastopol's roadstead had been well planned and proceeded in an orderly manner. As well as crossing the pontoon bridge, steamers and barges ferried the garrison and other of the city's inhabitants to safety. Key buildings and batteries were set on fire and magazines exploded. Several ships were also sunk. The Russians feared that they might be pursued and harassed during their departure, but only the occasional missile was directed at the pontoon bridge or the city. After the rear guard and last stragglers were across the roadstead, the temporary bridge was pulled over to the north side. The Russians soon began to redeploy and increase the fortifications for the defence of the Severnaya.

William Russell reported that at 00.30 hours on 9 September, the soldiers on duty in the trenches became aware of the unusual quietness of the Redan and volunteers crept inside to reconnoitre. The dead, dying and wounded were the sole occupants and nothing could be heard but the groans of the wounded. Fearing mines, they retired back to their lines. At 02.00 hours fires were seen to break out in various parts of the city and spread to the principal buildings. A violent explosion at the back of the Redan rocked the area at 04.00 hours followed by four others elsewhere. The magazines at the Flagstaff and Garden batteries blew-up at 04.45 hours with those at the Quarantine and Alexander sea-forts following at 05.30 hours. The air was filled with bursting shells emanating from these exploding strongpoints. Fort Paul was noticed to have been on fire at 07.10 hours with the pontoon bridge being disconnected from the south shore at 07.15 hours. A minute later Fort Nicholas was observed in flames and at 09.00 hours fresh explosions were heard in front of the French positions.

The first groups of Allied soldiers entered Sevastopol early on 9 September and found the streets deserted. The fires continued for a few days with the occasional explosion adding to the danger. The French and Turks began to plunder the buildings, but many British were held back by sentries and the cavalry. Those that entered found the Russian hospitals full of the dead and wounded, the latter left in appalling conditions. The Redan and Malakhov Bastions also become macabre attractions and the task of clearing way the bodies commenced. The Allies marvelled at Sevastopol's fortifications and contemplated how cleverly the well-thought-out Russian defences had held them in check for almost a year.

Mary Seacole visited Sevastopol on the first day after extracting a pass from Major General Robert Garrett of the 4th Division for herself and some companions so she could supply refreshments to officers and soldiers in the Redan and the city. She wrote in her autobiography:

Many parts of it (Sevastopol) were still blazing furiously – explosions were taking place in all directions – every step had a score of dangers, and yet curiosity and excitement carried us on and on. I was often stopped to give refreshments to officers and men, who had been fasting for hours. Some, on the other hand, had found their way to Russian cellars; and one body of men were gloriously drunk, and playing the wildest pranks. They were dancing, yelling, and singing – some of them with Russian women's dresses fastened around their waists, and old bonnets stuck upon their heads … . I was offered many trophies … . It was very hazardous to pass along some of the streets exposed to the fire of the Russians on the north side of the harbour. We had to wait and watch our opportunity, and then gallop for it. Some of us had close shaves of being hit. More than this, fires were still breaking out around, while mines and fougasses not unfrequently exploded from unknown causes. We saw two officers emerge from a heap of ruins covered and almost blinded with smoke and dust, from such unlooked-for explosion.

Mary entered the city again the next day and visited a hospital. She reported:

The very recollection of that woeful hospital, where thousands of dead and dying had been left by the retreating Russians, is enough to unnerve the strongest and sicken the most experienced. I would give much if I had never seen that harrowing sight. I believe some Englishmen were found alive in it; but it is well that they did not live to tell of their fearful experience.

Fanny Duberly also reports in her journal that she had heard of a wounded soldier of the 90th Regiment being found naked, yelling and mad under a pile of dead men in a hospital, where he had been placed by the Russians to die of hunger, fever and pain. This man had not had food for three days and died on the floor before his rescuers.

Fanny was not able to obtain a permit to enter Sevastopol until 13 September when she rode to the Redan and then into the city with her husband Henry. They cantered across the open space before the bastion and galloped up and over the steep parapet. Henry told her to look down at the partly-filled ditch where men who had died in the assault were buried. She was moved and wrote in her journal that 'the frowning battery was their grave and solemn monument'. Fanny described the Redan as follows:

What wonderful engineering! What ingenuity in the thick rope-work which is woven before the guns, leaving only a little hole through which the man laying the gun can take his aim, and which is impervious to rifle shot! The Redan is a succession of little batteries, each containing two or three guns, with traverses behind each division; and hidden away under gabions, sand-bags, and earth, are little huts in which officers and men used to live. Walking down amongst these (for we were obliged to dismount) we found that tradesmen had lived in some of them. Henry picked up a pair of lady's lasts the precise size of my own feet. Coats, caps, bayonets lay about, with black bread and broken guns. The centre, the open space between the Redan and the second line of defence, was completely ploughed by our thirteen-inch shells, fragments of which, together with round shot, quite paved the ground. We collected a few relics, such as I could stow away in my habit and saddle-pockets, and then rode down into the town.

Once in Sevastopol, Fanny was ecstatic:

Actually in Sevastopol! No longer looking at it through a glass … but riding amongst its ruins and its streets. We had fancied the town was almost uninjured – so calm, and white, and fair did it look from a distance, but the ruined walls, the riddled roofs, the green cupola of the church, split and splintered to ribands, told a very different tale.

After finding three Russian corpses, one of which was sitting with his hands in his lap as if looking at them, Fanny and Henry rode to the quay-side and saw the mastheads of sunken ships. Riding around the head of the dry docks they experienced a putrid and nauseating odour and soon afterwards find a pile of decomposing human bodies that had been flung into the street prior to burial. Moving on to the Little Redan, she described how the ground was covered with half-dried pools of blood, caps soaked in blood and brains, broken

Opposite top: Simpson's watercolour entitled *The Redan, and Advanced Trenches of the British Right Attack* shows the view north over the Vorontsov Ravine from the British Left Attack on the morning of 9 September 1855. Sevastopol is burning and Fort Alexander on the shore of the roadstead is exploding in the distance on the far left. The Redan, with a British flag, stands near the end of the Vorontsov Ridge to the left of centre. The line of the 5th Parallel runs across the ridge between the Redan and the white scar of the Quarries shown to the right of centre. There is a depression to the right of the Quarries, with the area of Egerton's pit on the opposite upward slope. The 3rd Parallel is the furthest trench line to the right crossing over the ridge. The hill beyond the depression at the centre right is the Malakhov. In the foreground, reliefs are returning to camp with prisoners. A rifle pit is to the right of the head of this column. (DeGolyer Library, Southern Methodist University).

Opopsite: The same view today was taken looking north from near the line of the 1st Parallel on the British Left Attack on Green Hill Ridge. As in Simpson's watercolour, the Vorontsov Ravine is the main feature with the Vorontsov Ridge beyond. The city of Sevastopol is in the distance on the far left with the Black Sea behind on the horizon. The Redan was located in the trees on the skyline to the immediate right of centre. The site of the Quarries was above the wooded side ravine seen descending into the Vorontsov Ravine on the right. A barrier was constructed across the floor of the ravine at this point to deter the Russians from making incursions through British lines.

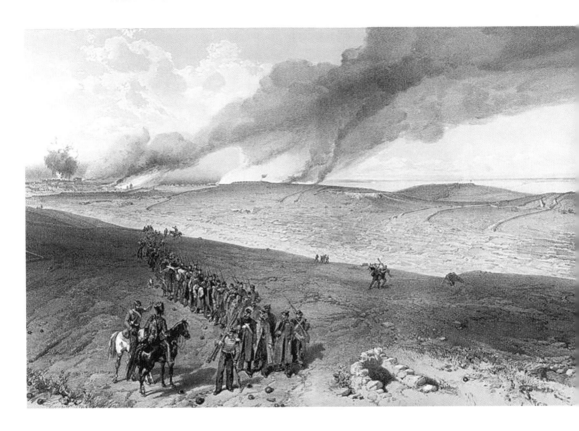

bayonets, shot and shell and four or five dead horses killed as they were bringing up ammunition for the last defence of the Malakhov. Fanny was very impressed with the design and construction of the Malakhov Bastion with its underground quarters and mess room. After again picking-up souvenirs, such as buttons, grape-shot, cards, a glass saltcellar and a screw from a gun, they made their way back to the cavalry camp.

Russell visited Russian bastions very soon after the fall of the city and wrote of the scenes of devastation. He described corpses in the ditch before the Malakhov as 'piled over each other in horrid confusion' with the ground on the right towards the Little Redan 'strewn with the bodies as thick as they could lie'. In the Malakhov, Russell found dead Russians lying 'in heaps like carcasses in a butcher's cart'. At the Redan, he saw the ditch 'piled up with English dead, some of them scorched and blackened by explosions and others lacerated beyond recognition'. He found a music book in a bomb-proof shelter with a canary and a vase of flowers outside.

Life after the Siege

Fort Paul was the only fortress completely destroyed in Sevastopol by the Russians. The others had been burnt in fires but their walls still stood even after their magazines had detonated. Work soon stared to construct new batteries facing the Russians across the roadstead. One British position was to the right of Fort Paul about 700 yards from Fort Catherine on the opposite side. The French erected a mortar battery behind Fort Nicholas to shell Russian working parties on the north shore. In the weeks after Sevastopol had fallen, Russell reported 'the silence in camp to be almost alarming' with little noise apart from the occasional exchange of shots across the roadstead However, with the construction of more batteries by the Russians and the Allies, this state of affairs did not last long.

A Commission was set up to divide the spoils of Sevastopol, such as artillery pieces, evenly between the Allies on the basis of respective troop numbers. Old batteries facing the Malakhov and Redan were disarmed and the men of the Naval Brigade were sent to rejoin their ships. Meanwhile improvements were made to transport corridors to and from Balaklava. A new all-weather road parallel to the military railway was being constructed to the camps by the Army Works Corp aided by soldiers. Locomotives to pull wagons on parts

Opposite top: Simpson's watercolour entitled *The Interior of the Redan, taken from the left face, looking towards the salient angle looking South*, shows the scene inside the bastion after its occupation by the British. On the left a rope mantelet designed to protect gunners from rifle fire hangs over an embrasure. Gabions, which were wicker cylinders filled with earth used for strengthening, can be seen lining parapets and traverses. Traverses were earth mounds designed to shield gunners from shells exploding in the Redan. In the middle distance on the left, a group of men approach the Redan across the open ground where the assaults took place on 18 June and 8 September 1855. (Library of Congress, Washington).

Opposite bottom: The scene today looking north from the angle of the salient along the low wall that marks the position of the parapet of the left face of the Redan. This image is the reverse view of that shown in Simpson's watercolour. The obelisk with an eagle on top is a Russian monument commemorating the valiant defence of the Redan.

of the railway instead of horses were expected to arrive soon. Construction was started on a branch line from Kadikoi to a depot under the Causeway Heights near No. 2 Redoubt to supply the Sardinian camp near Kamara. Even another line from the Col de Balaklava to the port of Kamiesch was under consideration though this never eventuated.

Fanny Duberly reported that Balaklava 'was no longer a heap of dirty lazar houses, infested with vermin, and reeking with every kind of filth', and its principal street 'was no longer crowded with ragged starving soldiers hauling along dying horses by the head, and making the horses echo back their curses and blows until one's heart grew cold'. Instead, she described the town 'as washed, dressed and fed' and 'fresh, healthy and even pretty'. Remarkably, rows of trees had been planted, roads raised and railings erected. In addition, the shallow water at the head of the harbour and the swampy ground beyond was reclaimed and the stream from Kadikoi to the harbour, which before had overflowed, now ran between high banks. Fanny put this down to Russell's indignant and influential articles for change published in *The Times* finally having some effect. Certainly, the Sanitary Commission had done much to improve conditions.

Russell himself had the following to say about Balaklava:

> Balakalava has ceased to exist. There are only some dozen of the original houses left scattered here and there amid iron storehouses, mountainous piles of wood, heaps of coal, of corn, of forage, of shot and shell, and of stores multitudinous. The harbour is trenched upon by new quays and landing places, and two long jetties project far into the waters at the shallow head of the harbour, and render good service in taking the pressure of the quays at the waterside.

French troops from the trenches had been relocated to the Baidar Valley and an expedition into the interior was rumoured, but nothing eventuated. The Russians still held the passes from the Black Sea coast through the mountains to the interior. The weather began to deteriorate and it was not expected that anything further would be attempted against the enemy until next spring. Supplies were increased so as to avoid the shortages and hardships that had been endured during the previous winter. Lessons had been learnt and the organisation within the army was improving. The construction of huts for the army was

Opposite top: A Robertson/Beato image entitled *Breach in the Redan* showing the angle of the salient where British troops entered the bastion and gained a foothold before being repulsed by the Russians on 8 September 1855. Men can be seen standing on the parapet to the right of the breach near where two flags fly. According to Simpson's watercolour showing the Redan, the smaller flag would have been a Union Jack and the larger one a White Ensign. The Vorontsov Ridge is on the skyline in the centre. (Royal Collection Trust/© Her Majesty Queen Elizabeth II, 2016).

Opposite bottom: Today's view looking south-southeast from the interior of the Redan towards the low wall that follows the line of the bastion's parapet. The angle of the salient is on the left where there is a gap in the wall. The apartment buildings in the distance on the far left are on the Vorontsov Ridge just behind the line of the 2nd Parallel on the British Right Attack.

Above and opposite: Two images by Robertson/Beato, both of which are entitled *Interior of the Redan,* form a panorama showing the devastation caused by the final bombardment. Wicker gabions are evident in the foreground and along the parapet wall. A rope mantelet still hangs in front of the embrasure on the left. (© Manuscripts and Special Collections, University of Nottingham).

a big priority. Sappers and miners began sinking deep mines that would destroy the dry docks, and soldiers on the quays burnt old Russian supplies. There was time to celebrate the first anniversary of the great victory on the Alma with many regiments holding 'Alma dinners'.

The Russians showed no sign that they would leave the Severnaya area north of the roadstead. They relocated a large magazine on the water's edge further inland probably because the old building had been a target of French mortars at Fort Nicholas. Another battery was constructed by the French between Fort Nicholas and the ruins of Fort Alexander to fire on Fort Constantine.

Mary Seacole recalled that there were cricket matches, picnics, parties, horse races and theatricals during this period. She wrote that her restaurant was always full and 'merry laughter was heard at many a dinner party held beneath the iron roof of the British Hotel'.

Military Excursions from Eupatoria

Soon after the fall of Sevastopol in September 1855, a French force consisting of 2,000 light cavalry commanded by General Armand d'Allonville and a number of infantry battalions were sent by ship from Kamiesch to assist 30,000 Turks under Ahmed Pasha operating in

the neighbourhood of Eupatoria. D'Allonville had led the brigade of Chasseurs d'Afrique as commandant at the Battle of Balaklava and, with the 4th Regiment, he had driven off the Russians that had fired on the Light Brigade from the Fedioukine Hills with two half-batteries. On 29 September, d'Allonville and three cavalry regiments were near the town of Sak, which was close to Lake Tuzla and not far from the beach where the British had landed just over a year ago. Aided by fire from Allied steamships off the coast, his force attacked eighteen squadrons of Russian cavalry supported by Cossacks. A hundred prisoners were taken together with six guns, fourteen wagons plus 2,000 horses and camels.

In early October, Pélissier requested that the British provide some cavalry to help carry out further reconnaissance missions to determine the strength of the enemy in the arid and desolate countryside around Eupatoria The 4th Dragoon Guards, the 6th Dragoon Guards, the 12th Lancers and the 13th Light Dragoons together with C Troop of Royal Horse Artillery under the command of Brigadier General Lord George Paget reached the port on 14 October with disembarkation complete by 20 October. They camped on the beach to the right of the town.

Their first expedition with the French and Turks left Eupatoria on 22 October returning on 24 October. The village of Karagut and the town of Sak were destroyed during this sortie. Russian cavalry encountered retreated before the Allies after being fired upon. The next expedition left on 27 October and returned on 29 October. On the first day, the Allies advanced rapidly after the Russian cavalry for four miles near Sak in an effort to get them to show their numbers and disposition plus unmask their guns. During this action, C Troop commanded by Captain Henry Thomas bravely advanced through an area ranged by heavier Russian guns to a position suitable for its three lighter field guns. The fire from C Troops guns was very effective, though this was not fully appreciated until Russians

A panorama formed from the merger of two images by Shaw-Lefevre entitled *The Glacis of the Redan from the Curtain of the Malakoff, shewing the ground over which the British Troops had to advance, on Sept 8th.* The view is to the southwest from the Russian defence line near the Gervais Battery and looks over the Middle Ravine towards the Vorontsov Ridge carrying the Redan, the earthworks of which are visible on the skyline left of centre. British troops advanced across the open ground on the skyline to the left of the Redan during assaults. (© Manuscripts and Special Collections, University of Nottingham).

The same scene today from the location of the Gervais Battery The low wall in the foreground follows the old defence perimeter. The Redan was located behind the apartment building seen on the centre skyline.

commented on the affair after the armistice. The Allies lost about thirty men killed or wounded as a result of cavalry clashes and artillery fire. They later retired to the neighbourhood of Sak for the night followed by the Russian cavalry. After a three-hour march inland the next day, a force of Russian cavalry twice as large as the Allies was encountered, but no action ensued. Just before noon, the Allied cavalry retired back to Sak shadowed again by Russian cavalry.

Squadrons of the British cavalry participated in an additional four one-day sorties in November. One on 2 November captured enemy cattle while another on 16 November brought in firewood. The British cavalry and C Troop embarked from Eupatoria for winter quarters at Scutari on the Bosphorus between the end of November and early December.

The Expedition to Kinburn

The British government wanted more to be done to humble Russia. The capture of Sevastopol now wasn't enough. Sir James Simpson was not seen back home in Britain as the man capable of undertaking what was required. He seemed more interested in making sure that the British army did not suffer as it had done in the winter of 1855-56 than to embark on another major campaign in the Crimea, such as driving the Russians from the north side of the Sevastopol Roadstead. Simpson tried to answer his critics, but pressure was mounting on him to do something and he did nothing.

France likewise would have liked more glory, but was aware of that the cost in terms of human lives had so far been high. The capture of Sevastopol and the destruction of its naval facilities had always been the main objective and this was now almost a reality. As a negotiated peace was in the offering, wouldn't it be wise to await its outcome? Pélissier was not particularly inclined to any more adventures because of public opinion in France was not in favour of further bloodshed.

The political pressure on Simpson eventually became too much and he resigned as Commander-in-Chief. Lord Panmure, the Secretary of State for War, accepted Simpson's resignation on 1 October 1855. Lieutenant General Sir William Codrington, the ditherer at the Redan, was chosen as his successor. This led to Lieutenant General Sir Colin Campbell, who had a better claim to the position, returning home in November in a huff.

While all this had been going on, the Allies, encouraged by their navies, decided to inflict some more damage on the Russians, but not on the garrison across the roadstead or the army in the hinterland of the Crimea. The targets were to be the two forts guarding Dnieper Bay into which the Bug and Dnieper rivers emptied and it was to be primarily a naval operation. The object was to deny the Russians access to the Black Sea from their important naval and warship building base of Nicolaev on the River Bug.

The Allied fleet under Rear Admiral Lyons and Vice Admiral Bruat consisted of six battleships with 583 guns, steam frigates, sloops, gunboats, mortar vessels, floating batteries and rocket boats. British ships carried 3,340 men of the 17th (Leicestershire), 20th (East Devonshire), 21st (Royal North British Fusiliers), 57th (West Middlesex) and 63rd (West Sussex) regiments plus 1,350 men of the Royal Marine Light Infantry, who had long been in camp on the 'Marine Heights' defending Balaklava. French ships carried 6,000 troops. The total contingent amounting to over 10,000 men was under the overall command of General François Bazaine.

The expedition sailed on 7 October 1855 arriving off Odessa, which was thirty-eight miles west of the main objective, the next day. The fleet caused much alarm to the

The Robertson/Beato image entitled **Tower of the Malakoff**, taken looking from the north. The French attack came up the slope of the hill on the far side of the tower. The French have constructed a hut and a semaphore alongside a flag pole on the ruins of the tower. A traverse strengthened with wicker gabions can be seen in the foreground. (Royal Collection Trust/© Her Majesty Queen Elizabeth II, 2016)

The Malakhov Tower, which is a major tourist attraction, as it looks today after restoration. The interior can be inspected for the cost of a small entrance fee.

inhabitants of Odessa, who thought that there would be a bombardment that would destroy their city. However, the Allied plan was to divert attention from the true objective and encourage the Russians to send troops to the aid of the city.

The armada remained anchored five miles off Odessa for five days delayed by fog and then a stiff breeze. During this time the Russians improved the fortifications of the city. Calm weather was necessary to ensure the success of the mission and, when this came, the fleet sailed for the fort of Kinburn, which was positioned on a spit that protruded northwest into the mouth of Dnieper Bay. The Allied ships anchored three miles from Fort Kinburn at 15.00 hours on 14 October. During the night, several French and British vessels forced the passage between the end of the spit and the fort at Oczakov on the opposite shore and entered Dnieper Bay.

The next morning, troops were landed about four miles below Fort Kinburn entrenching themselves on the spit while gun- and mortar-boats bombarded the strong point for three hours. On the 16 October, the works on the spit were continued so that one defence line faced the fort and another the mainland at the end of the spit. The Russians in the fort were now cut off by land from any reinforcements. The bombardment continued in the afternoon with the Russian batteries returning the fire though Russell reported that 'no apparent effect was produced by either side'.

Kinburn fell on 17 October after a short and desperate defence. Russell described the inevitable surrender:

> The storm of shot from this great ordnance is appalling. The very earth seems to be flying into dust and the fiery embers of the fort are thrown into columns of sparks. Still the Russians stand to the only guns they have left. The broadsides increase in vigour, and at last a white flag is waved by a single man from the rampart. Boats with flags of truce push off, and bring back the information that the garrison is willing to surrender. At 2.00 pm, the firing ceases and 1100 men march into our lines. Several of these are quite drunk; they carried off food and drink and the officers wore side-arms.

The North and Centre Spit batteries further along the spit from Fort Kinburn did not surrender immediately. Fire continued from one gun until its casemate was destroyed by shots from HMS *Terrible*. The attack was notable in that it was the first occasion that ironclads had ever been used in war. These were the French floating batteries the *Dévastation*, *Lave* and *Tonnante* that had arrived too late to participate in the siege of Sevastopol. They fired 3,000 rounds between them and, although receiving ninety-seven impacts on their iron sides, suffered no damage in this area. Russell described the Russian round shot bouncing off their sides and splashing in the water leaving no impression other than a slight dent. Their participation in the attack after being towed to positions about 800 yards offshore was deemed to have been a huge success.

The Russians lost forty-five killed and 130 wounded from their garrison of 1,400 men and, although some wanted to fight on, the Governor's reason prevailed and it was agreed that they should lay down their arms as the situation was hopeless. The Allies lost two dead and thirty-two wounded. The two killed and twenty-one of the wounded were members of the crews of the French floating batteries hit elsewhere other than their iron cladding.

The Russians evacuated and then blew-up the magazine at Fort Nicolaev at Ochokov on the opposite shore of the estuary the next day. However, this strongpoint was not occupied as was Fort Kinburn, because of difficulties of defence from the landward side. On 20 October, British gunboats and a survey vessel entered the Bug and met some French boats descending after going someway upstream and seeing nothing of interest. The British decided to look for themselves. The banks were found to be high and suitable for defence. Guard stations and look-out posts were seen here and there. The flotilla was shot at by a Russian battery on a cliff and after an exchange of fire the boats turned around to return to the estuary. The port of Nicolaev was further to the north, but considered too dangerous to approach. The next day, French boats went up the Bug and fired on the same battery. On 22 October, the settlement of Stanislav east of the moth of the Bug was reconnoitred as a strong body of infantry with field guns to its rear and a newly constructed battery on a spit was observed. Nothing much else was attempted or achieved.

Fort Kinburn was repaired enough to protect and support a mainly French garrison and ships' guns were hauled into place to replace those destroyed. Troops marched down the spit to lay waste to the country so as to deprive any attacking Russian land force of supplies. They brought back poultry, geese and pigs. The two outlying batteries on the spit were eventually destroyed. When the fleet sailed back to Sevastopol, enough soldiers were left to hold the fort and enough Allied ships to deter any enemy attack by sea or land. The area was held until June 1856.

Explosion at the French Siege Train

On 15 November 1855, a large explosion took place in a magazine of the French Siege Train, which was close to the British Right Siege Train, on the Chersonese Plateau. The blast was so great that pieces of debris and shells were flung far and wide. A stone was reputed to have hit the door of Mary Seacole's 'British Hotel' which was almost four miles away. As well as killing French soldiers, the explosion also caused deaths in the British Light Division and the British Right Siege Train.

A windmill, which was a landmark amongst the sea of tents in the camps east of the Vorontsov Road, was close to the explosion. The windmill itself was used to store 180 tons of gun powder and a fierce fire raged within 200 yards of the structure after the explosion. Brigadier General Charles van Straubenzee, commander of the 1st Brigade of the Light

Opposite top: An image by Robertson/Beato entitled *Magazine in the Malakoff* showing the interior of the bastion with magazines reinforced with gabions and topped with earth. The French storming party would have fought fiercely in this area for the control of Malakhov Hill. The semaphore and flag pole erected on top of the ruins of the Malakhov Tower by the French after its capture are on the right skyline. The Mamelon is the low flat-topped hill in the middle distance on the left with defensive earthworks running along its crest. The Vorontsov Ridge is on the skyline just left of the centre. (Royal Collection Trust/© Her Majesty Queen Elizabeth II, 2016).

Opposite bottom: The area of the Malakhov Hill immediately behind the tower is parkland today with a major walkway leading down a gentle slope towards its northern end where it overlooks the Karbelnaya district.

The Robertson/Beato image entitled *Interior of the Malakoff*, shows a Russian battery strengthened with gabions and sandbags. The Mamelon is seen on the left skyline with a battery stretching along its flat summit and another battery with eight embrasures dug in lower down the slope. Shaw-Lefevre took an almost identical picture entitled *Interior of the Malakoff – Guns flanking the Little Redan*, but without the Mamelon in the background. The location of both images was a few yards northeast of the Malakhov Tower. (Royal Collection Trust/© Her Majesty Queen Elizabeth II, 2016).

Guns in battery in the area to the immediate northeast of the Malakhov Tower today. Views from this location towards the Mamelon are now obstructed by mature trees that cover the Malakhov hillside to the southeast.

Simpson's watercolour entitled *Ditch at the Malakoff, Gervais Battery, and rear of the Redan* looks west from close to the Malakhov Tower and shows the captured defences in this area of the Malakhov Hill. The Gervais Battery is lower down the slope on the left and to the right of a horse and rider. The Redan is visible on the crest of the Vorontsov Ridge above the Gervais Battery. Sevastopol is in the distance on the right. The Great Barracks are below the city on the far right with the hospital to its left. (Library of Congress, Washington).

The view today to the west from close to the Malakhov Tower, showing the parapet sketched by Simpson as it looks today. The ditch would have been on the left. The land descends towards the location of the Gervais Battery beyond the trees in the background.

Right: A portrait of Mary Seacole taken after the Crimean War. (Public domain work of art).

Opposite top: Simpson's watercolour entitled *Ditch of the Bastion du Mât* shows the southwest face of the battery at the Flagstaff Bastion after its occupation by French troops following the fall of Sevastopol. The ditch was twice the ordinary width and flanked at its far end by a bomb-proof block-house containing two guns, which could enfilade any attacking troops. An entrance to a mine or underground passage propped by timbers can be seen on the left side of the ditch. Many mines were dug from the ditch to connect with outlying rifle pits or their ends packed with explosives to blow-up advanced French trenches. The Central Bastion is in the distance on the left. (Library of Congress, Washington).

Opposite bottom: The ditch before the southwest face of the Flagstaff bastion as it appears today. The entrances to old underground mines can be seen on the left side of the ditch. A monument to Leo Tolstoy, who served in the Flagstaff Bastion for a time during the Crimean War, is found in the interior of the bastion to the northeast. A reconstructed battery complete with guns occupies the southeast face of this strong defensive position that was never taken by force by the French.

Division hurried to the tents of the 7th (Royal Fusiliers) Regiment. Here he called for volunteers to climb the wall of the mill and cover the roof, which had been blown away, with wet tarpaulins and blankets as a protection against flying sparks and burning wood. Lieutenant William Hope and twenty-five men responded to the appeal of their brigadier together with a sergeant and some men from the 34th (Cumberland) Regiment. Within ten minutes of the explosion, Lieutenant Hope and others were piling wet blankets over the exposed gunpowder boxes despite the air being filled with exploding shells and burning debris. Others carried water to soak the blankets into the mill. In half an hour, the situation had been saved.

The Winter of 1855-56
The differences of opinion as regards policy on the future course of the war between Britain and France became more pronounced with Britain wishing to continue while France preferred a peace settlement. Many in Britain, did not regard the capture of Sevastopol

and Fort Kinburn as a fitting end of the conflict. However, with the winter closing in, nothing more could be done to pursue the war until the following spring.

Much had been learnt since the awful winter of 1854-55 when the British army suffered so much. This time, they were much better prepared than the French, who were not as badly affected as the British during the first winter and consequently were in a better position in the spring of 1855 to push forward the siege agenda. The second winter was weathered by the British much better than the first. The troops that were fresh when sent to attack the Redan had now been drilled and discipline had improved. Morale was high and the health of the army was good. Most were keen to start the offensive again when the weather permitted. However, cholera and dysentery were rife in the French camps. Many succumbed to illness with an estimated 40,000 dying of disease. As a consequence, when spring came they were not strong enough to be an active partner in any planned action against the Russians in the Crimea. In addition, it would require a major effort to dislodge the Russian army from its secure positions on the Mackenzie Heights.

Russia had been overly optimistic that it could reverse the situation in the Crimea, especially after the fall of the Turkish fortress at Kars on 26 November 1855. However, after the Austrians delivered a five-point ultimatum a few days after Chritmas in 1855, it came under pressure to accept peace terms. The first point was to give up the protectorates of Wallachia, Moldavia and Serbia, the second to remove all obstructions to free navigation on the Danube, the third to allow free trade on the Black Sea and the fourth was to relinquish claims as a protectorate over the Orthodox peoples of the Ottoman Empire. Austria threatened to enter the a war on the side of the Allies if these conditions were not met. This in effect meant that Prussia would also no longer sit on the fence and also join the Allies.The Russians knew that they could not really afford to continue the war as it was a drain on resiurces, both financially and militarially. They accepted the terms after internal debate, and a protocol was signed by most warring parties in Vienna on 1 February 1856. A peace conference began in Paris on 25 February 1856 and an armistice lasting until 31 March agreed to on 28 February. A peace treaty was signed on 30 March 1856. Kars was to be given back to Turkey while the capturted areas of the Crimea were to be handed back to Russia. It also stipultaed that neither Turkey nor Russia could maintain a military arsenal or naval dockyard along the shores of the Black Sea.

After the New Year, all the talk in the British camps was of going home. Even before the armistice, firing across the roadstead slowed and finally ceased. Mary Seacole advised that the Russians and Allies made overtures of friendship from either side of the Chernaya River. She herself went to the river's banks and exchanged some coins for 'a little metal figure of some ugly patron saint' and some white bread.

Work had been progressing on preparing the dry docks in Sevastopol for destruction and these were finally blown-up along with Fort Nicholas and Fort Alexander in early February 1856. There was a major review of 25,000 British troops from forty-six battalions on 24 February 1856, which was cold day with the wind blowing from the north. Codrington inspected a line of troops and Marshal Pélissier was also present. There was march past with many 'tattered and shot-rent banners' held aloft. Russell recalled that 'the colours of the 23rd Fusiliers were like a sieve, pierced by countless bullets, and telling the eloquent and bloody and elegant tale of the Alma and of Inkerman'. Some were even worse and could not be unfurled.

Mary Seacole's establishment, which was known to her as the 'British Hotel', served as a sutlers' store and restaurant, but did not provide accommodation and was never a hospital. It was located at Spring Hill on the land in the foreground to the left of the today's main road from Balaklava to the Col de Balaklava.

Soon afterwards, it became known that the war was coming to an end. At 08.00 hours on 28 February 1856, a Russian boat with a flag of truce left the north shore of the roadstead and was met half halfway by a French boat. Arrangements were made for a military meeting the next day at the Tractir Bridge. Russell wrote 'As if to celebrate the armistice, the White Buildings were blown-up in the afternoon'. Unfortunately, Major George Rankin of the Royal Engineers, who had commanded the ladder party at the last attack on the Redan, was killed when he returned to investigate a mine that had failed to explode.

At 10.00 hours on 29 February 1856, a white flag was hoisted at the eastern end of the Tractir Bridge. Twenty five Cossacks rode up to just beyond the flag with Major General Timofeev, Chief of Staff of the 4th Corps of the Russian army, and his staff. A few minutes after 10.00 hours, Lieutenant General Barnard and some staff officers rode down the road through the valley in the Fedioukine Hills and crossed over the bridge. The details of the armistice were arranged in two blue- and white-striped tents erected in the rear of the bridge. General de Martimprey, Major General Windham, and Colonel Count Pettiti, who were Chiefs of Staff of the French, British and Sardinian armies respectively, were also present. Russell reports a sort of fraternisation between the French, Sardinian and British officers present on one hand and Russian officers on the other. Bartering took place for Cossack whips. Some reconnoitred the terrain beyond the bridge

More Allied officers arrived as the day advanced. Many rode on the soft springy turf on the far side of the river. Hares were chased. A party of gallopers even went as far as a Russian battery and smoked cigarettes with the enemy of the previous day. Later, British, French, Sardinian and Russian Generals rode over the Tractir Bridge between a double line

Sketch by E.A. Godsall entitled *The Explosion of the Right-Seige Train, near Inkerman Mill* that appered in ***The Illustrated London News*** on 15 Decamber 1855. The windmill, which served as landmark in the sea of tents on the Chersonese Plataeu, is depicted to the immediate left of the explosion.

formed by spectators and out into the valley beyond. Taking leave of the Russians, the Allied Generals returned to the bridge. More spectators were arriving having heard the news and sentries were posted to prevent anyone else crossing the river.

The two sides again met at the bridge on the afternoon of 14 March 1856 to sign the conditions of the armistice. Although the weather was cold, a considerable number of Allied officers had found their way to the location. However, there was no fraternisation this time or rides across the bridge into the Russian side of the valley. Allied officers and men journeyed to the Chernaya every day after this to stare or communicate with the Russians, examine the new race course that had been prepared near the river just to the north of the Fedioukine Hills and pursue the wild fowl.

After the war had ended, there was an opportunity for those who were curious to explore the hitherto inaccessible Crimean hinterland. Various trips were made to locations as far as Simferopol and Yalta. Mary Seacole travelled with a large party that was full of fun. Her companions tried to persuade Russians that she was Queen Victoria by paying her 'the most absurd reverence'. It was also possible for the Roberston/Beato team to visit and photograph the Russian forts on the northern side of the roadstead.

From the end of April 1856, the British regiments began to leave the Crimea one after another. Mary Seacole and her business partner found themselves with goods on their hands that they couldn't sell because of a lack of customers. Towards the end, they had to get rid of their stores at give-a-way prices, which contributed to their bankruptcy on their return to England. The 'British Hotel' was pulled down and packed up for conveyance home, but the Russians got the outhouses and sheds together with costly kitchen fittings and stoves. Prime cheeses costing ten pence a pound were sold a penny a pound. For wines costing forty-eight shillings a dozen she was bid four shillings. In her disgust and without any friends left to make gifts of the drink, Mary poured much away determined that 'the old foes' would not benefit.

Many made last pilgrimages to battlefields and graves. Russell rode to the Alma on two occasions to reminisce. Plans were made for the long-term survival of British graveyards around Sevastopol.

Mary Seacole recalls standing on Cathcart's Hill looking out over Sevastopol for one last time. A few days later she stood on a crowded steamer on her way home. The last British troops, which was a detachment of the 50th (Queen's Own) Regiment, left Balaklava on 12 July 1856 when the port was formally handed over to the Russians. Although most of the old round shot littering the region had been collected and taken away, the military railway was left behind intact. In a final touch of irony, the track was sold to the Turks by the Russians soon after the evacuation. Visiting Balaklava in 1857, an Englishman noted that the railway wharf was still recognisable as was the old Post Office, which was the subject of the first photograph taken by Fenton after his arrival in the Crimea March 1855. Few other buildings remained.

Epilogue

Published figures on the number of casualties during the Crimean War vary and, therefore, the statistics below are approximations only. From the information available it appears that out of just over 111,000 British troops men sent to the Crimea, 2,755 were killed in action, 2,019 died of wounds and a further 16,323 succumbed to disease giving a total of over 21,000 dead. It has been estimated that out of 300,000 French troops sent to fight, about 95,000 died in the Crimea with 8,500 being killed in action, 11,750 dying of wounds and 75,400 dying of disease. The Sardinians contributed 15,000 men with 2,050 dying in action or through disease. The Turks, who also fought the Russians on the Danube, lost 19,100 in action, 10,800 through wounds and 25,500 of disease giving a total of 45,400. By far the greatest loses in the war were suffered by Russia with a possible 30,600 dying in action, 42,000 of wounds and 374,000 of sickness. In total, Russian losses may have amounted to 446,600 out of a total of just over 2,000,000 eventually in the field.

The peace treaty signed in Paris in 1856 did not succeed to curbing Russia's expanion as it began to annex land between the Black and the Caspian Seas three years later. Although on the winning side, the Ottoman Empire continued to decline in power and prestige. Over half a million muslims expelled from the Caucasus were shipped to Turkey's Black Sea ports which caused financial problems and civil disorder. The Treaty of Paris was finally repudiated by Russia in 1870 when Europe was preoccupied by the war between France and Prussia. The Turkish goverement was bankrupted in 1875 and incresed taxes on unhappy populations in the Balkans. This led to nationalist uprisings which were bloodily suppressed by irregular Turkish troops. In 1876, some Balkan states dclared war on the Ottoman Empire and Russia came to their aid in 1877 after assurances from the Austrain-Hungarian Empire that it would remain neutral. Russian militray intervention helped the independenace claims of Bulgaria and others with a back-footed Turkey offering a truce. Under pressure from the British, Russia accepted the truce in 1878, but continued to move towards Constantinople. Britain then sent a fleet of battleships to intimidate Russia into not entering the city which led to a treaty that forced the Ottoman Empire to recognize the independence of Romania, Serbia, Montenegro, and the autonomy of Bulgaria. Thus, Russia reasserted its influence in the Black Sea region and grew more powerful. The Crimean War resulted in the inevitable being delayed for just twenty years.

The war brought about a recognition that the British army was in urgent need of reform. It also highlighted the failings of its supply system and the lack of men for essential non-military duties, such as road building. In addition, it led, through the efforts of Florence Nightingale, to improvements in nursing care.

15

Sevastopol City and the South Harbour
After the Siege

Those areas of Sevastopol within range of the Allied guns suffered considerable damage during the siege and this was compounded by the deliberate destruction wrought by the Russians as they abandoned the city after the capture of the Malakhov Bastion. The scene of devastation was documented by those who ventured into the streets of the city after its fall.

Robertson/Beato's image entitled *Sebastopol from the Left Attack* looks down on Artillery Bay in Sevastopol from the high ground to the southwest. Damaged suburban houses lie just beyond the open foreground. Fort Nicholas with its two tiers of casemates is in the middle distance to the right of the entrance to Artillery Bay. Fort Michael is visible on the left in the far distance on the opposite shore of the roadstead. This image would appear to be inappropriately named as the view is not from the British Left Attack nor even the French Left or Town Attack. The site of the Quarantine Bastion on the Russian defence line around Sevastopol is some distance behind the camera. This bastion would have overlooked part of the area to the west where the French besiegers would have had their trenches, but the image is not a view any French soldier would have had before the city fell.

Today, Artillery Bay, which is to the left of the tall apartment block with the red-roof just right of centre, is only glimpsed from roughly the same position. The north side of the roadstead is visible in the far distance, but the view to Fort Michael is blocked by tall buildings in the left middle distance.

Robertson/Beato's image entitled *Church of St Peter and St Paul* shows the church with the top half of a front column missing. This landmark was built between 1840 and 1844 on Central Hill in Sevastopol and styled on the ancient temple of Theseus in Athens. The church today looks very much as it did when the Robertson/Beato took their photograph except that the half column is now complete again.

Simpson's watercolour also entitled *Church of St Peter and St Paul* looks north past the church over the entrance to the South Harbour and across the roadstead. The Church of St Michel the Archangel and the clock tower entrance to the Admiralty are in the middle distance at centre and partly obscure Fort Nicholas. Fort Michael can be seen on the far side of the roadstead above Fort Nicholas. The view today that compliments Simpson's watercolour, looks towards the Church of St Peter and St Paul from the end of Tereschenenka Street. The road on the right still turns as it drops down the east side of Central Hill. End of last sentence deleted

The Church of St Peter and St Paul in the Robertson/Beato image appears to have a roof. However, Simpson depicted the same church without a roof in his watercolour. As the

The Robertson/Beato image entitled *Sebastopol from the Left Attack.* (Royal Collection Trust/© Her Majesty Queen Elizabeth II, 2016).

The modern view of Sevastopol from an equivalent position on the slope down into the city from behind the site of the Quarantine Bastion.

The Robertson/Beato image entitled *Church of St Peter and St Paul.* (Royal Collection Trust/© Her Majesty Queen Elizabeth II, 2016).

The Church of St Peter and St Paul on Sevastopol's Central Hill today.

Simpson's watercolour entitled **Church of St Peter and St Paul.** (Library of Congress, Washington).

The view today looking from Tereschenka Street towards the Church of St Peter and St Paul.

The Robertson/Beato image entitled *Theatre, Sebastopol.* (Royal Collection Trust/© Her Majesty Queen Elizabeth II, 2016).

Robertson/Beato's first image entitled *Street in Sebastopol.* (Royal Collection Trust/© Her Majesty Queen Elizabeth II, 2016).

The Robertson/Beato image entitled *The Library* showing the Temple of the Winds. (Royal Collection Trust/© Her Majesty Queen Elizabeth II, 2016).

Only the Temple of the Winds remains at the site of the Library today.

Above left: The Robertson/Beato image entitled _Russian Tomb in Sebastopol_.

Above Right: 'The Kazarsky monument as it looks today'. Note that this is not a 'tomb' as Robertson/Beato thought – it is just a monument.

roof was reported destroyed in a fire during the siege, this suggests that the Robertson/Beato photograph may not have been taken immediately after the siege ended.

The Robertson/Beato image entitled _Theatre, Sebastopol_ shows the St Peter and St Paul Church without a roof on Sevastopol's Central Hill at upper right. This indicates that this particular image was taken soon after the city fell. The ruined building in the left foreground, which is described as a theatre, was on the west side of hill near Catherine Street, which is now Lenina Street.

The image _Street in Sebastopol_, which was again taken by Robertson/Beato, shows what look like government buildings gutted by fires. These fires were probably lit by the Russians as they abandoned the city. The street most likely ran north-south on Central Hill.

Robertson/Beato's image entitled _The Library_ shows the ruins of the Public Library on Central Hill built for the use of naval and military officers by Czar Nicholas I. It was set on fire by the Russians the night they abandoned Sevastopol. Simpson painted a watercolour depicting its destruction. The only part of the building standing today is the Temple of the Winds, which is located 50 yards from St Vladimir's Cathedral.

The Robertson/Beato image entitled _Russian Tomb in Sebastopol_ suggests that the photographers believed the subject of their picture was above where someone was buried. However, it was a monument made in 1834-39 to commemorate the action of the _Mercury_ and its crew under the command of Captain Alexander Kazarsky.

325

The Robertson/Beato image entitled **Church and Clocktower.** (Royal Collection Trust/© Her Majesty Queen Elizabeth II, 2016).

The site of the clocktower today is occupied by the Museum of the Black Sea Fleet.

The brig *Mercury*, which was designed for patrol service along the Black Sea coast, was built in 1820. The vessel had a shallow draft worsening its manoeuvrability and was armed with only twenty guns. On 14 May 1829, during the Russian-Turkish War of 1828-29, a Russian detachment of three ships, including the *Mercury*, ran into a Turkish squadron consisting of over ten vessels in the Black Sea off the Bosphorus. While the other two Russian ships were more agile and successfully fled the danger, *Mercury* was forced to face the Turks. Despite the superiority of the enemy, *Mercury* kept her flag flying and accepted battle. She managed to hold her own against two large Turkish warships - the 110-gun *Selimie* and 74-gun *Real-bei* – by damaging their rigging and masts. Finally, the Turks had to give up pursuit.

As the sound of guns from the south died away, the crews of the two other Russian ships, the *Standart* and the *Orfey*, which had escaped the battle, believed the *Mercury* had been sunk and lowered their flags to half-mast. In fact, only four of *Mercury*'s sailors were killed and six wounded. However, 133 holes were found in the sails and twenty-two breaches in the hull. The captain and crew were given a hero's welcome when they arrived back in Sevastopol.

The monument is situated at the top of a flight of steps that ascends the Central Hill in Sevastopol from Primorsky Boulevard near Nachimov Square. A garden lies behind the monument, which leads to today's Headquarters of the Black Sea Fleet.

Robertson/Beato's image entitled *Church and Clocktower* shows the church of St. Michael the Archangel on the left. The tower on the right, which was built in 1829, was the gateway to the Admiralty and carried an English clock. Both of these buildings were out of range of allied artillery and were not badly damaged during the siege. They stood on Catherine Street, which is now Lenina Street. The Museum of the Black Sea Fleet now stands on the site of the clock tower. The chapel, which can be seen in front of the church in the contemporary image, is the building with the green roof further down the street from the museum in today's view.

The Robertson/Beato image entitled *Maison Verte* shows the west-facing wall and the end south–facing wall of a girl's school on Central Hill guarded by French soldiers. Its name is derived from its green roof seen from afar by the Allies during the siege. The building today is located at the intersection of Serhjejeva-Tsens'koho and Suvorova Streets. It serves as government offices and now longer has its ornate spires. Trees surround the building making it difficult to reproduce the contemporary image in the summer months when foliage blocks the view of the facade.

A second Robertson/Beato's image entitled *Street in Sebastopol* shows the view north down the road seen on the far left in *Maison Verte*, which is now called Suvorova Street. Note that the side railings and pillars behind the sentry box on the right are identical to those in front of the west-facing wall of the building in *Maison Verte*.

A third Robertson/Beato image entitled *Street in Sebastopol* features buildings on either side of a grand thoroughfare that were either damaged during the siege or perhaps by fire as the Russians vacated the city. No indication is given of where this photograph was taken, but a glimpse of what is likely to be the ground on the north side of the roadstead as it descends towards Fort Constantine's promontory and other clues suggest that the view was to the north down what is today's Velyka Morska Street. This street is shown as it looks today. The slight dip in the road surface in the middle distance is believed to correspond with the dip seen in the image above. The modern building at

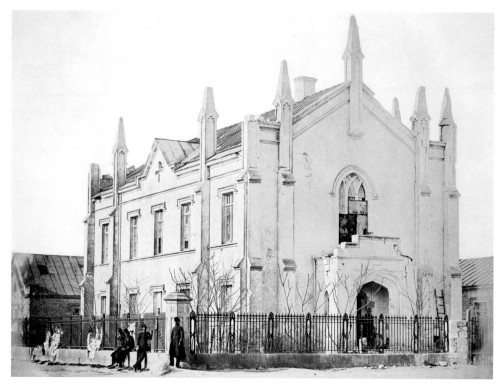

The Robertson/Beato image entitled *Maison Verte.* (Royal Collection Trust/© Her Majesty Queen Elizabeth II, 2016).

Robertson/Beato's second image entitled *Street in Sebastopol.* (Royal Collection Trust/© Her Majesty Queen Elizabeth II, 2016).

A third Robertson/Beato image entitled **Street in Sebastopol.** (Royal Collection Trust/© Her Majesty Queen Elizabeth II, 2016).

Velyka Morska Street in Sevastopol as it looks today.

Simpson's waterclour entitled entitled **Sebastopol from the rear of Fort Nicholas, looking South.** (Library of Congress, Washington).

Today's view was taken with the columned entrance to the Count's Quay on the left.

The Robertson/Beato image entitled *Sebastopol from the North.* (Royal Collection Trust/© Her Majesty Queen Elizabeth II, 2016).

the end of the street is on the western side of Artillery Bay and obstructs today's view over the roadstead.

Simpson's watercolour entitled *Sebastopol from the rear of Fort Nicholas, looking South* depicts the scene near the western entrance to the South Harbour after the siege. The Church of St Michael the Archangel with the entrance tower to the Admiralty to its immediate left are seen in the middle distance on the right with the church of St Peter and St Paul on the skyline a little further to the left. The Great Barracks with the Arsenal below are visible on the left across the South Harbour. The end of the Vorontsov Ridge that carried the Redan Bastion is on the skyline to its immediate right.

The actual location where Simpson made his preliminary sketch is now within a ferry terminal. Today's equivalent was taken with the columned entrance to Count's Quay, where steps lead down to the waterfront, on the left. This entrance to the quay-side was further away and seen on the right above the figure with the white baggy trousers in Simpson's watercolour.

South Harbour
The South Harbour, which was also called the Man-of-War Harbour or Dockyard Creek on some maps, is an inlet from the south side of Sevastopol's roadstead that separates the city from the district of Karabelnaya, It was overlooked by many of the principal buildings in the city of Sevastopol and by the Great Barracks and hospital, known collectively as the White Buildings, on the Karabelnaya side.

The Robertson/Beato image entitled *Sebastopol from the hut of the Russian General.* (Royal Collection Trust/© Her Majesty Queen Elizabeth II, 2016).

The modern view over the South Harbour from the slope behind the Redan.

The Robertson/Beato image entitled **Valley of the Cemetery**. (Royal Collection Trust/© Her Majesty Queen Elizabeth II, 2016).

Today's view towards the head of the South Harbour from the end of the Green Hill Ridge.

The Robertson/Beato image entitled _Military Harbour._ (Royal Collection Trust/© Her Majesty Queen Elizabeth II, 2016).

The view of the South Harbour today from near the site of Crow's Nest Battery.

The entrance to the harbour from the roadstead lay between Fort Nicholas on the city side and Fort Paul on the Karabelnaya side. Just to the east of this entrance is a side-inlet that led to the Karabelnaya dry docks. The harbour, which varies in width from 280 yards to 120 yards, extends inland in a southerly direction for almost one and a half miles and twists slightly to the west at its far end. The outer perimeter of fortifications protecting Sevastopol during the siege ran very close to the waters at the head of the South Harbour where there was an artillery position, known as the Creek, Strand or Peressip Battery. At its head, the land is flat and low-lying land with the Vorontsov Ravine exiting at its southeast corner and the Great or Picket House Ravine exiting from its southwest corner. To the south is the Green Hill Ridge, where the trenches and batteries of the British Left Attack were located in 1855.

Sevastopol within its defensive perimeter, consisting of the city proper to the west and the Karbelnaya district to the east, was virtually cut in half by the South Harbour. However, communications between the two sections was possible by means of a pontoon bridge, which left the Karabelnaya side close to the Great Barracks. This bridge was set adrift after Sevastopol was abandoned by the Russians.

Robertson/Beato's image entitled *Sebastopol from the North* looks south-southeast from Fort Paul on the end of the promontory that extended to the entrance of the South Harbour from the Karabelnaya side. Russian boats, one a paddle steamer, lie wrecked near the shore in the foreground with the mast of a larger sunken ship visible above the water further away at centre. The side-inlet that extended to the dry docks is on the left with the ruins of the Arsenal on the promontory beyond. Behind the piles of earth to the right of the Arsenal ruins, a road climbs up the high ground on the other side of the South Harbour to near a location known to the British as the Crow's Nest. A Russian battery at the end of this spur looked across the flat land at the head of the harbour to the Green Hill Ridge. The Central Hill of Sevastopol is on the right. The building with the dome just above the sailing ship on the extreme right was the church of St. Michael the Archangel. The Admiralty was to its left.

Robertson/Beato's image entitled *Sebastopol from the hut of the Russian General* looks to the northwest over the South Harbour from the slope behind the Redan. The buildings in the foreground have been destroyed by allied round shot overshooting the bastion. The pontoon bridge that connected both sides of the harbour can be seen in the middle distance with the city of Sevastopol on the left. Another picture, which is not shown here, was taken later by Robertson/Beato showing the same bridge adrift. The domed church of St. Michael the Archangel is on the top of the bluff just right of centre. To its left is the tower that formed the entrance to the Admiralty. Fort Nicholas is the long low building to its right with the north shore of the roadstead beyond.

A similar view over the South Harbour today was taken from a location further down the slope behind the Redan believed to have been just beyond the ruins seen at the centre in the Robertson/Beato image.

Robertson/Beato's image entitled *Valley of the Cemetery* looks northwest towards the head of the South Harbour from the end of Green Hill Ridge. The Vorontsov Road and the entrance to the Vorontsov Ravine and are on the right. The defence works shielding the Creek Battery run in a straight line across the head of the harbour. The road into the city of Sevastopol climbs the steep slope on the west side of the harbour in the distance to the right of centre. The title given to this image would not seem apt unless it refers to the

The Robertson/Beato image entitled **The Woronzoff Road from Sebastopol.** (©National Army Museum, London).

Looking towards the head of the South Harbour from near Sevastopol's Opera House today.

cemetery at the end of the Great Ravine captured by Major General Eyre's men on 18th June 1855, which is off the picture on the left.

The view today from the same location shows the entrance to the Vorontsov Ravine on the right. The waters at the end of the South Harbour can be glimpsed to the right of the tall poplars seen at centre.

The Robertson/Beato's image entitled *Military Harbour* looks north-northeast over on the head of the South Harbour from near the Crow's Nest Battery. Houses lie in ruins on the hillside. The line of defence works protecting the Creek Battery runs along the end of the harbour. The road into the city of Sevastopol is seen below and is again visible climbing obliquely up the steep slope of the headland on the left. The Great Barracks stand on the top of the far bluffs on the right above where the pontoon bridge meets the Karabelnaya side of the harbour.

The head of the South Harbour as it looks today was taken from near the site of the Crow's Nest Battery. The road into Sevastopol still follows the same route obliquely up the headland on the left with red-roofed university buildings occupying the ground on the far bluff on the right where the Great Barracks was once located. The railway from Simferopol now rounds the spur on the right. The north shore of the roadstead is visible in the far distance at centre.

The Robertson/Beato image entitled *The Woronzoff Road from Sebastopol* shows the view to the southeast over the head of the South Harbour from the high ground seen in the centre of their picture entitled *Valley of the Cemetery*. Green Hill Ridge where *Valley of the Cemetery* was taken is to the right of centre in this photograph. The British Left Attack was situated on the Green Hill Ridge with the most advanced trenches at the end before it drops steeply on to the flat land at the head of South Harbour. The Creek Battery lies along the shore at the end of the harbour with the Vorontsov Road beyond crossing flat land before entering the Vorontsov Ravine. The Redan was on top of the high ground on the left. The British Right Attack facing the Redan was on the section of the Vorontsov Ridge seen on the skyline to the right of centre.

The view towards the head of South Harbour today was taken from the terrace near the Opera House. The end of the Green Hill Ridge is beyond the harbour at centre with the Vorontsov Ravine to its left. The row of apartment buildings seen on the Vorontsov Ridge on the far left skyline are located between the sites of the 1st and 2nd Parallels of the British Right Attack. The flat land, which lay beyond the Creek Battery in the image above, is now occupied by Sevastopol's railway terminus.

16

The Karabelnaya, Roadstead and Sea Forts

The Karabelnaya was the district of Sevastopol that lay to the east of the South Harbour. It was effectively contained behind the fortified defense line that ran from the Barrack Battery on the end of the Vorontsov Ridge to the Redan Bastion, the Malakhov Bastion, the Little Redan Bastion and the shores of the roadstead at Careenage Creek. The main hospital, barracks, arsenal, dry docks and quay-side storage buildings were all situated within its boundaries. Many of those who worked servicing the needs of the Black Sea fleet and army also lived in the area.

Malakhov Hill dominated the Karabelnaya. The importance of this hill and its bastion in the defense of Sevastopol has been discussed previously. All the important buildings and structures in the district were within range of any heavy artillery mounted on its summit, which sloped gently to the north. In addition, the centre of the city of Sevastopol to the west of the South Harbour was also vulnerable. The Russians knew that it was important to hold the Malakhov at all costs. After its fall, Sevastopol was no longer tenable.

The first of three Robertson/Beato images, which are all entitled *Sevastopol from the Malakoff,* shows the view to the west-northwest from the northern end of Malakhov Hill. Ruined houses lie on the slope in the foreground with the depression that holds the dry docks on the right in the middle distance. The complex of impressive buildings beyond the depression is the Great Barracks. The South Harbour lies unseen behind the barracks with the city of Sevastopol beyond. The Black Sea is on the horizon.

Today's view also looks west-northwest from the northern end of Malakhov Hill. Trees on the slopes of the Malakhov Park partly obscure views of the streets below and, together with buildings in the Karabelnaya, prevent the depression where the dry docks were situated from being seen. However, the university buildings in the middle distance can be seen occupying the land where the Great Barracks once stood. The city of Sevastopol on the skyline lies beyond the South Harbour.

The second of Robertson/Beato's images entitled *Sebastopol from the Malakoff* shows the view to the northwest over the Karabelnaya from the northern end of Malakhov Hill. Piles of empty wicker gabions lie strewn on the slope in the foreground. Damaged houses and other buildings can be seen in the middle distance with the characteristic conical shaped, quay-side hoist known to the British as the Shears to the left of centre. Fort Nicholas lies on the western side of the entrance to the South Harbour with the city of Sevastopol to its left. The church of St. Michael the Archangel in Sevastopol that featured in *Church and Clocktower* is on the extreme left. Fort Paul is in ruins on the near side of the entrance to the South Harbour. Fort Constantine is visible at the end of what appears

The first in a series of images taken by Robertson/Beato entitled *Sebastopol from the Malakoff*. (Royal Collection Trust/© Her Majesty Queen Elizabeth II 2016).

The modern view looking west-northwest from the northern end of Malakhov Hill.

The second of Robertson/Beato's images entitled *Sebastopol from the Malakoff.* (Royal Collection Trust/© Her Majesty Queen Elizabeth II 2016).

Today's view looking northwest from the northern end of Malakhov Hill.

The third of three Robertson/Beato images entitled _Sevastopol from the Malakoff._ (©
Manuscripts and Special Collections, University of Nottingham).

as a long, low promontory on the other side of the roadstead. The Black Sea is beyond.
Fort Michael is on the north shore of the roadstead on the far right. This photograph shows
how Malakhov Hill dominated the area and how whoever held it controlled Sevastopol.
Malakhov Hill is now a park.

The modern equivalent of the second of Robertson/Beato's views shows the scene today
from the top of a flight of steps that lead down the northern end of the hill to the park's
main entrance. The promontory that carries Fort Constantine can be seen over the
roadstead at centre with the site of Fort Nicholas just behind the crane at centre.

The view in the third image entitled _Sebastopol from the Malakoff_, which forms a
panorama with the preceding two, shows the view to the north-northwest over the
Karabelnaya from the top of the slope at the northern end of Malakhov Hill. Defensive
earthworks are visible on the slope in the foreground. Four rows of ruined cottages can be
seen below the hill. It is likely that these were destroyed by round shot overshooting the
Malakhov Tower located 450 yards behind the camera to the south-southeast. The open
ground on the right falls away into the small Ouchakov Ravine before it rises again towards

Robertson/Beato's image entitled **Little Malakoff and Curtain.** (© Victoria and Albert Museum, London)

The park on the site of the Little Redan today. The low wall that marks the line of the parapet runs across the background at the high point of the ridge. The ground drops down towards the Careenage Ravine beyond this wall.

the Point Battery, which is out of the picture. Part of a viaduct that carried the aqueduct from the upper Chernaya Valley to the dry docks over the ravine can be seen at the water's edge on the far right. The roadstead with the north shore beyond is in the background. This view in his direction today is obscured by trees growing on the slopes of Malakhov Hill.

The Little Redan, or Bastion No. 2, was an important strongpoint bewteen the Malakhov Bastion and the Point Battery, which was a component of Bastion No. 1 close to the shore of the roadstead. All three sites were linked by curtain wall earthworks that were in themselves a formidable barrier. These defences were opposite the area of the French Right Attack in 1855. The battery on Malakhov Hill that provided flanking fire to the ground in front of the curtain between the Malakhov and Little Redan can be seen in the Robertson/Beato image *Interior of the Malakoff* in Chapter 14.

The Robertson/Beato image entitled *Little Malakoff and Curtain* in the Victoria and Albert Museum's collection in London, but also known as *The Little Redan* and *The Little-Redan after the Siege* in other collections, shows gabion-reinforced fortifictions of a battery where dislodged guns and a mortar lie in the foreground. In the background, the curtain wall with a distinctive dog-leg also seen on contemporary maps extends from the Little Redan, which is partly visible on the extreme right, to the Point Battery in front of the the long low building visible on the left. Fortifications associated with Bastion No. 1 run further away to the right of the Point Battery towards Sevastopol's roadstead visible in the distance. The modern view from near where Sevastopol's semi-circular defence line met the roadstead at the entrance to Careenage Creek is shown as the first image in the next chapter.

The depression in the middle distance before the curtain and Point Battery is the Ouchakov Ravine. Off the picture to the left lay a viaduct that took the aqueduct that supplied water to the dry docks over the ravine. Part of this viaduct is seen on the third of the Robertson/Beato images entitled *Sebastopol from the Malakoff* reproduced earlier in this chapter. Just to the left of cente, a long mound of earth lies close to the Ouchakov Ravine. This is depicted on contemporary maps as a L-shaped, six-gun battery with four guns facing southeast towards the back of the curtain earthworks between the Malakoff and Little Redan basions and two facing northeast towards the back of the curtain earthworks between the Little Redan and the Point Battery. Mortars here may have lobbed shells over the Curtain at French positions.

The north-northeast view in the Robertson/Beato image indicates that the battery close to the camera must have been halfway along the eastern edge of Malakhov Hill. A position with similarly arranged fortifications is found in detailed plans of the Malakhov Bastion roughly 150 yards to the north of the Malakhov Tower. This position is not named on plans, but may have been known to French soldiers and Robertson/Beato as the Little Malakoff.

The Dry Docks

The massive stone dry docks in the Karabelnaya district of Sevastopol were completed just before the war began to service Russia's expanding Black Sea Fleet. They were described at the time as amongst the greatest and most magnificent works of their kind in the world. There were two rows of docks separated by a large basin. The row furthest from the inlet had three dry docks capable of taking ships drawing eighteen feet of water while the one nearest the inlet had two capable of taking ships drawing twenty-one feet of water. The

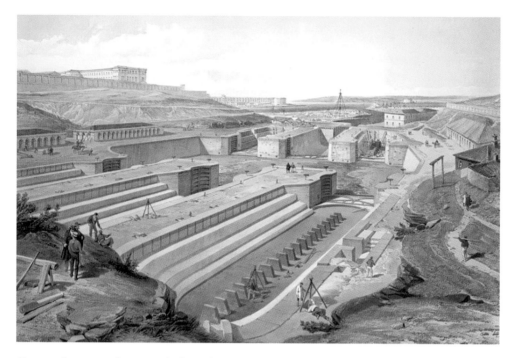

Simpson's watercolour entitled **Docks at Sebastopol, with Ruins of Fort St. Paul.** (Library of Congress, Washington).

The view looking northwest over the site of the dry docks today.

Robertson/Beato's image entitled *The Docks.* (Royal Collection Trust/© Her Majesty Queen Elizabeth II 2016)

Robertson/Beato's image entitled *Docks after the Explosion.* (Royal Collection Trust/© Her Majesty Queen Elizabeth II 2016)

basin, which was above the level of the Black Sea, was joined to a side-inlet from South Harbour by a series of three large locks, each with a rise of ten feet. The last lock was between the two deeper dry docks to the north of the basin. The water for supplying the basin, filling the docks, and working the locks, was brought by an aqueduct twelve miles long from the headwaters of the Chernaya River.

The dry docks were an essential component of the development of the city as an important naval base and, as such, became a prime target for destruction by the Allies. The correspondent of the *Daily News* described the docks prior to their destruction as follows:

> They are built of carefully cut white limestone, edged with a close-grained fine granite … At certain intervals where openings have been left in the sides of the docks to admit of descent by flights of stone steps, are seen some highly polished blocks of red granite, magnificent in size and quality … The iron gates, of enormous size, and the machinery by which they are opened and closed, are all of the most careful workmanship.
>
> Close to the docks themselves is a large engine-house, and near it is seen the termination of the aqueduct … The docks were filled from this source, and the pumps are so arranged that each dock could be filled or emptied irrespective of the remainder … Since the stream flowing along the aqueduct was diverted by the Allies, the docks have remained dry, and many fragments of shells as well as round shot are now to be seen scattered about them and over the floor of the great basin.
>
> Alongside of the docks are spacious wharves, and all the various workshops, sheds, and houses used by the artisans and laborers in the dockyard employ. These wharves are continuous with those of the Karabelnaia harbor, terminating at Fort Paul, where the lofty store buildings … were partly converted into hospitals when the barrack hospitals were no longer tenable, and when so many dead and wounded were left on the 9th of September 1855. Looking down on the docks of the Karabelnaia from the high ground near the entrance, there appears such a perfect unity in their design, the scale on which they are built is so magnificent, the execution of the work so perfect, that it is impossible to watch the operations of the miners for their destruction, without a feeling of regret that so vast an expenditure of wealth and labour, such toil of mind and ingenuity of thought, should have been employed and exercised to so little good result.

When the last section of the dry docks was finally blown-up during the first week of February 1856, it was reported that the sky became clouded with smoke, stones and rubbish with masonry of considerable size rising perpendicularly upwards.

Colonel John E. Upton, who was British, was the engineer in charge of the construction of the dry docks and his son William Upton was his primary assistant. As well as the dry docks, William and his father designed and built the bridges and tunnels that carried the aqueduct. The father and son team were also involved in the construction of local fortifications as well as prestigious buildings. All in all, they played a vital role in increasing Russia's military capabilities in the region as part of a 25-year project costing £1,500,000. At one point the Uptons had crews of 30,000 men under their command.

William Upton had become a Russian subject prior to his father's death in 1851. Unfortunately, he underestimated the effect the war would have on his family and country

The Robertson/Beato image entitled *Fort Nicholas.* (Royal Collection Trust/© Her Majesty Queen Elizabeth II 2016).

The same view today looking north-northwest from the University's grounds.

The Robertson/Beato image entitled *The Shears.* (Royal Collection Trust/© Her Majesty Queen Elizabeth II 2016).

16.15. Today's view looking north-northeast over the site of the Shears from the University's grounds.

The Robertson/Beato image entitled **Sebastopol from the Redan.** (Royal Collection Trust/© Her Majesty Queen Elizabeth II 2016).

Today's view looking over Careenage Creek towards the Inkerman Ridge from the headland that carried the Point or Bastion No. 1.

Simpson's watercolour entitled *Head of the Harbour, Sebastopol.* (Library of Congress, Washington).

The view of the head of Sevastopol's roadstead as it looks today.

Simpson's watercolour entitled *The North Side of the Harbour of Sebastopol from the Top of the Harbour, 22nd June 1855.* (Library of Congress, Washington).

Today's equivalent view looking west down Sevastopol's roadstead.

The first of two of Robertson/Beato images entitled *Valley of Inkerman.* (Royal Collection Trust/© Her Majesty Queen Elizabeth II 2016).

The same view over the Chernaya Valley today with the ruins of Kalimata Castle on the ledge at centre.

The second of two Robertson/Beato images entitled *Valley of Inkerman.* (Royal Collection Trust/© Her Majesty Queen Elizabeth II 2016).

The same view today over the head of Sevastopol's roadstead looking towards the Inkerman Ridge.

estate outside Sevastopol. On the afternoon of the day when Balaklava was first occupied by the British, Upton was captured by the cavalry at his farm and taken before Lord Raglan. In a tense meeting, Upton was unable to convince Raglan and his staff that he was loyal to Britain. Aware that he had no choice but to co-operate, he managed to negotiate the assurances for his family's safety in return for information on Russian fortifications. He also acted as a translator in a hospital.

Upton was detained with his wife and daughters and there was some debate about whether or not legal proceedings should be brought against him. However, the family eventually moved to England, where he could not find work because of his reputation, and then to Canada, where he built a homestead and farm. He died in 1893. His diaries are on file with the National Archives of Canada.

Simpson's watercolour entitled *Docks at Sebastopol, with Ruins of Fort St. Paul* shows the five basins that served as dry docks with the entrance to the complex on the far side at centre. The Great Barracks is shown on the high ground to the left with Fort Nicholas on the western side of the entrance to the South Harbour in the distance at centre. The ruins of Fort Paul are on the eastern side of the same entrance with the Shears dock-yard hoist to its left on the shore of the side-inlet from South Harbour that leads to the dry docks.

The same view today is obscured by buildings and trees that now stand on the site of the old dry docks. A gantry carrying overhead electricity cables for the Sevastopol to Simferopol railway, which runs along the slope seen in the foreground above, is at lower right. To the right of the trees at centre, the superstructure of a ship is visible in one of two current dry docks situated at the head of the inlet beyond where the old dry docks were found.

The Robertson/Beato image entitled *The Docks* looks northwest over the dry docks. The Shears hoist can be seen in the middle distance on the promontory that carried the Arsenal. The South Harbour is to the left of the hoist and the side-inlet that led to the dry docks to the right. Beyond the hoist is the entrance to the South Harbour from the Roadstead with Fort Nicholas on the promontory to the left and the remains of Fort Paul on the promontory on the right.

A later image taken by Robertson/Beato entitled *Docks after the Explosion* shows the dry docks sometime after they were blown-up. The hoist on the shore of the side-inlet from South Harbour is beyond at centre. The first storehouse of a row that was constructed on the opposite side of the inlet and which can also be seen above and in Simpson's watercolour, is on the far right

The Arsenal and the Shears
Robertson/Beato's image entitled *Fort Nicholas* looks north-northwest through the entrance of the South Harbour to the north side of the roadstead from behind the Great Barracks. Ships can be seen on the Black Sea in the far distance. Fort Nicholas is the long low building on the left side of the harbour. The ruins of the Arsenal lie in the foreground.

The same view today was taken from the north-facing terrace of the university, which now stands where the Great Barrack buildings were once located. The white building on the promontory that once carried Fort Nicholas is a terminus for ferries from the north shore of the roadstead.

Robertson/Beato's image entitled *The Shears* looks north-northeast from behind the Great Barracks across the side-inlet from the South Harbour. This inlet led to the dry docks, which are off the picture to the right. The Shears, which has been seen in other images

The Robertson/Beato image entitled *Fort Constantine.* (Royal Collection Trust/© Her Majesty Queen Elizabeth II 2016).

Fort Constantine today from the same position.

presented in this chapter, was the Russian hoisting apparatus used for the masting and demasting of naval vessels, fitting and removing boilers, and mounting and dismounting guns. Storehouses line the quay on the far side of the inlet to the right of the Shears. The land here curves to the left to form the promontory at the eastern entrance to South Harbour. The hills on the skyline are on the north side of the roadstead. This picture forms a panorama with *Fort Nicholas*.

The modern view looks north from a terrace behind today's university buildings. The old storehouses still line the quay on the right, but the view of the side-inlet from the South Harbour is obscured by the dockyard structures seen in the foreground. The high ground on the skyline covered with dachas and apartments is on the north side of the roadstead.

The White Buildings

The White Buildings were so-called because they were constructed with white stone taken from the Quarry Ravine below the battlefield of Inkerman. They comprised the impressive buildings that made up the Great Barracks and the main hospital. Allied round shot overshooting the Redan destroyed the hospital and forced the Russians to use the storehouse beside the inlet from the South Harbour that led to the dry docks as makeshift accommodation for the sick and wounded. These unfortunates were abandoned by the retreating Russians when the Sevastopol fell and found in appalling sanitary conditions by the Allies. Both the damaged Great Barracks and hospital were destroyed by the British on 28 February 1856 as a means of reducing the future military capabilities of the Russians.

A Robertson/Beato image taken following the fall of Sevastopol entitled *Sebastopol from the Redan* looks to the north-northwest from the north-eastern slope behind the bastion. The ruins of the hospital are on the left in the middle distance with the Great Barracks beyond at centre. The South Harbour is on the left with Fort Nicholas at its entrance. The conical-shaped hoist on the quay-side of the inlet that led to the dry docks from the South Harbour is visible to the right of the long barrack building. The north side of the roadstead is in the far distance with the Black Sea on the skyline. The long, low promontory that carried Fort Constantine on its point is on the far left. Ships can be seen on the roadstead on the far right. Urban development and trees on this slope today prevents a modern equivalent image being taken.

Careenage Creek

Careenage Creek or Careenage Bay was the name given to an inlet on the south side of the roadstead that was overlooked by the Point or No.1 Bastion, which lay near the north-eastern end of the semicircle of defences around Sevastopol. No views of this area exist from the Crimean War, which was an important location historically.

The photograph here shows Careenage Creek with its entrance to Sevastopol's roadstead just off the picture on the left. The view is to the southeast towards the head of the inlet with the Inkerman Ridge in the right background and the Careenage Ravine on the extreme right. The aqueduct that carried water to the dry docks in Sevastopol from the upper Chernaya Valley ran along the slope on the far side of the inlet and then along the slope on the near side, where the railway can be seen below, before entering a tunnel. The Sappers' Road, which allowed the Russians access to Sevastopol from the hinterland during the early stages of the siege, crossed the Careenage Ravine at the end of the inlet on a viaduct. Russian troops from Sevastopol marched over this viaduct on their way to the Battle of Inkerman. The viaduct no longer exists, but must it have been closer to the end of the inlet than today's railway embankment.

The Selenghinsky and Volynsky Redoubts, known collectively as the White Works, which were captured by the French on the 7 June 1855 after the third bombardment of Sevastopol, were situated on the high ground to the right of centre. The Zalbalkansky Battery, which also fell to the French on the same day, but relinquished as untenable, was on the end of the high ground to the left of centre. The headland was under French control by the time of the final bombardment and assault on the city on 8 September 1855.

Sevastopol's Roadstead

The Sevastopol Roadstead is an elongated seawater inlet that runs from the Black Sea in the west to the estuary of the Chernaya River in the east. It is three quarters of a mile in width near its entrance, but gradually tapers as it extends about four and a half miles distance inland. The roadstead served as shelter and an anchorage for the Russian Black Sea Fleet, which was well protected by a series of forts situated at either side of its entrance and along its north and south shores. The centre of the city of Sevastopol is situated on its southern shore about one mile from its entrance. To the south of the head of the roadstead lies the Inkerman Ridge, where the Battle of Inkerman was fought. It was here that William Simpson sketched views of the roadstead from spurs of high land before the siege ended.

Simpson's watercolour entitled *Head of the Harbour, Sebastopol* looks northeast over the end of the roadstead and the estuary of the Chernaya River from a spur on the Inkerman Ridge that carried St Laurent's Battery. The Battle of Inkerman took place on high ground off the picture to the right. The Volovia Ravine, up which some Russians regiments marched onto the battlefield of Inkerman after crossing the Chernaya River at the Inkerman Bridge, lies below to the right. A British-built mortar battery sits on the spur beyond the gorge and is visible on the extreme right. It faces Russian batteries on a headland across the water on the far left near the Inkerman West Lighthouse and another on the hill seen to the left of centre. Smoke issues from artillery firing at both locations. The mortar battery spur runs back to the south and joins East Jut.

The same scene is recognisable today. The main differences are that houses are now found in the Volovia Ravine and on the lower slopes of the spur from the Inkerman Ridge opposite and land has been reclaimed for development from the roadstead under the headland on the far left where Russian batteries were located. The photograph was taken further down the slope than where Simpson was positioned when he made his preliminary sketch because the thick brush higher up now obstructs the view.

Simpson's watercolour entitled *The North Side of the Harbour of Sebastopol from the Top of the Harbour, 22nd June 1855* looks west down the roadstead from the same spur from the Inkerman Ridge where he sketched *Head of the Harbour, Sebastopol*. The 1st Parallel that ran across the Inkerman Ridge had its northern end on this spur. French batteries, which sat on the crest of the next spur on the left, are at the end of the 2nd Parallel across the Inkerman Ridge. Above this spur and another glimpsed further away, the promontory that ends at Fort Constantine can be seen in the distance at the entrance to the roadstead. The track along the shoreline below is the East Sapper's Road taken by Russian regiments that marched from the Inkerman Bridge to the battlefield of Inkerman via St George's Ravine, which cuts inland behind the near headland on the left. A side track from the road is seen crossing a bridge over the aqueduct that carried water to the dry docks in the Karabelnaya district. In the right foreground, French riflemen crouch behind rocks waiting for a target that may present itself within range. Simpson reported that the limestone cliffs on the north side of the roadstead were 'dazzling and painful to the eye' on a sunny day.

The same view today shows a coastal road below servicing industrial developments running parallel with the Sevastopol to Simferapol railway. Large floating docks are visible in the middle distance with the grey shapes of warships lining the opposite shore beyond. The promontory at the entrance to the roadstead that carries Fort Constantine can be seen in the far distance on the left.

The first of Robertson/Beato's images entitled *Valley of Inkerman*, which has been enhanced because of poor quality, looks south up the Chernaya Valley at the head of Sevastopol's roadstead. It was taken after peace was declared in 1856 from the slopes of the spur where smoke issuing from a Russian battery was depicted to the left of centre in Simpson's *Head of the Harbour, Sebastopol*. The darker area in the foreground was a swamp at the head of the roadstead. The ruins of Kalamita Castle are beyond on the ledge above a cliff. The Inkerman cave church was below this cliff under the castle. The hills on the left form the western end of the Mackenzie Heights.

Today's modern view looking south up the Chernaya Valley was taken from a slightly higher position on the same headland and shows how the swamp has either been reclaimed for industrial use or dredged and made into an extension of the roadstead. In the middle distance, the ruins of Kalamita Castle are on the ledge at centre while the Chernaya River can be glimpsed on the left.

The second of Robertson/Beato's images entitled *Valley of Inkerman* shows the view from the same headland only this time to the south-southwest. This photograph forms a panorama with the last picture and looks over the swamp at the head of the roadstead and the course of the Chernaya River below a cliff face to the Inkerman Ridge. The road across the swamp in the right foreground was built on a straight causeway and led to the unseen Inkerman Bridge. The Post Road seen winding up the side of East Jut in the middle distance on the right disappears as it turns into the Quarry Ravine, which is identified by the exposed limestone cliff running obliquely upwards. Beyond Quarry Ravine is the Inkerman Tusk spur. The high point on the skyline at right is Mount Head at the northern end of the Fore Ridge on the Inkerman battlefield.

In the modern photograph taken from the same position, the area of swamp in Robertson/Beato's image is today part of the headwaters of Sevastopol's roadstead extended as a harbour. On the right, the main road from Inkerman to Sevastopol follows the same line as the old Post Road as it winds up the eastern face of East Jut, which now carries communication towers. The steep-sided spur from the Inkerman Ridge known as the Inkerman Tusk is left of centre across the Chernaya River and beyond the Quarry Ravine. Mount Head on the Inkerman battlefield is the high point of the Inkerman Ridge on the skyline to the right of centre. The slope down from Mount Head seen before it disappears behind the Inkerman Tusk is the Kitspur.

Forts on the Roadstead

A number of forts built on the shore around the entrance of the roadstead protected Sevastopol from attack by enemy warships. These forts and the line of ships sunk across the roadstead's entrance prevented allied ships from getting within firing range of Sevastopol during the war.

The Robertson/Beato image entitled _Fort Michael._ (Royal Collection Trust/© Her Majesty Queen Elizabeth II 2016).

Fort Michael as it looks today.

Klembovsky's photograph of Sevastopol's roadstead in the early 1900s with Fort Catherine on the left. (Royal Collection Trust/© Her Majesty Queen Elizabeth II 2016).

Today's view over Sevastopol's roadstead with the site of Fort Catherine on the left.

Robertson/Beato's image entitled *Fort Constantine* looks west-southwest towards the strongpoint that sits at the end of a promontory at the northern entrance of the roadstead. This fort also appears in the distance on many images taken looking out over the roadstead from the south side and shown earlier in this chapter. Fort Constantine was complimented on the south side by Fort Alexander. Both were attacked by the allied fleet the first day of the first bombardment of Sevastopol on 17 October 1854. This view was taken from the next fortified headland to the east after peace was declared and visits to the north side of the roadstead or Severnaya, were permitted.

Today's scene was taken from a dacha garden on the same headland that was fortified in the 1856 image. The fort is still of military importance and cannot be visited. A breakwater now extends further across the roadstead's entrance from the fort. Locals swim in the roadstead at lower left.

Robertson/Beato's image entitled *Fort Michael* was taken looking east from the same fortified headland that was used as platform to photograph *Fort Constantine*. Fort Michel was another formidable fortress with guns mounted in two layers of casemates and on the roof. Today, Fort Michael is a museum and easily visited from Sevastopol by a regular ferry, seen at the jetty in today's image, that leaves Artillery Bay. The north side of the harbour is now a dormitory suburb of Sevastopol.

The pointed obelisk seen on a headland beyond Fort Michael in the modern view is one of the few remaining monuments that celebrate the former USSR. The next headland along seen on the left was the site of Fort Catherine, which was not built of stone as were Forts Constantine and Michael, but had earthworks for protection.

Colonel Klembovsky's image taken from the north side of the roadstead in the early 1900s looks south-southwest towards the city of Sevastopol. Fort Catherine's earth parapet with gun embrasures can be seen on a promontory in the foreground. The site where Fort Paul stood is in the distance on the extreme left above the number '3'. The site of Fort Nicholas on the other side of the entrance to the South Harbour is above the bow of the one-funnelled steamship just right of centre and indicated with a '2'. Further to the right, the site of the Artillery Fort on the high ground west of Artillery Bay is identified with a '1'. The dome of St Vladimir's Cathedral is on the skyline above the two-funnelled warship on the left.

The site of Fort Catherine, which is still a military installation and thus out-of-bounds, is on the left in the modern photograph. The sites of the forts on the south side can be found in the same locations as they were seen in Klembnovsky's image. The dome of St Vladimir's Cathedral still dominates the skyline on Sevastopol's Central Hill.

Appendix I

Profiles of the Principal Artists Whose Work Appears in This Publication

WILLIAM SIMPSON

William Simpson in 1859 aged 36 years. (© Adrian Lipscomb).

William Simpson was born in Glasgow on 28 October 1823. He was the son of James Simpson, a shipyard labourer, and Ann (née Johnstone). He was fond of his mother, whom he turned to for comfort and support, whilst his father was frequently drunk and abusive. His formal education was rudimentary but, by the age of fourteen, Simpson had earned an apprenticeship in lithography. He was interested in both the arts and sciences, and attended free lectures at the Andersonian University and the Mechanics Institute. However, it was art that was his main interest and he would often use money meant for food to buy colours at the art supply shop.

When aged twenty-seven in 1851, Simpson moved to London and worked for the lithographers Day & Son. Lithography was becoming important and the technology was being utilised to illustrate newspapers. When the Crimean War broke out in 1854, Simpson was commissioned to prepare a drawing of the anticipated fall of Sevastopol in the expectation that it would be on hand for immediate use when the city was actually captured. He found this difficult, as there was little in the way of accurate representations of Sevastopol available in London at the time. However, when it became apparent that an extended siege was likely, he was sent to the Crimea to make sketches on the spot.

Simpson arrived in the Crimea in mid-November 1854. He had missed the earlier battles of the Alma, Balaklava and Inkerman, but he was able to record events from the siege lines before Sevastopol. During the winter, he was struck by the plight of the common soldier, who he described as 'miserable looking beings … covered with mud, dirt, and rags'. While in the Crimea in early 1855, he met Roger Fenton, who took his photograph. He associated

363

with many senior officers including Lord Raglan. He went on the expedition to Kertch, which was captured on 24 May 1855, but was back in time to observe the major attack on Sevastopol on 18 June. He was still at the front when the city was abandoned by the Russians on 8 September 1855. Simpson left the Crimea later that autumn.

Throughout his time in the Crimea, his sketches were made with pencil, and coloured later from memory. He sent back his work to London where they were transferred to stone by his lithographers. He was paid £20 for each picture. Some of the watercolours were exhibited by the art dealers Colnaghi, who also produced two large portfolios containing over eighty lithographs entitled *The Seat of the War in the East*. Two thousand copies of the complete set were produced. Simpson dedicated the series to Queen Victoria, whose patronage he enjoyed for the rest of his life, and he became a frequent visitor to Windsor Castle and Balmoral. So popular were his pictures that he became affectionately known as 'Crimean Simpson'.

The Great Indian Mutiny of 1857 had turned the British public's attention to India, and Day & Son believed that the production of a large format book of tinted lithographs of Indian scenes would be profitable. As a consequence, Simpson visited India from 1859 to 1862 and became enamoured of its cultures and its contrasts. Indian architecture, archaeology and the daily life of the people were the subjects of his prolific sketches. Unfortunately, while away from Britain, Day & Son failed financially and Simpson's watercolours of India eventually became part of their liquidated stock. Simpson had paid his own expenses while in India and on his return to London he was left almost penny-less. A small book entitled *India, Ancient and Modern*, was later produced, but was of poor quality.

Simpson accompanied the British Army to Abyssinia in 1868 and was sent by the *Illustrated London News* to sketch the opening ceremony of the Suez Canal in 1869. While in the Middle East, he also visited Jerusalem to make detailed drawings of ancient water tunnels and caverns. He covered the Franco-German war in 1870 and in 1871 was sketching Paris under the Commune. Simpson was commissioned by the *Illustrated London News* to travel to China in 1872 to sketch the marriage of the emperor. He took the opportunity to extend this trip to a round-the-world journey. He published his account in *Meeting the Sun: A Journey All Round the World*, which was published in 1874. In 1877 Simpson visited the eastern Mediterranean to sketch archaeological excavations at Mycenae, Troy and Ephesus, a trip he particularly enjoyed, and, in 1878, he accompanied a military expedition to Afghanistan.

Simpson married Maria Eliza Burt in 1881 when he was fifty-seven and bought a large house in Willesden, London. He became a father of a daughter Ann when he was sixty. In 1885, he undertook one last major expedition through Persia and Afghanistan with the Afghan Boundary Commission, which was to survey the border between Russia and Afghanistan. The task involved a 1,000 mile trek, but presented Simpson with opportunities to sketch desolate locations and the cultural sites, such as the tomb of the poet Omar Khayyám. In Tehran, he met the Shah of Persia.

Simpson sketched the funeral of Kaiser Wilhelm in Berlin in 1888 and also visited the International Exhibition in Glasgow. However, a trip back to Scotland in 1890 to sketch the opening of the Forth Bridge by the Prince of Wales led to major decline in his health because of the bad weather. He died on 17 August 1899 at his home in Willesden with his wife and daughter by his side. He was aged seventy-five. He had never fully recovered from the attack of bronchitis he caught while sketching in Scotland in 1890. He was buried in his mother's grave in Highgate Cemetery in London.

(The above account of the life of William Simpson is adapted from *William Simpson, Prince of Pictorial Correspondents*, by Adrian Lipscomb (1999) at *The Victorian Web - Literature, History and Culture in the Age of Victoria*, http://www.victorianweb.org/painting/simpson/bio.htm).

ROGER FENTON

Roger Fenton's portrait taken in a professional studio in February 1852.
(Library of Congress, Washington)

Roger Fenton was born into a very wealthy family at Crimble Hall in Lancashire in March 1819. His father, John Fenton, had inherited property, in addition to a half interest in the family bank and cotton mill. He also served as Member of Parliament for Rochdale. In 1838, Roger Fenton and his brother began studying at University College London. After being awarded a Master of Arts degree, he became a pupil of an historical painter. In the early 1840s, Fenton moved to Paris and trained in a studio where photography was encouraged as a new art form. Realizing that he would never make a great painter, he returned to London in 1844 and studied law. Fenton qualified as a solicitor and married Grace Maynard in about 1847. They had three daughters with two becoming painters.

Fenton did not give up painting and had canvases accepted by the Royal Academy three years in a row. He also kept up-to-date with advances in photography and became one of the dozen founder members of the Photographic Club in London when it was formed in 1847. A more widespread interest in photography developed in England after the Great Exhibition of 1851 when some patents on photographic processes, which were hampering progress, were relaxed. Fenton then became a front runner in attempts to create a Photographic Society. He visited Russia to document work in progress on a new suspension bridge over the River Dnieper, but took advantage of the trip to visit and photograph Kiev, St Petersburg and Moscow.

An exhibition of 800 photographs from various sources was organized in London at this time. It was a great success and led to the inauguration of the Photographic Society on 20 January 1853. Fenton graciously accepted the post of Honorary Secretary. The first issue of the *Journal of the Photographic Society* appeared on 3 March 1853. On 3 January 1854, another exhibition of almost 1,500 photographs was organised. Fenton's dreams concerning the advancement of photography had now been realised.

Fenton had had friendly relations with Prince Albert since he and the queen consented to be patrons of the Photographic Society in May 1853. Fenton was commanded to

Buckingham Palace on several occasions between 1853 and Prince Albert's death to photograph the royal family.

Fenton embarked from the East India Docks in London en route to the Crimea on 20 February 1855 aboard *Hecla* under the patronage of Queen Victoria and Prince Albert, and the Duke of Newcastle, the Minister for War, However, he was financed by Thomas Agnew & Sons who wanted images of people and scenes of interest to sell to the public. He took with him a photographic van and two assistants. Both helped with his photographic work, but they were specifically employed as handyman and cook, and driver and groom. Unfortunately, they were both unreliable and liked to drink. Marcus Sparling, who was photographed sitting on the box of Fenton's photographic van, died five years later of

Marcus Sparling, who was Fenton's assistant, on the box of their photographic van. (Library of Congress, Washington)

inflammation of the liver. The van was fitted-up for living, cooking, sleeping and darkroom work, as plates had to be developed immediately after being taken. Unfortunately, the horses Fenton brought with him from Gibraltar turned out to be unsuitable for their duties. Others had to be borrowed from artillery units and those working on the military railway.

Fenton became quite exasperated at the time it took to get organised after his arrival in Balaklava on 7 March 1855. It wasn't until 15 March, that the first picture, which was of a villa that had served as a Post Office, was taken. For the next two weeks he photographed the sights of Balaklava. At the end of March 1855, he moved out of Balaklava and began photographing individuals, groups and views at the cavalry camp near Kadikoi. Up until this time, Fenton lived on *Hecla*, but when he later moved up onto the Chersonese Plateau, he relied on the food and hospitality of those he met.

Thanks to a letter of introduction from Prince Albert to Lord Raglan, Fenton enjoyed privileges not usually available to other civilian visitors to the Crimea. He took portraits of high-ranking officers of the British Army, such as Lord Raglan, General Sir James Simpson, and lieutenant generals Sir Harry Jones, Sir John Pennefather and Sir James Scarlett. Also photographed were Marshal Pélissier, and generals Beuret, Bosquet. Cissé, Labousiniére of the French Army. Omar Pasha and Ismail Pasha featured in photographs of the Turkish Army. Many lower ranking officers were also included in his collection, plus the artist William Simpson, the newspaper reporter William Russell, Croat labourers, a French *cantinérie*, the postmaster and others. Portraits of a few individuals were taken more than once and some, such as Sir George de Lacy Evans, the Duke of Cambridge and Prince Napoleon, were likely photographed in a studio after he had returned home.

Fenton often dined with generals and officers drinking champagne and smoking cigars. He was comparatively mild in his observations regarding of the running of the war, possibly because he saw himself as a guest. Fenton has been criticised for not documenting the lives of ordinary soldiers in the trenches and it has been suggested he was class-conscious, and that he did not want to expose himself to any real danger. It has been argued that even when he took his famous photograph entitled *The Shadow of the Valley of Death* on 24 April 1855, the risk of being hit by shot and shell was exaggerated in his communications.

After ideal photographic conditions in the spring, the light conditions deteriorated and the heat increased in summer making it more difficult for Fenton to get successful pictures. The time of exposures became longer and cleaning the plates under the hot conditions more exacting. Also, the collodion on his plates would sometimes dry before the liquid spread evenly over the plate. Another significant problem was that the collodion was only sensitive when wet and this restricted how far the plates could be taken after being prepared in the dark room in the van. In addition, the van became hot and stuffy to work inside.

The failure of the British attack on the Redan on 18 June 1855 depressed Fenton, as a number of his officer friends were killed. He left for home soon afterwards, sick with cholera. However, his assistants looked after him on the voyage and he was well on the way to recovery by the time he reached England. On his return, he was immediately summonsed to Osborne House on the Isle of Wight to see Queen Victoria and the Prince Consort and asked to recount his adventures. Later, he showed all his Crimean photographs to Napoleon III in Paris. His work as a war photographer in the Crimea was exhibited, published and widely acclaimed.

In February 1856, Fenton relinquished his post as Secretary of the Photographic Society to a paid official, but remained on the Council until May 1856 when he was forced to resign after becoming a council member of the Photographic Association, which was a commercial organisation. However, he was elected Vice-President in 1858, remaining a member until 1862.

At the height of his fame in 1862, Fenton announced that he was going to retire from photography. This came as a surprise to most of those who knew him and was never officially explained. It has been suggested that it was because he saw no future in the art because of the problem of fading prints. He sold all his equipment and went back to his former occupation in the City of London. He died on 8 August 1869 at the age of fifty after a short illness caused by his hurrying to catch a train.

His career in photography only spanned eleven years, but he was one of the most prolific and versatile photographers of the nineteenth century. His fame rests chiefly on his photographs taken of the Crimean War, but his endeavours in other areas are noteworthy.

JAMES ROBERTSON and FELICE BEATO

Less is known about Robertson and Beato's time in the Crimea than Fenton's because, unlike Fenton, none of their letters, if any where written during this period, have seen the light of day. It is known that Robertson travelled to the Crimea in 1855 and 1856 with Beato, who was his senior assistant and protégée at the time, and they worked together. Their roles seemed to have been interchangeable, although Robertson seems to have signed the plates. Although they concentrated on landscapes and fortifications, the two-man photographic team did take some pictures of groups of soldiers possibly because of their commercial potential. As well as covering some of the same ground as Fenton in Balaklava and on the Chersonese Plateau, they were also able to document the destruction of Sevastopol's buildings after the city's fall. These images of the result of war showed the substantial damage caused by Allied bombardments during the siege.

Above left: James Robertson photographed in Constantinople in 1845. (Public domain work of art) **Above right: Felice Beato circa 1866 – believed to be a self-portrait.** (Public domain work of art)

James Robertson was born in Middlesex in 1813, the son of Thomas Robertson, a Scot who made military caps for the British Army. He trained as a coin and medal engraver at the Royal Mint in London from 1833 to 1840 under William Wyon. In 1841, he was appointed Chief Engraver at the Imperial Mint in Constantinople with a mandate from the Sultan to improve the coinage. In 1851, the Sultan awarded him the Order of Glory, a decoration usually presented to foreign technicians after ten years exemplary service to the Ottoman Empire. It was while in Constantinople that Robertson took up photography, probably through an interest in watercolours and engraving. He began by taking photographs of Constantinople and selling them to wealthy travellers. His first recorded sale was on 4 July 1853 to the Earl of Carlisle. Later that year, he published twenty photographs in the album *Photographic Views of Constantinople*. Possibly in 1853, but certainly in 1854, he made one or more visits to Greece to photograph classical antiquities. Forty-eight views were published later in 1854 as an album entitled *Grecian Antiquities*. During this period, Robertson engaged Felice Beato as an assistant and on 19 April 1855 married his sister Leonilda Maria Matilde. They had three daughters.

Robertson's involvement with the Crimean War began in April 1854, when he crossed the Bosphorus at Constantinople to take pictures of the British regiments assembling at Scutari. His first confirmed visit to the Crimea began in June 1855 when photographs were taken of Balaklava and environs with the help of Beato. The images of views of the siege lines, and of ruined Sevastopol buildings after the city had been abandoned by the Russians in September, are classics and provide documented evidence of the topography of the battlefield and the effects of the Allied bombardments.

Another excursion to the Crimea was made in March to May 1856. After the armistice, it was possible to visit areas that had previously been out of bounds. Images were made of groups of regimental personnel and scenes on ground previously held by the Russians.

It has been argued that only Beato took photographs during this last visit while Robertson concentrated on selling their work to Army officers.

Soon afterwards, Robertson went into partnership with Felice Beato. They went on a photographic mission to Malta in 1856 and took a series of photographs that were endorsed by both their signatures. In spring the next year, Robertson travelled with Felice Beato and Felice's brother, Antonio, to the Holy Land and Egypt. Another visit to Greece followed. Robertson seems to have given up photography in the 1860s with the firm of *Robertson & Beato* being dissolved in 1867.

Robertson retired as an engraver at the Imperial Ottoman Mint in 1881. In that year he left with his family for Yokohama in Japan, arriving there in January 1882. He was presumably visiting his brother-in-law Felice Beato, who was living in the city at the time. Robertson died in Yokohama in April 1888. Robertson earned his place in the history of photography with his coverage of the Crimean War and for his photographs of historical Mediterranean sites. He was an outstanding contributor to the new art form of photography.

Felice Beato, Robertson's co-worker in the Crimea, was born in Venice in 1832, but the family later moved to the island of Corfu, which was under British control. As a British subject, Beato was registered as a 'ten-year-old' with the British Consulate-General in Constantinople in 1844. Beato must have been about twenty-one when he first went to work for Robertson. Their business and social relationship was cemented when Robertson married Felice's sister.

Beato accompanied his brother-in-law Robertson as his senior assistant on his visits to the Crimea in 1855 and 1856. As Robertson scratched his signature into most of the plates taken by the two-man team at this time, it is uncertain how many were actually taken by Beato. However, there is a strong argument for Beato being responsible for many of the photographs of the ruined city of Sevastopol taken in 1856.

Beato travelled to India in 1858 to record the aftermath of the Indian Mutiny. He took pictures of the mutiny's main sites at Delhi, Cawnpore, and Lucknow, which were sequenced and captioned to re-create events. Rebel corpses were included in some views to increase the effect. At Lucknow, he arranged disinterred bones in the foreground of a photograph in order to dramatically depict the massive slaughter that had occurred. Basing himself in Calcutta, he also spent two years photographing architectural sites in present-day Agra, Varanasi and Amritsar.

Beato then went on to photograph the Second Opium War in China in 1860 and also took architectural views of the cities of present-day Beijing and Guangzhou. He then spent more than twenty years in Japan (1863–84), his longest residency in one country, and the most prolific period of his career. He made hundreds of ethnographic portraits and genre scenes.

Beato was hired in 1871 to document an American punitive expedition to Korea, which was a response to an incident in 1865 in which an American-owned trading vessel, the *General Sherman*, was captured in Korean waters and its entire crew killed. As well as portraits of American military crews and views of the American fleet, he also took pictures of the Korean people and local views. Beato was appointed as the Consul-General of Greece in Japan in August 1873.

Speculative ventures in Japan financially ruined Beato and he moved on in 1884. He covered the Anglo-Sudan war in 1885 and lived in Burma from 1887 until 1905. Landscapes, architectural views, and portrait studies made at that time, offer a glimpse into Burmese life at the end of the 19th century. While in Burma, he opened a curio business selling, in addition to photographs, Burmese works of art in wood, metal, ivory and silk as souvenirs to Western tourists. He died in Florence in 1909.

Felice Beato had a much longer career in photography than did James Robertson, his mentor and teacher. His work in India and the Far East is among the earliest from that part of the world. Breaking a taboo, his photographs are believed to be the first to show bodies on a battlefield. He will be remembered as one of the first truly great war photographers.

VLADISLAV KLEMBOVSKY

In 1904, an album was published by the Museum of the Defence of Sevastopol in Russia containing 119 photographs of battlefields and monuments of the Crimean War taken by Colonel Vladislav Napoleonovitch Klembovsky of the Russian Army. Klembovsky's pictures had explanatory captions in Russian and French giving information on the historical significance of the scene and indicated the location of important landmarks. Maps indicating where the images were taken with arrows showing the direction the camera was pointing were also included as a guide to readers. For its time, it was an advanced work of art and still serves as a unique illustrated guide to the battlefields of the Crimean War

A close inspection of the images in the book shows that little had superficially changed in the geography of the area of conflict between the time of the war and the

Portrait of Vladislav Klembovsky. (Public domain work of art)

early 1900s. In addition, many of the original monuments were still standing. Most importantly, urban development and intense agriculture were not yet intruding upon the battlefields. The photographs show a unique view of the terrain before it was to change forever.

After taking his photographs in the Crimea, Klembovsky went on to distinguish himself in the 1904-05 war against the Japanese by leading his regiment in a successful night attack in Liaoyang Province in Manchuria. He eventually became Commander–in-Chief of the Northern Front during the First World War and recipient of the imperial award 'Order of Saint George IV Class'. Klembovsky was later appointed Supreme Commander-in-Chief of the Russian Army in August 1917 by Alexander Kerensky, the leader of the Provisional Government, following the overthrow the Tsar and after a rebellion by General Kornilov. Klembovsky became a leading figure in the Red Army in 1918 after the communist coup, but was later arrested. General Klembovsky died in prison on 19 July 1921 aged sixty-one years, a tragic end for a Russian patriot.

GEORGE SHAW-LEFEVRE

George Shaw-Lefevre in later life.
(Reproduced with permission from Darryl Lundy)

George Shaw- Lefevre was born in Battersea on 12 June 1831, the only son of Sir John Shaw-Lefevre and Rachel Emily. He was educated at Eton Public School and at Trinity College, Cambridge, and was called to the Bar in 1855. Also in 1855, he travelled to the Crimea as a guest onboard a yacht belonging to Sir Edward Colebooke as a 'war tourist', arriving before the fall of Sevastopol. Unlike others of his ilk, Shaw-Lefevre brought with him a camera and took a number of photographs. One showed HMS *Leander* at the entrance to Balaklava Harbour and others views of the Redan and Malakhov bastions after the Allied occupation of Sevastopol.

On his return to England in April 1856, he selected twelve of his best albumen prints and engaged, at his own expense, the print-seller J. Hogarth to bind and publish them under the title *Photographic Views of Sebastopol taken immediately after the Retreat of the Russians, September 8, 1855*. How many were sold is not known. His idea was to have the proceeds go to the Nightingale Fund, which had been launched on 29 November 1855 with the aim of raising enough money for the establishment of a training institute for nurses.

After this brief dalliance with photography, he seemed to have put away his camera to pursue a life in politics. He became the Member of Parliament for Reading in 1863, a seat he held until 1885. He served under William Gladstone as Parliamentary Secretary to the Board of Trade from 1868 to 1871, as Under-Secretary of State for the Home Department from January to March 1871, as Parliamentary Secretary of the Admiralty from 1871 to 1874 and again in 1880, and as First Commissioner of Works from 1881 to 1885.

Shaw-Lefevre lost his seat at the 1885 general election, but was elected for Bradford Central in a by-election in April 1886 , which he represented until 1895. He again became First Commissioner of Works and a member of Gladstone's Cabinet in 1892. When Lord Rosebery became Prime Minister, he was appointed President of the Local Government Board from 1894 until 1895. In 1897 he was elected a member of the London County Council. In 1906, he became Baron Eversley, a revival of the title held by his uncle. He made his last speech in the House of Lords in 1913.

He married Lady Constance Moreton in 1874, but they had no children. He died in April 1928. His contribution to the documentation of the Crimean War was not great, but some of his images are still classics and, unfortunately, are often attributed to Robertson and Beato.

Appendix 2
Maps From Aerial Images

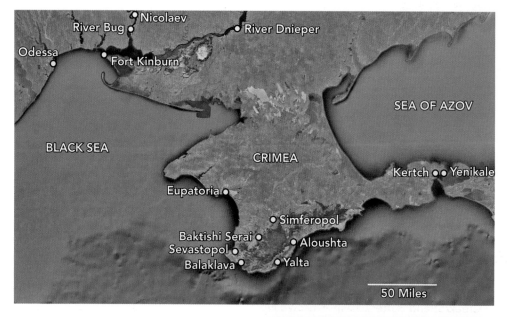

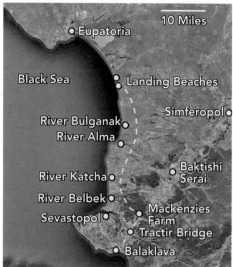

Above: Crimea and surrounds showing important locations. North is to the top of the image. (Adapted from Google Earth™ image)

Right: Southeast Crimea with the approximate route of the Allied army's march from the landing beaches to Balaklava shown as a yellow dashed line. North is to the top of the image. (Adapted from Google Earth™ image)

Above: The Chersonese peninsula showing battlefields and other locations mentioned in the text with the route of the Vorontsov Road shown as a yellow dashed line. North is to the top of the image. (Adapted from Google Earth™)

Right: Sevastopol showing the location of bastions and batteries towards the end of the siege on the modern cityscape. The defence lines around Sevastopol are shown as a solid yellow line. North is to the top of the image. Key: A = Arsenal, AF = Artillery Fort; BB = Barrack Battery; BL = Belkine Lunette; BLA = British Left Attack; BoB = Boulevard Battery; BRA = British Right Attack; CB = Central Bastion; CBa = Creek/Strand Battery; CNB = Crow's Nest Battery; CH = Sevastopol's Central Hill; DD = Dry Docks; FA = Fort Alexander; FC = Fort Constantine; FB = Flagstaff Bastion; FCa = Fort Catherine; FLA = French Left Attack; FN = Fort Nicholas; FM = Fort Michael; FP = Fort Paul; GB = Garden Batteries; GBr = Great Barracks; GBa = Gervais Battery; GR = Great Ravine; H = Hospital; LR = Little Redan Bastion; M = Mamelon; MB = Malakhov Bastion; PB = Point Bastion; Q = Quarries; QB = Quarantine Bastion; QC = Quarantine Cemetery; R = Redan; RR = Rostislav Redoubt; S = Shears; SB = Sviatoslav Battery; SH = South Harbour; SR = Schwartz Redoubt; VR = Vorontsov Ravine. (Adapted from Google Earth™ image and Map VII in Jocelyn, 1911).

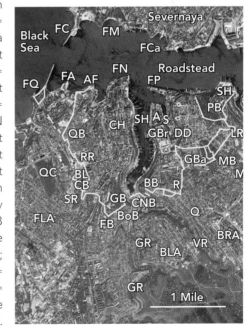

Sources of Information
and Additional Reading

Adkin, M., *The Charge – The Real Reason Why the Light Brigade was Lost* (Pimlico, London, 1996).

Beatty, J., *Position of the British Army Before Sevastopol Showing the Line of Railway*, Map of an area north of Balaklava, also showing vineyards, the position of French and Ottoman forces, redoubts, entrenchments, roads and contours. Signed James Beatty, Civil Engineer, 13 April 1855; Item WO 78/1028/4, The National Archives, Kew (TNA).

Brine, F., *Map of Sebastopol and Surrounding Country showing the Russian Defences, Positions of Allied Armies and their Trenches, together with the British Military and Naval Burial Grounds. Captain Frederic Brine, 1857*; Item MPH 1/427, TNA.

Caldwell, G. and Cooper, R., *Rifle Green in the Crimea* (Bugle Horn Publications, Leicester, 1994).

Cooke, B., *The Grand Crimean Central Railway* (Cavalier House, Knutsford, 1990).

Elphinstone, H.C., *Outline Plan of the Left Attack*, Lithographed and printed in the Topographical Depot (Southampton), War Department, 1858; Item ZMAP 1/130, TNA.

_____, *Outline Plan of the Right Attack*, Lithographed and printed in the Topographical Depot (Southampton), War Department, 1858; Item ZMAP 1/130, TNA.

_____, *Plan of the Defensive Position of Balaklava*, Lithographed and printed in the Topographical Depot (Southampton), War Department, 1858; Item ZMAP 1/130, TNA.

_____, *Plan of the Siege of Sevastopol by the Allied Armies in 1854-5*, Lithographed and printed in the Topographical Depot (Southampton), War Department, 1858; Item ZMAP 1/130, TNA.

Fletcher, I. and Ishchenko, N., *The Crimean War – A Clash of Empires* (Spellmount, Staplehurst, 2004).

_____, *War in the Crimea – An Illustrated History* (The History Press, Stroud, 2008).

Gartlan, L., 'James Robertson and Felice Beato in the Crimea: Recent Findings.' *History of Photography*, 29, 2005 (1), pp.1-9.

Gernsheim, H. and Gernsheim, A., *Roger Fenton, Photographer of the Crimean War* (Arno Press, New York, 1973).

Henisch, B.A. and Henisch, H.K., 'James Robertson and his Crimean War Campaign.' *History of Photography*, 26, 2002, (4), pp.258-68.

_____, 'George Shaw-Lefevre, Crimean Photographer', *The War Correspondent*, 23, 2005, (2), p.15.

Hibbert, C., *The Destruction of Lord Raglan – A Tragedy of the Crimean War* (Longmans, London, 1961).

Jocelyn, J.R.J., *The History of the Royal Artillery (Crimean Period)* (John Murray, London, 1911).

Keller, U., *The Ultimate Spectacle – A Visual History of the Crimean War* (Harwood Academic Publishers, Newark, 2001).

Kelly, C. (Ed.), *Mrs Duberly's War* (Oxford University Press, Oxford, 2007).

Kinglake, A.W., *The Invasion of the Crimea; its Origin, and an Account of its Progress down to the Death of Lord Raglan* (W. Blackwood and Sons, Edinburgh and London, 1863-1887).

Klembovsky, W., *Vues des Champs de Bataille de la Campagne de Crimée 1854-1855*, Edition du Musée de la Défense de Sébastopol, Expedition pour la Confection des Papiers d'État, St Petersbourg, 1904.

Lambert, A., *The Crimean War: British Strategy Against Russia 1853-1856* (Ashgate Publishing Ltd., Farnham, 2011).

Lysons, D., *The Crimean War from First to Last* (John Murray, London, 1895).

Massie, A. (Ed.), *A Most Desperate Undertaking: The British Army in the Crimea 1854-56* (National Army Museum, London, 2003).

Mawson, M.H. (Ed.), *Eyewitness in the Crimea – the Crimean War Letters of Lieutenant Colonel George Frederick Dallas* (Greenhill Books, London, 2001).

Mercer, P., *Give Them a Volley and Charge! – The Battle of Inkerman 1854* (Spellmount, Stroud, 2008).

Öztuncay, B., *Robertson, Photographer and Engraver in the Ottoman Capital* (Vehbi Koç Vakfi, Istanbul, 2013).

Paget, G., *The Light Cavalry Brigade in the Crimea* (John Murray, London, 1881).

Ponting, L., *The Crimean War: The Truth behind the Myth* (Vintage G Digital, London, 2010).

Raines, J., *Balaklava, its Lines and Harbour. Relief map showing fortifications and buildings in Balaklava and surrounding district. Reference table. Compass indicator. Scale 10 inches to 1 mile. Drawn by Julius Raines, Captain of the 95th Regiment, Assistant Engineer, July 1855 – copied by J.G. Kelly, Quartermaster General's Office, Horse Guards. July 1856*; Item MPH 1/121, TNA.

Reilly, W.E.M., *Siege of Sevastopol – An Account of the Artillery Operations Conducted by the Royal Artillery and Royal Naval Brigade before Sebastopol in 1854 and 1855* (Her Majesty's Stationary Office, London, 1859).

Robins, C. (Ed.), *Romaine's Crimean War* (Sutton Publishing, Stroud, 2005).

Ross-of-Bladensburg, J., *The Coldstream Guards in the Crimea* (The Naval and Military Press, Uckfield), a facsimile of 1897 edition.

Russell, W.H., *The War from the Death of Lord Raglan to the Evacuation of the Crimea* (G. Routledge and Co., London, 1856).

Russell, W.H., *General Todleben's History of the Defence of Sebastopol 1854-55, A Review* (Tinsley Brothers, London, 1856).

_____, *The British Expedition to the Crimea* (G. Routledge and Son, London, 1877).

Seacole, M.J., *Wonderful Adventures of Mrs Seacole in Many Lands* (James Blackwood, London, 1857).

Simpson, W. and Brackenbury, G., *The Seat of the War in the East from Eighty-one Drawings made during the War in the Crimea* (Day and Son, London, 1902).

Spratt, T.A.B., *Plan of the Heights, River and Bays of Alma Surveyed by the Officers of HMS* Spitfire *under the direction of Captn. Spratt R.N., September 23rd, 1854*; Item FO935/352, TNA.

Sterling, A., *The Story of the Highland Brigade in the Crimea* (Remington and Co. Ltd., London, 1895).

Whinyates, F.A., *From Coruña to Sevastopol: The History of 'C' Battery, 'A' Brigade (Late 'C' Troop), Royal Horse Artillery* (Allen, W.H., London, 1884).

Windham, C.A., *The Crimean Diary and Letters of Lieut.-General Sir Charles Ash Windham* (Kegan Paul, Trench, Trübner & Co., Ltd., London, 1897).

Index

INDEX OF 1854-56 IMAGE TITLES

William Simpson

INDEX OF VLADISLAV KLEMBOVSKY'S IMAGES PUBLISHED IN 1904